Donald Hume

Donald Hume

Notorious Bank Robber
and Double Murderer

Jonathan Oates

Wharncliffe True Crime

PEN & SWORD
TRUE CRIME

First published in Great Britain in 2020 by
Wharncliffe True Crime

An imprint of
Pen & Sword Books Ltd
Yorkshire – Philadelphia

ISBN 978-1-52676-966-4

Typeset in 11/13 point Minion Pro by Lapiz Digital

Printed and bound by 4edge Limited

Pen & Sword Books Ltd incorporates the imprints of Pen & Sword Archaeology, Atlas, Aviation, Battleground, Discovery, Family History, History, Maritime, Military, Naval, Politics, Social History, Transport, True Crime, Claymore Press, Frontline Books, Praetorian Press, Seaforth Publishing and White Owl.

For a complete list of Pen & Sword titles please contact

PEN & SWORD BOOKS LTD
47 Church Street, Barnsley, South Yorkshire, S70 2AS, England
E-mail: enquiries@pen-and-sword.co.uk
Website: www.pen-and-sword.co.uk

Or

PEN & SWORD BOOKS
1950 Lawrence Rd, Havertown, PA 19083, USA
E-mail: Uspen-and-sword@casematepublishers.com
Website: www.penandswordbooks.com

Contents

List of Plates

Preface

Donald Hume is usually presented as being one of a number of particularly vicious killers to emerge in war battered Britain in the decade immediately after the end of the Second World War; ranking alongside Neville Heath, John George Haigh, Ronald Chesney and John Christie. This is because he is stated as having killed and dismembered Stanley Setty, a murder he was tried for (and acquitted of) but later confessed to in 1958. Yet, he was the only one of those listed to escape, if not scot free, at least with his life at a time when the death penalty could be awarded to murderers. Furthermore, having got away with one murder, Hume went on to kill in Switzerland in 1959 and so another man lost his life. Once again Hume saved his own skin as this murder was committed in a country where capital punishment had been abolished. Unusually amongst the killers of the 1940s and 1950s who were exposed, he died peacefully in relatively obscure old age at the end of the century.

It is always stated – after 1958 – that Hume was a double murderer. Although he certainly confessed to murder in a newspaper, repudiating an earlier statement made to the police, he also made another admission whilst in prison. This has never been produced in public or even alluded to (the document in which it appears was closed until 2015). The two contradict each other. He also made an additional statement at a later trial. At least two must be incorrect. This book does not assume that the customarily accepted view of the case (that Hume killed Setty after a fierce fight due to annoyance at the latter's treatment of his dog) is necessarily correct. Instead, the reader is presented with all statements at the times that Hume made them, with analysis, rather than a linear narrative of what is assumed to have happened.

The case also exposed the way, in a manner that no other case of this era did, in which the press operated as regard to those tried for murder. Whilst it was usual for Sunday newspapers to pay a defendant's legal costs in exceptionally notorious cases – in order to gain their exclusive stories to boost circulation figures, this usually applied to men who were about to be hanged. In Hume's case, not only did he provide a newspaper with an edited autobiography after his trial, but also, after he had served a prison sentence as an accessory to murder, he then confessed to the same newspaper, for money, but could not be charged with murder under double-jeopardy laws. Hume's statements in the press also led to a number of court cases against various newspapers in the late 1950s. The press also gave their readers the impression of Hume as a monster, without noting the shades of grey and even white that made up his character and we will see how misleading an impression was given of the man (albeit with his active co-operation).

Hume may have been vicious, but he was also quite imaginative. He claimed he chopped up his first victim's body, apparently without any compunction or hesitation. Then, and there is no doubt about this, he dropped the pieces out of an aircraft which he was piloting over the sea, a method of disposal that was novel. The victim was reported missing immediately after his absence was noted and so a manhunt ensued and the press avidly reported each step of the search and various theories were discussed and discarded. When Hume was on trial, crowds flocked to the court each day.

To date there has been one full-length study in English of Hume, by John Williams in 1958, and in 1976 a volume of *Celebrated British Trials* was devoted to the case. The case has also featured in chapters of numerous true-crime books and in magazines. Yet, writers have chiefly relied on what has already been published, especially Williams' book which is at times uncritical of Hume's confession and so fails to discuss certain aspects of his murderous career, or even whether that confession was truthful. His family life, his time in Switzerland and later crimes are usually downplayed, as is his trial in Switzerland and life after sentencing (some of the latter is inevitable as Hume lived for four decades after Williams' book was first published). This work draws on a wider range of sources, including files at The National Archives of the Metropolitan Police and the Department of the Public Prosecutor, contemporary newspapers and sources often used by a genealogist when investigating a family's or individual's history.

The treatment is roughly chronological, with Chapter 1 covering Hume's youth prior to the Second World War, Chapter 2 looking at his experience of wartime, petty crime, business and marriage. The next chapter takes a step back to examine the career of his associate and his first victim, Stanley Setty. Chapter 4 details the disappearance of Setty and Hume's subsequent actions to dispose of the corpse, its partial discovery and the police investigation. Chapter 5 focuses on how Hume was arrested and brought before the courts. Chapters 6 and 7 detail the trial at the Old Bailey and Hume ultimately evading the noose. Chapter 8 concerns Hume's initial prison career, his differing confessions and his finding new romance in Switzerland. Chapter 9 details his bank robberies in England and Switzerland in 1958–9, leading to shootings, an undoubted murder and his eventual arrest. The next chapter discusses his trial in Switzerland. Finally, the last chapter surveys his three decades in custody, his repatriation to England and his mysterious demise.

Pre-decimal currency is often referred to throughout the book. For those unfamiliar with it, 12 old pence (abbreviated to *d.*) made up 1 shilling (abbreviated to *s.*) and 20 shillings was a pound note. In the 1940s, when much of the narrative in this book is set, a working man could expect a weekly wage of between £5 and £8, and a middle-class employee about twice that. At this time, £1,000 per year was a comfortable salary, but many men had to exist and support their families on less than half of that amount.

Acknowledgements

This book could not have been written without the assistance of numerous individuals, most of whom, being employed in archives and libraries (chiefly The National Archives and British Library), must remain anonymous. Family and friends have accompanied me on trips to take of some of the photographs featured. Lindsay Siviter has kindly provided me with photocopies of pertinent information from various sources and advice on the content, as well as commenting on the text and accompanying me on research and photographic trips. Paul Lang and Charles Bronson have been good enough to share their reminiscences of the elder Hume with me. John Curnow kindly translated an article in German for me. John Gauss read over the text and helped improve it. Dr Anna-Lena Berg provided me with a relevant article and introduced me to a book on the case in German, from which she translated relevant extracts and as well as reading through this book and making relevant recommendations. She has been a tower of strength throughout and a constant source of aid and encouragement.

The pictures of Hume and Setty on pp. 4 and 13 of the plate section are reproduced courtesy of the Mayor's Office for Policing and Crime.

This book is dedicated to Lindsay, who is a modern-day walking Newgate Calendar.

Chapter 1

A Little Bastard, 1919–39

Most of what is known about Hume's early life is derived from his confession made to the *Sunday Pictorial* newspaper in 1958. Previous authors writing about him have largely accepted this account, occasionally with some scepticism, but have not made much effort to investigate Hume's background in order to corroborate any of it. In many cases, though, such verification is impossible. There was no one from his early years who brought forth an account of his youth and nothing was written at the time. This chapter will draw inevitably on Hume's account, but will also, where possible, use other material as well as a healthy dose of suspicion about the words of Hume, who was a proven liar and known fantasist.

Usually very little information is given about Hume's mother, who is only named as 'Aunt Doodie', the name given to her by Hume and she comes across – because of uncritical acceptance of Hume's account – entirely negatively. Using sources often employed in genealogical research, we can now learn far more about her and her background.

Hume's mother was Bessie Emily Whiddington (also known as 'Doodie'). She was born in Marylebone, north west London, on 1 October 1889. Her parents, Richard (1859–1927) and Ada Ann Fitzgerald (1855–1933), were both teachers, employed by the London County Council's schools department. Ada was quite a remarkable woman, who had been born in Ireland but came to London aged 19 and went on to become the headmistress of a girls' school on Mornington Crescent in London. She was a devout Christian and is thought to have written two hymns, 'Not I but Christ' in 1891 and possibly 'Always Together' in 1904, and may have been a member of the evangelical Keswick Convention. Bessie was their third and last child; the others being Richard (1885–1970) and Bertha Ann Fitzgerald (1888–1959). In 1891 the family lived at 41 Argyle Square, St Pancras, in north London. From 1894–1902, they were in the same district, albeit at 86 Mansfield Road, sharing the house with another family and from 1904–10 were at 11 Bartholomew Road. In 1905 Bessie enrolled at the North London Collegiate School in order to train to become a teacher.[1]

By 1911 the family was certainly socially upwardly mobile. They had moved to the newly established Hampstead Garden Suburb, in the district of Hendon, Middlesex. This was part of the suburban expansion of north London, with the opening of Golders Green station on the Northern Line, but was also a co-partnership community aimed at the idealistic lower middle class (including the family of the future author of *Brideshead Revisited*, Evelyn Waugh). Similar suburbs existed at Letchworth and at Brentham in west London. There would be no shops, cinemas or pubs on the estate but there would be an Evening Institute for talks and classes. No one would own their homes, but they would share in the management of the estate.[2]

The Whiddingtons now lived at a house called Rossville, 8 Bigwood Road. It was a seven roomed semi-detached house with the privacy of a privet hedge, the same as the other houses in the street. They also had a live-in general domestic servant, 19-year-old Pheasant Bertha; a sure sign of being middle class. All this could be paid for, because, despite the younger Richard being a university student (albeit in receipt of various scholarships), both his parents and both his younger sisters were all employed as school teachers. Bessie was employed by Hendon Urban District Council and so worked locally.[3]

Bessie was an Assistant at the Hampstead Garden Suburb School, which was then located at the Institute on Central Square, close to the newly consecrated St Jude's Anglican Church. She began her employment in March 1911, but had ceased working there by June 1912. She was paid £4 11s. 8d. per week by August 1911; a good salary for a young woman at this time.[4]

In 1912 Bessie married one Percy John Hume (1886–1919), educated at St John's College, Cambridge (as was her brother, both had won scholarships in science subjects, and undoubtedly the two met through Richard). On 3 May 1910 Percy entered the Indian Civil Service as a junior stores clerk, initially on £150 per year. The couple were wed on 19 July 1912 at St Jude's Church (the same place of worship attended by the Waugh family; it is possible that the future novelists brushed shoulders metaphorically with the mother of a future criminal). Her occupation is not noted on the marriage certificate, for she had resigned her teaching post, as was required for female teachers on marriage. It was a big wedding, with a reception at her house for 80 guests and 100 gifts were received. Bessie's sister was one of the four bridesmaids.

It does not seem that Bessie and Percy had their own house, but by late 1916 a daughter, Margaret Fitzgerald Hume (1916–92), was born. It is probable that Bessie and Percy had split up by 1918 because in that year she is listed as residing alone in The School House in Hooke, a tiny Dorset village with a population of 141, and was the village schoolmistress, teaching 60 children at the Elementary School. In any case, Percy suffered from consumption and was permanently retired from his job on 23 August 1916 and this condition probably accounts for his premature death on 20 October 1919 in a hostel on 29 North Side, Clapham. His will left £263 18s. to his widow.[5]

Two months later, on 20 December, his widow gave birth to a son, Donald, at 'Rest Harrow', a nursing home on Ulwell Road in the Dorset town of Swanage, which had a population of 7,112 in 1921. There is a blank on the birth certificate where the father's name is usually inserted. Bessie could have put her late husband's name there for as he was dead, he could hardly object. Many women were single mothers at this time because their husbands had been killed in the First World War. Furthermore, rates of illegitimacy soared during the social upheaval of war (from 37,329 to 44,947 between 1914 and 1918). In 1919–20 Bessie was living in the newly renamed Armistice House, in Toller Porcorum, a small village in Dorset not far from Hooke. However, mother and baby returned to her parents' house in Bigwood Road because the birth was registered from there on 27 February 1920.[6]

Hume later said that being without a father had a major impact on his subsequent life. Writing in 1958, he stated:

> Fantastic . . . that's how my life has always been. That's how the stars were stacked for me. I was born in Swanage, Dorset, with a chip on my shoulder, large as an elephant. I've got a grudge against society. All my life I've had to fight the shame and degradation of not knowing who my father was.[7]

Being illegitimate was certainly a great social stigma at this time, but Hume's reactions to it were probably exaggerated.

Yet, it seems that he did know who his father was; his uncle, Richard Whiddington, attested in 1942 that his father later married his mother and he certainly told Dr John Campbell McIntyre Matheson (1892–1972), Principal Medical Officer of Brixton prison, in 1949 that he knew who his father was. He was Reginald Duncan House (1894–1953?). Little is known about him. He was one of five sons (and nine children) of Tom House (1851–1920), a builder and farmer, and Martha Greening Home (1852–1925), his wife. He was baptised at the parish church of Powerstock, Dorset, on 21 October 1894. The family lived at Glebe Farm at Powerstock, with two servants. Reginald worked with his family on the farm in the 1910s. Powerstock was just 4 miles from where Bessie Hume lived.[8]

The next few years are unclear. The Whiddingtons had left 8 Bigwood Road by 1921 (by now all three children had married). Hume later stated, 'I was sent to an orphanage at Burnham on Sea, Somerset, until I was eight.' His wife later recalled that Hume had told her he was in an orphanage as a lad. Yet, there was no orphanage at Burnham in the 1920s; it was a small seaside town and most orphanages were in large towns and cities. Possibly it was a small private house which took in young children and was never listed officially (children's homes were meant to be registered with the council). Or maybe Hume was inventing this story.[9] Possibly Hume was put in an orphanage because after his birth his mother was unwell, either physically or mentally, and had no one else who could provide full-time care for him; in any case she had two daughters to look after. But postnatal depression does not last for six years and so if Hume did live apart from his mother there must have been other reasons for this that we do not know about.

Dr Matheson, when talking to Hume in 1949, related what Hume told him, 'His early life and environment were not good. He was illegitimate and his mother, a schoolmistress, to protect her reputation, placed him in an orphanage.'[10] All we know about this is taken from John Williams' book about Hume. Williams did not meet Hume but he had the assistance of journalist Victor Sims who carried out lengthy interviews with Hume. How accurate Hume's tales are is another question. They may have been exaggerated. Hume's uncle, in his account of his nephew's life in 1942, does not mention any time spent in an orphanage, so as with Hume's claiming he did not know who his father was, this may well be another invention, told in 1958 to gain sympathy with a reading public. The orphanage he claimed to have been sent to was on the sea front and run by three old women who did not show any kindness to their charges. Children slept eight to a bed, had to rise at 4 in the morning and were fed sparse and unappetising food. Discipline was strict and children wore rough brown jerseys and darned trousers. School holidays were spent digging holes in the sand. On one occasion, Hume alleged, he and a little girl were shut in a cellar and a woman dressed in a green cloak and bonnet came down, reciting strange oaths and brandishing a stick. Hume realised that this was actually a member of staff and saw a chopper nearby. Grabbing hold of it he chased their tormenter away. There was a parrot which screeched 'Bastards!' at the children. Hume apparently lived here from the age of 2 to 8, or so he said, but why he was still there after his parents' marriage is uncertain.[11]

Hume claimed, that some years later, 'I was put in the care of a kindly grandmother – my own mother's mother. For the first time in my life someone was kind to me. I was allowed to go to the pictures, and to mix with normal kids. Gran lived in Hendon, London.' Gran, of course, was Ada Ann Whiddington, now in her seventies. Her husband had died in 1927 in Norfolk and she was now living at 26 Addison Way, not far north of Bigwood Road, with her elder daughter, whose marriage was short-lived, and a servant. There were happy memories of these times, mixing with other children, playing freely with other children in London streets, seeing gangster films at the cinema and having a loving adult to care for him. Hume then stated, 'But after six happy months with her, I was put on a train for the country . . . to my aunt.'[12]

Meanwhile, Bessie and House, described as an engineer (later a salesman in cattle foods and a lorry driver), had a daughter, Betty Fitzgerald House, born in Sherborne, Dorset in 1921. Two years later Bessie was school mistress at the village school of Mapledurwell, a few miles from Basingstoke in Hampshire; as with the schools in Dorset at which she had taught, it had less than a hundred children and she lived in the accommodation provided (although unmarried on appointment she stated her name as being Mrs Bessie House). According to Anne Pitcher, a local Hampshire historian, 'Mrs House was totally wrapped up in her pupils. She brought with her all sorts of ideas.' She was both ambitious and determined for her school and her charges, with the result that she organised Christmas pantomimes for the whole village (which were great successes), assisted several of her pupils to gain scholarships for higher education and gave her pupils music lessons. She was a capable pianist and on the piano that she used in lessons was a framed picture of a small boy. When her pupils asked 'Who's that Mrs House?', she replied 'Oh, that's my Donald.' Whatever Hume thought, his mother had not forgotten him and did at the very least display some maternal affection towards him.[13]

Meanwhile, in 1925 Hume's parents married, doubtless in a quiet civil ceremony in a place far removed from anyone who knew her as a headmistress in Hampshire; namely south London. Three years later she applied for another job, this time at Herriard village school. Herriard was a small straggling village of 345 people and 9 farms dominated by the Herriard Park estate belonging to Major Francis Jervoise (one of the managers of the said school), a few miles to the south of Basingstoke. On 20 April 1928 the managers for that school appointed Bessie as headmistress given the impending retirement of the current incumbent in June. Mrs House had clearly made a good impression for she had beaten eight other candidates to the job and duly began work there on 5 September 1928. This was the Church of England village school established in 1837 and extended in 1850 and 1897. Both boys and girls attended it.[14]

Hume, in 1958, bitterly recalled, 'My mother made me call her "Aunt". She used to tell me "I only adopted you as a companion for my daughter".' The family lived in the school house provided with the job, which was next door to the school, on the road from Basingstoke to Alton. It was a middle class household, with at least one live-in servant. He recalled, 'It was brought home to me with stark reality that not only was I unwanted, but I was a sheer embarrassment to my aunt.'[15]

When Bessie arrived at the school she found much to dismay her that due to an outbreak of measles and scarlet fever only eight children were present. It was very cold and stoves had to be lit. The older children were backward because of frequent absences and an inadequate supply of books. Anne Pitcher described Mrs House as 'very capable and steady' and that she sought to improve matters. She was outspoken and lobbied Jervoise and the vicar for funds, gave the children individual attention, introduced handicraft lessons and obtained a piano. Once again she did much for the school and its pupils; Pitcher declaring 'Mrs House had really uplifted it.'[16]

From 1928–33 his mother was assisted by another teacher, Miss Dorothy Dicker. In 1929 Mrs House was appointed as petty cash keeper, too. It is not known how proficient Mrs House was as a teacher (the school log books for all the three Hampshire schools she taught at are closed for public inspection) but a reference in the school managers' minute book in 1934 states that she had not been efficiently supervising the assistant school teacher, Miss Taylor. Hume, now known as Brian Hume for the first time, was one of several pupils, which included his sister, Betty, who entered the school at Easter 1929. He claimed that he was caned in front of the whole school (presumably by his mother as she was the headmistress) so his mother could demonstrate that no favouritism would be bestowed upon him. He later told Dr Matheson, 'he was made a drudge and was frequently beaten for trivial offences and held up to ridicule before the pupils of the school.' There was gossip amongst the children about his parentage and finally a servant told him that 'You are Auntie's son. She is your mother.' Hume stated, 'I felt my dislike for the woman who didn't want to be known as my mother turning into hatred.'[17]

When the rest of the family went on holidays to the seaside, he was forced to stay at home to look after the poultry. Naturally, he resented this. He claimed, 'One day I took my mother's small bore gun and shot the cockerel. Then I threw the cockerel into the cess pool and pretended it had drowned. It was the first thing I ever killed. But I knew that it began to shape my fighting philosophy.'[18] Whether this incident happened is, of course, unknown. It is certainly at odds with his comments as an adult that he loved animals.

Hume passed the entrance exam to attend Basingstoke grammar school (other well-known killers from the 1940s such as Heath and Haigh also attended grammar schools). Founded in 1556, it was then located on Worting Road, which it had been since 1870, and was 'a gaunt three story reddish-dun brick building.' The uniform included a black cap with a silver dove emblem and boys attending the school were sometimes known as tits. A famous old boy was Gilbert White, a noted eighteenth-century naturalist.[19]

In 1927 120 boys attended the school, some having gained scholarships. It was a day school and some boys cycled there from outlying villages and these may have included Hume. The headmaster was Charles Wilhelm Percivall, MA, who had studied at Cambridge. According to John Arlott, later a respected cricket commentator, who attended the school in the 1920s, Percivall 'had all the traditional characteristics of those people', meaning Prussians. He was also asthmatic and taught maths. Perhaps more sinister was that he always carried a cane with him and enjoyed doling out punishments to boys; either in the wash-basin room or before the whole school in the main hall. Arlott hated him for this and detailed his later verbal revenge on the man. On the whole, though, the teaching standard was good, and there was a strong emphasis on games, especially cricket and football.[20]

In January 1933 Hume is recorded as being in Form III, as he is in the September of that year. He left school the following year – the register lists him in Lent 1934, but with his name crossed out; schooling then being compulsory to the age of 14. Yet, he was not particularly bright, 'the records show that he was somewhat backward as a pupil.' His unsatisfactory progress led him to leave. Of his time there we know nothing for he did not choose to record it in his autobiography which he retold to Victor Sims and there are no known sources which would indicate any particular interests or aptitudes he had or any friends he made there. It may well have been an experience he was eager to forget. Similarly unhappy at home, he left to make his own living. Apparently he obtained a job as a kitchen boy to a Hampshire family on the coast; the lowest of the low. He did not like it and so returned to his mother's house. 'But not for long', he recalled.[21]

One night in 1934 he packed his belongings into a suitcase and left his bedroom by a window. One version has it that he planned to run away to sea and to become a cook on board a ship. In this he failed. Another account claimed he hitch hiked to London and slept on Barnes Common one night and left his few belongings there – including model aircraft he had built. He then went to Somerset House, on the Strand, where the civil registration records of births, marriages and deaths were then stored. He paid the required fee and was shown his birth certificate. It confirmed what he had already been told; that he had been born outside wedlock and, what was worse, that his father was apparently unknown, as the section for father's name was blank. He stated in 1958 that, 'From that moment I knew I would have to fight the world on my own. And woe betide anything or anybody who got in the way. I wrote to my mother telling her what I had discovered. She never answered – and I have never seen her since.' Bessie had no further part to play in her son's life. On 21 December 1939 she left her job at Herriard school and became headmistress at Longparish village school, where she remained for another decade. She was still there in 1950 but had left by the following year, presumably having retired from the school now that she was just past 60 years of age. She was the beneficiary of her sister's will in 1959 and was apparently still alive four years later. Her two daughters married in Longparish in 1944 and 1950 and she acted as witness on both occasions. There is no evidence that Hume attended either celebration.[22]

It is hard to assess Bessie's character. She was clearly well educated and intelligent, competent enough to hold down a demanding job. Her parents and sister were teachers, too, and her brother became a distinguished academic and scientist. Thomas Duncan Webb (1917–58), a well-known crime journalist on the *People* newspaper, wrote, though on whose authority is not known, that she was 'loved by her pupils, respected by all who knew her.' This is backed up by Anne Pitcher's books which include many favourable references to her. But an excellent teacher may not have been an excellent mother too. Yet, all we know about her as a human being is what Hume tells us, and she appears cold-hearted and unloving towards him. She was certainly in a difficult situation in 1919, albeit one presumably of her own making, with an illegitimate son and no husband. If she did send him to an orphanage, we should not condemn her out of hand, though conditions there would probably have been far from easy for a young boy. Illegitimacy was frowned upon socially as were women who bore children out of wedlock – very much in the minority in the early twentieth century, despite the rise in extra-marital sex during the First World War. We just do not know enough about her and her exact family and social circumstances to be able to judge and establish how accurate Hume's harsh verdict of her was. Yet, to disown one's own son seems to have had a powerful effect on the young lad. If he could not trust his mother, then who could he trust other than himself?[23]

There had certainly been a failure for mother and son to form a natural bond. Why he lacked any bitterness towards his father is unknown, however. His parents do not seem to have made any effort to try and bring their son home. After all, he was alone in the big city and its numerous dangers for young and lonely people. Their behaviour towards him was hardly normal and so the impact on him may well have led to him becoming insecure and so prone to boastfulness.

He needed to work to live, however. On his return to Barnes Common to collect his belongings, he thumbed a lift and was picked up by Frederick George Fox, builder of 27 Chilwell Street, Paddington, who was driving a lorry. He was sympathetic and found lodgings for Hume with Mrs Mary Ann Clare (1871–1966), who was childless, in Praed Street, near Paddington. Fox's wife paid for the teenager's lodgings and gave him some new clothes and it was verified that his mother did not want him back. Initially, he was trained as an electrician, which paid 25s. a week. Fox then employed him as an electrician's mate. Yet, on 11 November 1937 he was sacked because he would not attend night school, as Fox wanted him to. He was not without work for long and on 16 November took a job as a polisher at the British Metal Engraving Company at St Margaret's, Middlesex. He received £2 10s. per week. At this time he still lodged with Mrs Clare, now a widow and living at 16 Ashleigh Road, Mortlake, not far from his employment. He also joined the King Street branch of the Hammersmith Communist Party, aged 17, which probably fuelled his sense of grievance against others who had what he desired. It does not seem that he joined the party out of an ideological commitment to socialist ideals, but, as we shall later note, extremist politics had an appeal for him on some level. 'I suppose it was because I believed I would get something for nothing', he said. It led to him selling Communist literature, fighting Fascists and the police, but being turned down to fight in the Spanish Civil War (he later claimed he went out to Spain at this time to fight). In 1937 he was noted by MI5 as being an active Communist.[24]

Hume also took to pilfering as a teenager. This began by stealing from a chemist's shop where he worked part-time and selling the items on to teenage acquaintances. From then on he and others graduated to stealing motorcycles and cars and racing with them, often leaving the vehicles smashed up on the south coast or elsewhere. Speed was his passion; going at 80mph on a motorcycle through London and splitting up with his first girlfriend were early experiences. He was never caught, however.[25]

Then there was his interest in gadgetry and experimentation. This included using his lodgings in Mortlake to make a large firework in a tin canister to 'shake things up a little' at an old people's home. It blew up prematurely and destroyed some of the house. He and a friend experimented with a primitive breathing apparatus on the Thames near Kew Bridge, but an oar from a passing boat fouled the breathing tubes and the experimenter nearly drowned.[26]

International events, though, were soon to alter this young man's life considerably, as they were for millions of others.

Chapter 2

Hume in War and Peace, 1939–49

When the Second World War broke out in September 1939, Hume was initially apathetic. He later recalled, 'The way I felt, the country was not worth dying for. What had it given me? If the ruling classes wished to preserve their wealth, let them. I'd fight for mine when I got it.' This was echoing the Communist Party line, of course, for in 1939 the Soviet Union and Nazi Germany were allies. Yet, ideology and his own personal bitterness were not enough, and he decided to enlist. 'The excitement war could bring outweighed everything.' He chose the RAF, which was the most popular and glamorous of the three armed services. It had been expanding throughout the 1930s and was equipped with the latest technology as funds had been pumped into the aerial service rather than the army or navy. Hume already had an interest in flight, so it was the natural choice for him and doubtless he had high expectations of becoming a pilot and a fighter ace.[1] Another man who would become infamous for his later misdeeds was Neville Heath and he also served in the RAF during the war, albeit with distinction.

Another reason why he chose the RAF was that he may well have known of his uncle's career in that branch of the armed forces in the First World War. Richard Whiddington had been a captain in the RFC and finished the war as a major in the newly formed RAF. Whiddington had become an esteemed academic afterwards and possibly Hume was impressed by his achievements (his father is not known to have served in any combat role in the First World War). Whiddington was also on the RAF officers' selection board at the outset of the war and Hume may have thought that this could have worked to his career advantage.[2] It did not.

Hume began his service career at RAF Uxbridge, where, in the 1920s, Lawrence of Arabia and, less well known, John Christie, had also been employed. It was used as a training depot and he was there from 7 September–15 December. At this time he was still living with Mrs Clare in Mortlake, though claiming he was born on 3 March 1917, thus adding nearly three years to his age. His ration card entry lists him as a trainee pilot with 902 Squadron. He then was sent to RAF Debden in Essex for twelve days and then to the Hastings Initial Training Wing. He was eager to fly. Although he trained as a pilot and then as an air gunner, he failed the necessary exams and so did not qualify for either. He later claimed that he had flown for about 40 hours and that he had had a few hours training in flying. Despite his later pretensions, Hume was only an aircraftsman in the RAF, one of the lowliest of the low (John Christie had been an aircraftsman in 1923–4). The rank is the equivalent to being a private in the army. He was later stationed at 7 Anti-Aircraft Co-operation Unit, until 21 January 1940.[3]

His RAF service was short-lived, however, for he became very unwell (again as with Christie). From 22 January–2 March 1940 he was at the Hastings Sanatorium. He seemed to make a recovery for from 3 March–26 November he was at 7 Anti-Aircraft Co-operation Unit once again. On 27 November he was sent to 10 (S) RC Blackpool. It was here that he decided to rename himself as Terrence B. Hume and as T.B. Fitzgerald Hume, the third name being inspired by that of his beloved grandmother. His health gave way again and on 18 March 1941 he was sent to Matlock Hospital for a month.[4]

Hume seems to have contracted cerebro-spinal meningitis (spotted fever), was treated and then recovered. He was also seen as being mentally unstable, for he described himself as being pro-Nazi and detailed adventures in Germany and Spain that he had not in fact experienced. He went before a medical board examination on 7 April 1941 where 'he was then considered to be a psychopathic personality and to suffer from pseudo-parkinsonism.' This is where a patient exhibits some of the symptoms of Parkinson's disease, including tremors, slowing down and forgetfulness. His character, though, was deemed to be 'very good', which means that when in uniform he obeyed orders. He was thus discharged on health grounds on 13 May. He applied to the medical board for a pension and was examined on 11 July 1941. They then declared him as a psychopath but could find no evidence of pseudo-Parkinsonism and that the after effects of cerebro-spinal meningitis had cleared up. They thought that his personality was 'constitutional in origin' and had not been aggravated by RAF service. No pension was granted.[5]

A specialist in psychological medicine at Clifton Military Hospital at York stated that: 'having suffered from meningitis, he has developed a degree of organically determined psychopathy, as a result of which his mentality, particularly as evinced by his political opinions, has lost its plasticity, thereby rendering permanent what might have been an otherwise purely transient, adolescent phase in the social maturation of a Bolshie.'[6]

These psychiatric assessments hardly seem professional. There is no link between extreme political views and being a psychopath and no link between the latter and meningitis.

On 7 September he left the RAF, deemed 'physically unfit for Air Force service, although fit for employment in civil life.' His character, though, was stated as being 'very good'; a similar verdict was given on Christie two decades previously.[7] Other than this, virtually nothing is known for certain about his short-lived RAF career, for his service records at the Ministry of Defence Records Section (RAF) are currently closed.

This failure in the RAF may have had a psychological impact. Dr Matheson later stated that it might have led to embitterment and a sense of inferiority, especially as he never qualified as either pilot or even gunner. It may have led to him boasting and to later criminal behaviour. On leaving the RAF, he often suffered from hay fever and headaches, which he had treated.[8]

Back in civilian life, he turned to what he described as 'spivery.' His first venture was to sell home-brewed gin, using either distillate from potatoes or surgical spirits, to night clubs and he made £60 from the venture. He had no qualms, claiming that everyone was doing it. On 21 April 1941 he took a job as a night air raid spotter at Napiers' aircraft engineering works on Acton Vale, west London, receiving £6 10s. per week. This job entailed reporting bombs which dropped on the factory or nearby and attempting to extinguish any fires which resulted, if practicable. Whilst employed there he spent an evening in the Irish Shamrock Club in Hammersmith and met an IRA man, who sold him two guns. Hume recalled, 'They just made me feel good.' Guns tend to give the bearer a feeling of power over his fellows and this Hume probably quite enjoyed, though he had no bullets for them. However, police investigating possible espionage at the factory found Hume's guns and questioned him about them. They also found in his possession sensitive photographs of the parts of the planes that the men in the factory were working on, but Hume declared, probably correctly, that he was not a spy but an aircraft enthusiast. He was believed and released. The job lasted six months and he was dismissed on 6 October 1941 for being absent from duty on three consecutive nights and being quarrelsome. He also stole three knives and four forks, too (valued at 10s. 6d.). On the following day, he moved on to become an aero engine fitter at Sunbeam Talbot Ltd, which had been a motor car manufacturer at Barlby Road in Notting Hill, being paid £8 per week.[9]

Hume tried to re-enter the RAF again, so was released from Sunbeam under an essential works order on 26 November. A week later he was before the Aviation Candidates Selection Board of the RAF. However, his entry was deferred on educational grounds. So, on 5 December he became an aero fitter again, this time at London Aircraft Products, but only lasted a month before absenting himself on 22 January 1942 on the grounds of having a medical certificate stating he was unfit for such work.[10]

For the next three months he was officially designated as being unemployed. Of course, he was far from inactive. Failing to re-enter the RAF, he did the next best thing in his eyes. It was at this time, in January 1942, that Hume embarked on his first known criminal enterprise. A former RAF pilot, who was lodging with him, sold him an RAF officer's uniform with a DFM ribbon denoting a flying hero for £5 and Hume recalled, 'I could see the possibilities.' He could now play out some of his fantasies of make-believe and appear to have achieved what he had been unable to in reality. He stated that wearing it 'worked like a charm. It was a great thrill to have everyone saluting a bastard like me.' He renamed himself as 'B.D. Hume', but also called himself Donald, Terry, Brian and Terrence. But it was not only this which attracted him to using it, but practical, financial benefit, too. He wrote, 'Cocksure and confident I breezed into maintenance units and stores.' He forged identity cards and stole tyres and motor accessories and sold them on. He passed dud cheques too; after all, who then would not trust a hero of the Battle of Britain? Roald Dahl, himself an RAF pilot, noted in his memoirs, 'An RAF uniform with wings on the jacket was a great passport to have in England in 1941. The Battle of Britain had been won by the fighters and now the bombers were beginning seriously to attack Germany.' It enabled Dahl to persuade a hotel manageress to let him use her telephone and then when drunk soldiers went to attack him they veered off because, as one of them said, 'Ee's RAF! Ee's a pilot! Ee's got ruddy wings on 'im.' All in all Hume had made £300, but there was a price to pay.[11]

In his disguise as an RAF officer and with a forged identity card, Hume visited at least two RAF bases. Between 31 January and 5 February he was at RAF Speke, near Liverpool. Here he stole a scarf, flying boots, jacket and a flying helmet, valued at £14 2s. 6d., from Flight Lieutenant Douglas Turley-George. On 4 February he took £5 from Flight Lieutenant Clarke, secretary of the RAF Officers' Mess. He also took the opportunity to fly two aircraft there. On 30 March he was at RAF Padgate in Cheshire and at the medical centre there was examined and given a certificate to state he was unfit for duty. He then travelled southwards and at Staines in Middlesex, on 2 April, met one William Frederick Archer of La Bagatelle, Penton Hook, Staines and pitched a hard-luck story to him. Archer took him home and the next day found that Hume had stolen a page from his cheque book. Hume had also taken out loans with others, presumably trusting RAF officers, which he never planned to repay.[12]

Hume's masquerade came to an end at RAF Northolt on the afternoon of 3 April when he tried to call on the adjutant to cash a cheque for £25 at the South Barrier. Unbeknownst to him, officials at RAF Speke had circulated a description of him. It was noted that his identity card was a forgery and he was refused entry and then arrested by officers of the RAF Special Branch. On his arrest it was noted that he was 5ft and 5½in in height, with grey eyes, dark-brown hair and a chest measuring 32in. He had a round, smiling face, curly, unkempt hair, a large and slightly hooked nose and a left shoulder slightly lower than his right. Hume was sent to London and into DC George Helps' custody at 6 that evening at 47 Grosvenor Square. Interestingly, Hume gave his address as that of Professor Richard Whiddington of Ashley Court Hotel, 199 Queen's Gate in South Kensington. Whiddington gave the police a brief account of his nephew's life; born out of wedlock, though his parents later married; brought up by his mother claiming she was his aunt, attended Herriard school and then Basingstoke grammar school, left aged 14, took unsatisfactory jobs and ran off to London in 1934. He was never able to cash Archer's cheque.[13]

Hume spent a month at Feltham Borstal, Bedfont Road, Middlesex, where he was examined by a psychiatrist and the prison's medical officer who concluded that there was 'no evidence of insanity or feeble mindedness was found but that he was a psycho-neurotic due to probably the effects of his early upbringing.' Hume, known as Brian Donald Hume, was charged on 13 May 1942, but confessed and was bailed on recognisances for £5. He appeared at the Old Bailey on 24 June. He was charged with falsely suggesting he was in the RAF, wearing an RAF uniform to gain false entry and for forging false entry documents. The witnesses against him were Frank Charles Faiers, Edward Lennox Scott-Atkinson, Patrick Pullen and DC Helps. The counsel at the court was rising barrister Christmas Humphreys, who, as we shall see, went on to play a key role in Hume's later life. Here Hume was deemed 'an undesirable and unreliable character', but was given a lenient sentence, probably in part because of his youth and because it was his first known offence, in being bound over for two years. He was also fined the token sum of £5 and was ordered to undergo psycho-therapeutic treatment but never went.[14]

At the end of 1942 Hume began to live in Golders Green, north London, and opened an account with the Midland Bank branch there. In 1943 Hume resided at Flat B, on the second floor of 620 Finchley Road, Hendon, close to the Golders Green Tube station and not too far south from where he had lived with his grandmother at Addison Way. This address was used as the headquarters of his new business as an electrical engineer and plumber. He alleged that he could tackle jobs that big firms would not deal with and bribed employees of other firms to work for him, for there was a labour shortage due to the war. Often he would learn as he went on and would say whatever he needed to when dealing with customers. Lacking lead piping for a plumbing job, he used rubber and told the elderly client, 'I assure you these pipes will never freeze.' One Mr Preston (who was also Hume's landlord) and a Professor Winnington (possibly his uncle Whiddington is meant) went into business with him under the name 'Hume Electric Ltd.' The business was registered on 11 August 1943 with certificate 382158. The workshops were at Elektron Works, 18 Church Road, Leyton, in East London, and were described as radio and general engineers, manufacturers and importers.[15]

Business initially went well. By 1944 Hume had two new vans and was making an incredible £100 per week when the average wage was less than a tenth of that. He designed and sold 50,000 Little Atom toasters, electric towel rails and walking mechanical men. Orders worth thousands of pounds were taken from one firm. In 1947 he alleged he was worth £20,000, had a Cadillac worth £2,000, rented a £10 per week house in Denman Drive, Golders Green, had two shops and a staff of fifty. There is no way of knowing if these figures for Hume's income and wealth are genuine or not, and it is probable that he exaggerated the figures to boost his ego. In 1948 he did business with Jack Soneya, MD of Homeshade Company, who sold electrical goods and appliances. He apparently supplemented his legitimate income by working with others in stealing lorry loads of eggs, pepper and chocolate for resale, not because he needed the money but because he wanted the thrill of putting one over the law. Yet, as a former employee stated, 'he was not a good employer, but he did get things done.'[16]

Life was not all business deals and skulduggery for Hume. He was also a very sociable fellow. Webb once wrote of him, 'He was a jolly sort of chap, not unlikeable, as line shooters go. It was his affability, his ability to tell tall stories, which attracted my attention.' He continued, 'somewhere in that squat, fattish frame there must have been some good somewhere in that broad head must have been a kindly thought . . . somewhere in that demented and warped mind there must have been some feeling.' He was a member of various clubs in London such as the RAF Officers' Club and the Brevet Club; he was known at others, too; the M Club, the Spotlight Club, the Cleveland Club on Duke Street, the Hollywood Club on Old Quebec Street and the Light Club. His obsession with flight remained and he was known in the RAF Club as 'the Flying Cavalier' because he was an obvious liar. According to Webb, 'The uniform, the glamour, the excitement of war fed his insatiable ego', though he was also 'a coward and a liar' and full of 'hard luck stories.' He also used aliases such as Brian Fitzgerald (his mother's maiden name and the middle name of his half-sister) Hume and Terrence Brian Hume. He often visited Paris and stayed in hotels such as the Crillion and the California. He lived well, dressed well, went to expensive hotels and clubs and drove luxury cars. As time went by, 'one of the mysteries about him is how he obtained the money to indulge his extravagancies', assuming that he was not inventing tales of his own wealth.[17]

Hume was a fantasist. Inspector Grant of the Special Branch noted, 'Hume has a vivid imagination and has always endeavoured to create an impression that he has been engaged in exciting adventures.' Apart from posing as a former RAF officer, he also claimed to be a racing driver and used Canadian and South American accents. There were photographs and pictures of him in his flat in these guises. He also alleged that he had been tortured by the SS. Grant added that he was 'a plausible liar who has not only defrauded people who have befriended him but has stolen from them.'[18] Hume may well have been a fantasist because he was insecure, suffering low self esteem due to his miserable childhood.

Little is known about Hume's love life in his early years, apart from the unnamed girlfriend he went joyriding with in the later 1930s. He was certainly not immune to feminine charms, however, and in 1942 it was stated that he was 'Fond of women and dog racing and the company of RAF personnel.' He recalled romances with one Diana from Stratford-upon-Avon and with a brunette who was a cashier in a bank (perhaps the Midland Bank) on Finchley Road. There was another girlfriend who was a cinema usherette. However, he stated that he was 'just fond of them'. In fact he found another object for his affections, as he recalled, 'Around this time I fell in love at first sight – with a dog. He was a half husky, half Alsatian, that I bought for £1. I named him Tony. He was no ordinary dog. We had a mutual understanding.' Many people love dogs and have them as pets; and this does not exclude serial killers such as John Haigh and John Christie. Dogs give an unconditional and uncomplicated love which fellow humans are not always capable of.[19]

Someone new – and very important – entered Hume's life in 1947. He was in the M Club in Welbeck Road, having a drink. There he saw Renato Kahn, 'a sallow skinned importer.' With him was his wife of three years, Cynthia Mary (née Wright, just over a year Hume's junior, of 96 Clifton Hill, Marylebone), whom Kahn introduced to Hume, though another version suggests the two met in Hay. Cynthia was described as being a 'slim, attractive brunette.' She had been born in King's Norton, Warwickshire in 1921 and her father, Henry Grocott Wright (1880–1969), was an accounts controller of the Birmingham and Municipal Savings Bank and lived at Castle Hill Cottage, Kington, Herefordshire by 1949. Her mother was Beatrice Emily Mary Wright (1888–1974). Cynthia had two sisters; Margaret, born in 1914 and a bank clerk by 1939 (married in 1945 to Leonard Norris), when the family were living in 3 East Pathway, Birmingham, and Beatrice (1916–2002), who married in 1937 and became Mrs Fenwick. Cynthia had left home by that time and may have been at university. Rebecca West (1892–1983), a feminist and a journalist, gave a more detailed description of her in 1950:

> She was 29 and looked six years younger. She had soft dark hair, gentle eyes, a finely cut and very childish mouth, and an exceptionally beautiful creamy complexion. Her fault was that she appeared colourless . . . . she had a low pitched and very lovely voice, and a charm . . . she was infinitely kind and tender and simple and helpless . . . not intellectual but she was shrewd . . . she could survive some catastrophe.

She had been a sergeant in the WAAF during the Second World War and now worked as a shorthand typist, a skilled occupation.[20]

The Kahns liked Hume and often went out together. Thomas Lee Barry, a mutual friend, later stated, 'Kahn and his wife were never very happy. He was a play boy and I believe there were quarrels over money.' Cynthia told Hume that she was unhappy. She later said, 'My first marriage was not working out. As a young girl I was expecting so much more from marriage – a comfortable home, security, the love of a trusted man. My first marriage failed. I thought I would find these things with Donald.' Of Hume, she reported, 'My first impression of Donald was of a happy man. He was so convincing – in his company the world was full of sunshine.' He boasted to her that he was a Battle of Britain fighter pilot, that his dog had been rescued from Germany, a country he had never visited, during the war. The two began to live together. Hume recalled, 'Cynthia wanted the gay life. She was fond of night clubs, parties. I went everywhere with her. But I paid too much attention to her.'[21]

The two were married at Hendon Registry Office on 29 September 1948, though she had been living at 620b Finchley Road since late 1947. The witnesses were her parents and it is interesting to note that on the marriage certificate Hume did not mention his father's name or occupation, though he claimed elsewhere he was not ignorant of him. There are differing accounts about how this short-lived marriage fared. Both come from Cynthia, save for some savage comments from Hume about her alleged infidelity. In January 1950 she painted their relationship in glowing colours, 'When he had money he was the most generous man on earth . . . I have always had a trusting nature . . . . I never dreamed that the man who gave me so much happiness was what he really was.' However, she did not know all there was to know about him, 'He was forever romancing about his exploits as a fighter pilot. His knowledge of planes was incredible', and she assumed he was a 'pilot for an airline company . . . I had no reason to doubt it.' Yet, the two did not see much of one another as Hume was frequently away from his wife due to 'business.' He never spent much time at home except using it as somewhere to sleep.[22]

However, it appears that Cynthia may have seen the other side of Hume's character, although this was only revealed in 1951 when she was in the process of divorcing him. Apparently, 'up to the time of Hume's arrest there is a history of violent outbreaks of temper and other incidents in which he physically assaulted his wife. Serious blows with the fist were inflicted on her at a time when she was just six months pregnant [in early 1949] and just after the birth of the child.' Hume later insinuated that Cynthia had been having an affair with another man or even men. Yet, he was probably not wholly faithful to her as it is said he was seen in the company of other women whilst he was married. It is quite possible that both accounts are true; we know that Hume could be charming and also that he could be violent; the point being that Cynthia only chose to reveal the vicious side of her husband's nature when she needed to.[23] However, Cynthia may have been exaggerating her ex-husband's violence towards her as there was no evidence before 1949 that Hume was a violent man, more a fraudster and a thief, but not physically aggressive.

The Humes paid £5 8s. rent per month to Martin Collins who ran the greengrocers on the ground floor, though he lived elsewhere. Alfred Spencer, a headmaster, and Rosalinde, his wife, lived in flat 620a, on the first floor. Rebecca West described the property's immediate environs:

> It was a duplex flat in a line of houses, with shops underneath, that hugs one angle of a busy cross roads . . . it is the heart of a suburban shopping centre. The intersection is dominated by Golders Green station, and Golders Green Theatre stands besides it. At the end of the line of houses where Hume lived there is a cinema. A tram line links this spot with the further suburbs, many bus routes run through it, it sees more than suburban traffic in the way of automobiles, for this is a short cut between west London and the Great North Road. The shops round about serve a wide district, in which German is heard as often as English, for many refugees from Hitler's Germany have settled here; and perhaps for this reason it keeps later hours than most London suburbs. At all times a policeman on point duty stands 50 yards away.[24]

On 17 July 1949, a daughter, Alison Cynthia Hume, was born in a nursing home in north London. She was delivered by Dr Keith Blatchley, who was also a police surgeon, and who later visited the newborn. Tragically, Cynthia was carrying twins and Amanda did not survive.[25]

Flying continued to interest Hume. Describing himself as a director, he began taking flying lessons and on 31 March 1949 obtained his Royal Aero Club aviator certificate whilst learning at Elstree aerodrome, Hertfordshire, only a few miles north of his home. Although it had been used by the RAF during the war, it was released for civil operation in 1946, and was often used by aero clubs and private pilots using single- and twin-engine planes. In October 1949 he stated:

> About nine months ago I joined the United Service Flying Club. Elstree Aerodrome. My reason for doing so was to become an efficient pilot. My instructor at Elstree was Mr Keats. He trained me and eventually I was able to fly solo. I have only had one hour's instruction in map-reading. In fact if I was flying in bad visibility I would have difficulty in finding my bearings.[26]

Yet, Hume had a fascination with flight which bordered on fantasy, as he decorated his flat, as this statement made in 1949 shows:

> There is little doubt that Hume is very imaginative and likes to create an impression on people. His flat is decorated with several alleged RAF war trophies and photographs and caricatures of himself as a flying officer and racing motorist and he has even deceived his own wife in the belief that he was a pilot with an adventurous career during the late war.[27]

One wonders if Hume had read the short story by American humourist James Thurber, *The Secret Life of Walter Mitty*, which was made into a film in 1947 starring Danny Kaye and Virginia Mayo. The story concerns a very ordinary man who has daydreams about being a hero, including being a heroic RAF pilot during the Second World War. Unlike the story's hero, who keeps his daydream fantasies to himself, Hume tried to pretend to others that they were real.

Hume alleged in 1950 that he had been involved in smuggling and was known as 'the flying smuggler.' He had traded, so he said, in all forms of illegal commodities from aircraft to refugees. There is no evidence that he had done so except for his own word in a newspaper article in 1950, though previous writers relay this as undoubted fact. Having said that, there was never any investigation into this and no one would be likely to come forward voluntarily to admit their own part in the smuggling. Furthermore, did Hume have the necessary experience and ability? He can only have been involved in such from

April to September 1949. Fellow flyers doubted his flying skills and he himself admitted he had little navigational ability and could not fly in the dark.[28]

If we believe his story, he was engaged in flying over pound notes into Eire and flying a man from Britain to France without the need to trouble the immigration or passport authorities. Although he usually made £250 per trip, he made £400 on his greatest alleged coup. That was when he was contacted by a Frenchman in Mayfair, asking him if he could help in his scheme. Hume said yes and he found an engineer and an experienced pilot to help out. They met another conspirator in Paris, an American colonel with access to an American airbase near Munich. They took four American military planes to Palestine via France, Italy and Yugoslavia. Hume was the wireless operator.[29]

Hume was also apparently involved in shipping out aircraft to Indonesia and tried to sell aircraft to Pakistan, albeit unsuccessfully in the latter case. He also helped smuggle arms to Singapore. He supplied mustard gas bombs to Israel. Hume wrote, 'People approached me to get certain things, and to do certain things, and I obliged because that was my way of earning a living.' He disliked being termed a racketeer. In all he made thousands of pounds through these deals cumulatively and being known as being a useful man.[30] Yet, there is no evidence that he did any of this, though, as with many of Hume's stories, it is not impossible as he did possess a pilot's licence, but as he admitted and others confirmed, he lacked certain aviation skills. It is possible that all this is as much part of his fantasy life as was being an RAF hero.[31] Certainly, smuggling was a growth industry at this time of high taxes, shortages and rationing.

Hume was making a good income for himself and Cynthia, for in the first nine months of 1949 about £2,400 went into his bank account – and most left it, too. Whether this was due to his black-market dealings at home or abroad is unknown.[32]

Politically speaking, Hume began to flirt with Sir Oswald Mosley's Union Movement, a far right organisation which believed in a united states of Europe and the repatriation of black immigrants. Yet, as with his involvement in the Communist Party a decade before, this was probably not out of any deep political motivation and may have been because both organisations advocated violence. He read the *Daily Telegraph* – as did two notorious killers of this era, Heath and Haigh.[33] This suggests a degree of intelligence, too.

Hume also took time off; in June 1949 he was staying at a hotel in Torquay, driving down in his American car. He took part in a mile-long carnival procession, wearing a red and gold braid uniform, with the carnival chairman Mr Chapman and the carnival Queen Miss Dorothy Hartington and her two attendants. It all happened because Chapman saw Hume's car outside the hotel. Locating the owner, he later recalled:

> I asked him if we might borrow it for the carnival. He readily agreed, but made a condition that the car must not be decorated. Naturally the vehicle was pulled about quite a bit by the huge carnival crowds, but I must say that he was very good natured about it all. The carnival queen and her attendants liked him very much. He used to tell us about his experiences as a pilot. He had a striking Canadian accent.[34]

Hume's business began to have some difficulties from October 1947 and he filed for bankruptcy in the following month, with debts of £4,647 12s. 10d. and assets of £1,413 15s. 8d. He had already started up another business elsewhere. This was the Little Atom Electrical Products Ltd, located at Castle Factory, Market Street, Hay in Herefordshire, registered on 8 September 1947. It manufactured small plastic and Bakelite articles, accessories for electric light appliances. Initially, he said that it would employ 100 people, but at most only 6 worked there. Hume briefly lived in a hotel in Hay, and then in a flat on the firm's premises. Yet, his visits were 'always of a very brief character, rarely more than a day in duration', though he arrived in a luxurious American touring car. He knew few people in the town. In January 1948 this business was in difficulty, too, with arrears to the extent of £1,167. He was pressed for the money by his creditors and managed to pay off £500 by 16 March 1948. He had to sell parts of his plant to meet the payments and was taken to court in October. The company was finally wound up on 20 July 1949, but there were still further demands for payment on various outstanding invoices for Johnson Matthey and Company (London) for bi-metal strips supplied, and these occurred up until October 1949 and Hume was desperately looking for money to stave off his creditors. Hume said that his premises in Hay had burnt down and so payment was difficult.[35]

There had been two fires at the factory. The first had been found at 6 in the evening on 21 May 1948 by Hume and his works foreman. Apparently, Hume, in his RAF uniform, 'was conspicuous for the manner in which he helped to fight the fire.' It had apparently been caused by the fusing of electrical wires and cost £4,267 1s. 11d. in damage. The Sun Insurance Company paid up on 10 July. On the evening of 17 January 1949 the caretaker's wife noticed a fire which had begun with faulty wiring between the works' ceiling and the floor of the caretaker's flat. Although this time the insurance company was not happy about this apparent accident, they could not prove any wrongdoing and so on 9 March paid £4,711 16s. 6d.[36]

Writing in 1958, Hume blamed his business failure on his wife, whom he had hated from about 1950, 'I paid too much attention to her and not enough to my business. Soon it began to slip. I wasn't getting the orders, and the boodle I had made was going up in smoke.' He returned to the shady side of business, 'So I returned to London once more and became a super spiv.'[37]

Post-war London – indeed Britain – was not a wholly happy land. Despite victory in war, the aftermath comprised a period of heavy taxation, especially on goods deemed 'luxuries', shortages, rationing of petrol, food and clothing, queues, housing shortages, a worse state of affairs than had existed during the war itself. For many the outlook was grim and gloomy. All these were imposed by the new Labour government which needed to raise money to pay for the war and for an increasingly interventionist domestic policy. All this was at a time when the Metropolitan Police's numbers were well below those needed to combat an increasing black market which had developed as criminals sought to profit by selling highly priced goods to consumers who could not have them by other ways. Opportunities existed, therefore, for those who wanted to make money quickly and did not possess any moral scruples about the means to secure such ends. These criminals were known as spivs.

Hume had already had a few scrapes with the law following his conviction in 1942. In October 1944, a customer arrived after closing time and Hume sold him a second-hand American wireless set called a Westinghouse Midget for £12 5s. The customer later complained to the Board of Trade that the price was excessive and that the device was faulty. PC Monkton arrested Hume on the morning of 25 April 1945. Hume appeared before Hendon Magistrates' Court on 14 May 1945, but the case was thrown out because of insufficient evidence.[38]

On 13 June 1947, Hume sold an Atlanta saloon car to Brooklands, motor car dealers, of 103 Bond Street for £1,250. He did not, however, tell them that the car was not his to sell and that he still had outstanding hire-purchase debts on the car. Yet, it was not until 4 June 1948 that he was arrested, by one DC Tebell on Saville Row. He was charged at the Marlborough Street Magistrates' Court on 30 July, but the prosecution was withdrawn because Hume scraped together the money to pay the firm. He was also suspected of breaking the currency regulations, presumably by taking more than £25 abroad.[39]

He also became involved with a firm of car dealers on Warren Street, north London. He stated in October 1949 that:

> About three years ago I bought an Allard car. It was new when
> I bought it and after I had had it about four months, I sold it to

two traders in partnership in Warren Street whose names are, Mr Mansfield and Mr Roy Salvadori. These men, I believe, saw the car in Saunders Garage in Golders Green. He, Mr Salvadori, paid me £1,200 for the Allard motor car in £5 notes. There was trouble about me selling the car whilst it was under covenant. There was no civil action taken against me in respect of this deal.

About seven months ago I had another motor car, a 1940 Cadillac, which I also sold to Mr Salvadori for £700. He paid me in cash. I had purchased this car under the Hire Purchase System and still owed the Hire Purchase Company about £250. Salvadori deducted this amount and as far as I am aware settled with the H.P. Company. During these transactions I visited Salvadori's Offices in Warren Street on several occasions.[40]

The expanding black market opened up possibilities for Hume, who certainly needed money, and this was becoming increasingly problematic. In August 1949 he had to sell his dark-red Cadillac to William John Mansfield, a director of Mansfield Autos, a car dealer of Fitzroy Road, London, for £775 less outstanding hire-purchase payments. Martin Collins commented about this period from November 1949, 'Round two months ago he started to spend more time at home and since then has always appeared nervous as if he was avoiding somebody.' Collins added that until July 1949 Hume had always paid rent by cheque, but in August and September paid in one pound notes. Occasionally he had been a late payer and had needed reminding.[41]

On 27 September 1949 he was £78 5s. overdrawn at the bank (he only had an overdraft facility for £70). The bank stopped honouring his cheques between 24 and 30 September. He asked Mansfield, on 30 September, for 18s. 6d. apparently so that he could complete his football pools postal order; Mansfield refused. Roy Francesco Salvadori, Mansfield's co-director, was also asked and he said no too. He also claimed to be able to sell the latter two vans. Hume also owed his hairdresser £9, his newsagent £5 4s. 3d. and businesses who had supplied his now defunct firm wanted over £800 from him. Although in the first eight months of the year he had put over £2,000 in his bank account, his income was drying up for from 11 August to 4 October and he had deposited a mere £24 5s. 2d. Some assets were pawned; on 26 September he obtained £4 from John Long Ltd of 51 Kilburn High Road for a suit; five days later the same business gave him £6 for a three-stone ring. Clearly, Hume was seen by all as being in need of ready cash and as a very poor credit risk. The Humes, who had previously enjoyed a good income and the spending habits which went with it, were now forced to adjust to having a minimal income and this cannot have been easy for them, especially with a baby and Mrs Hume being unable to work.[42]

Hume was not wholly destitute, but clearly had very little spare cash. What he had was spent on outstanding bills. On 3 October Dr Blatchley called at the flat and was paid his fee; £30 in 5 pound notes. The police later thought that he must have borrowed this money from someone, but this mystery lender was never identified.[43] He did have an alternative and illegal source of income, yet one which contained within it the germs of great peril and we will learn more about this in the next chapter.

Chapter 3

Enter Stanley Setty

Stanley Setty was to play an important part in Hume's life. As with Bessie Hume and Cynthia Hume, he is a figure shrouded in mystery, but at least he made a greater impression on contemporary records than they did, though this is scarcely to his credit. Had Hume and Setty never met it is highly probable that Hume would have continued his relatively obscure life and would never have come to the attention of criminologists.

Setty was born in Baghdad, then part of the decaying Ottoman Empire, on 3 October 1903, under the name Salman Salih. He had dark-brown hair and brown eyes. His father was Saleh Salih (possibly born in 1872) and his mother (possibly stepmother) was Khtoun Shashoua, later anglicised to Katie (1881–1935). At birth he had one brother; David (1894–1961). The family was quickly added to with Max (1908–65) and a sister, Eva. It is not known why the family moved from their home country. Perhaps, being Jewish, they had suffered anti-Semitism and perhaps they thought that there might be better opportunities for them both socially and commercially in England. It is not known when they arrived in England, but as his second brother, Max, was born in Baghdad on 4 March 1908 and his third brother, Jack Setty (1910–83), was born in Chorlton, Lancashire in 1910, they probably arrived in Britain in about 1909. Initially, the family lived at 8 Oak Road, Manchester, but they do not appear on the 1911 census, probably because they, or at least some members, were in Canada or the USA at the time.[1]

The family later returned to Manchester, then the English city with the largest concentration of Jews after London and Leeds. His father ran a business at 47 Mosley Street, S. Setty and Co., merchants, in 1913 and 1914 (they seem to have anglicised their names quickly). In 1920 the business resurfaces, on Quay Street, Deansgate, and Setty senior is described as being a grey cloth merchant. Setty's schooling may have been minimal and certainly by the age of 15 he was working for his father in the cloth trade (the minimum school leaving age was then 14). He continued working in the family buisness until 1920, when his father deserted his mother and went abroad, never to return (it seems Setty probably saw his father again as he went on Continental holidays). Setty had attended junior school in Ramsgate and then briefly attended the Manchester Jewish School on Cavendish Road, Manchester (5–29 October 1915). He was then living with his mother at Whittington Road. In June 1920 Stanley and David Setty went into partnership and are listed as shipping merchants of 11 St Mary's Buildings, Quay Street, Deansgate, but were at 24 Brazenose Street in the following year. They were termed textile agents and exporters. At this time Setty was living at 23 Queen's Road, Didsbury, a well-known Jewish quarter of the city. He travelled to New York and back in 1921, and described himself as a shipper, so presumably this trip was for business.[2]

However the Setty Brothers business, which began with a capital of £1,800, ran into difficulties and in early 1922 went bankrupt. They had £14,719 of debts but only £5 worth of assets. At this time his elder brother was in the USA. As Setty was still deemed, legally, 'an infant', the bankruptcy sentence did not apply to him.[3]

Setty was soon in business again, travelling across the Atlantic in 1922 and 1923, described as a shipper and, later, as a merchant. In 1922 he lived at 77 Oxford Street in Manchester, and was at 31 Sandeleigh Crescent, Withington in Manchester in 1923. He started out on his own, selling goods on commission and by 1926 had saved between £300 and £400 and so had a small capital sum to help him on more ambitious ventures. In 1926 he found an office address in a Manchester packing house, and though nothing was ever packed there, it did give his clients false confidence in him. In 1927 and 1928 his business premises were at 44 Princess Street, whilst he resided with his mother at 17 Circular Road.[4]

It seems he dealt in cloth, as his father had, and there is a reference to him buying and selling poplin, crepe-de-chine and warp satin. He sold goods at a loss; of 30 per cent, 15 per cent, 13 per cent, 19 per cent and 25 per cent. In 1926–7 he made about 200 deliveries.[5]

Business was bad, but became worse and he found he could not sell the items he had at any price. Setty was now (April 1927) buying goods for future delivery, but he could not sell them and so used them to advance money upon. When he could not pay the men he bought from they took the goods back. He could only obtain goods because he had dealt with the same suppliers previously and so had retained some sellers' confidence. In order to recoup his losses, he gambled on dog racing in April 1927, but was unlucky and had lost £2,000 by June of that year.[6]

With mounting debts (£7,263), Setty left the country in December 1927, by which time his tenancy of his business premises had been terminated and he had been termed 'a useless tenant', with £180 from the sale of goods. He went to Milan to see his father, before visiting relatives in Paris. On both occasions he did so in part because he wanted to raise money. In this he was unsuccessful. He then returned to England in March 1928, and to Manchester, then presented himself to the authorities and petitioned for bankruptcy.[7]

Disaster struck again. At the Manchester Bankruptcy Court on 27 April 1928, Setty faced numerous charges. He owed £7,267 to creditors and had £2,000 betting losses. He had kept no books of account and there were no copies of invoices to his customers. The Senior Official Receiver, Mr F. Murgatroyd, and the Solicitor for the Trustees, Mr Chapman, questioned him closely on this point but he had no satisfactory answers. The only invoice book that could be found was far from adequate, for both the original invoice pages and the duplicates which should have recorded the transactions had been torn out. Setty could only state that he had passed both to the customers. As the Official Receiver said, the fixed leaves should have been retained.[8]

Setty declared that to describe himself as a shipper was not misleading, even though he had not done any shipping, but that he had meant to do so and had sold goods to men who were shippers. Chapman showed him a list of transactions he had made, to the total value of £23,659, buying goods at set prices (presumably on credit) and then selling them on the day of purchase at lower prices, thus generating income but incurring an overall loss. Setty admitted that he might have done this several times. Only eight of his purchases had resulted in a profit, but most had not. Setty did not accept this. The examination was temporarily closed.[9]

On 9 May Setty was before the Manchester City Magistrates' Court, having been arrested by Detective Inspector Haughton. Setty remarked, 'I don't wish to reply until I have seen my solicitor.' Magistrate Percy Macbeth (1878–1938), representing the Department of the Public Prosecutor, told the court that the case was a very complicated one and would need a great deal of inquiry. The charge was currently that Setty had obtained cloth goods on credit for £160 from Messrs Burgess, Leeward and Co. Mr Barrow Scree, defending, said that Setty had returned from Italy for the purpose of attending the legal proceedings against him. He was remanded for eight days and bailed for two sureties with £100 each.[10]

The next hearing was on 13 June at the same court. Macbeth told Setty there were twelve charges against him, under both the Bankruptcy Act of 1914 and under fraud legislation. Patrick Redmond Barry represented Setty. Then, on 21 June, he was in court again, when John Wellesley-Orr (1878–1956) was the stipendiary magistrate. He was charged under the Debtors and Bankruptcy Acts. Setty pleaded guilty and was told he would be bailed on the same conditions as before to appear at the next Manchester Quarter Sessions.[11]

The final hearing was on 1 August at the Court of Manchester Quarter Sessions before Sir Walter Greaves Lord (1878–1942), Recorder of Manchester since 1925. He stated that there were twelve counts of obtaining credit through fraud, nine counts of disposing of property obtained on credit and not paid for, one count of leaving the country when he owned property legally to be divided with creditors and he had also increased his insolvency by gambling. Setty, described as 'a native of Iraq', pleaded guilty.[12]

Macbeth was prosecuting. He recounted Setty's unfortunate business history, which has already been detailed here. Apparently Setty alleged that he had had to sell at a loss due to falling prices, but this was a lie because price fluctuations were then very minimal. Setty could only name one of the bookmakers he had dealt with when gambling. A Mr Jackson did his best to defend Setty. He argued that Setty was very young and was under baleful influences. With his father having deserted the family there had been no strong parental control of the boy. He did not have the mentality to deal with large sums of money and should have been an employee not a master. And he had returned to England of his own free will, 'There was no question of his being arrested. The whole of this prosecution is built up on his own statement made before Receiver.'[13]

Lord said he would take into account the undesirable influences on Setty but he could not accept his mentality as an excuse. A man of his nationality and training, he stated, matured quickly and knew just as much about business as an older man. If it were not for his poor upbringing he would sentence him to penal servitude (i.e. prison with hard labour). For the first twelve offences against the Debtors' Act, he gave Setty twelve months in the second division; for disposing of goods, another six months. These sentences would run concurrently. He added another six months for Setty having left England owing money. The sentence was thus eighteen months in prison. Once the verdict was given, Katie Setty shouted, 'Oh my poor innocent boy. Take me with him.' Struggling and screaming, she was led from the court by four police officers. Once in prison he had his fingerprints taken and these were sent to the Criminal Records Office in London. They were to have a future importance which could not then have been foreseen.[14]

Setty was admitted to Manchester prison on 8 August 1928, number 7327, and was discharged on 31 October 1929. Nothing is known of Setty's residence in prison, though clearly he behaved himself for he was released four months before the end of the term to which he had been sentenced. Afterwards, Setty became an employee; as an undischarged bankrupt he was no longer legally able to start up in business. He worked for his uncle, Benjamin Jack Shashoua, in the textile business and then (the latter left for Paris due to trouble with his mother-in-law – and because he was deported) went to London, a great place for anyone wishing to be anonymous, and worked in the car business. From 1934 he worked in Great Portland Street, presumably buying and selling, probably for another party. Quite possibly this was in the car trade, which his brother Max was working in from 1935 (Albermarle Motors, operating from Queen Anne's Mews). Apparently he earned between £2 10s. and £3 per week. If he was living with Max at this time, as he was in 1939, then the two led a peripatetic existence staying at over a dozen addresses in west and north west London and Lewisham in a decade.[15]

Setty appeared before the Manchester Central Court again, on 3 October 1938, this time as an applicant to have his bankruptcy conviction discharged. He was before Judge Thomas Bowes Leigh (1867–1947), judge of the court since 1925. The Official Receiver, Mr F.H. Langmaid, recited Setty's former misdemeanours. Setty pleaded that he wanted a discharge in order to clear his name and to get on in business. He did not want to start up a new company immediately on his own account, but might well wish to do so in a few years time. James Worden Stansfield (1906–91), a barrister, spoke on his behalf, arguing that Setty had been very young when convicted ten years ago and had been under bad influences. He only wanted the stigma of bankruptcy to be lifted from him. The judge acknowledged the stigma and the inability to begin again in business, and that these must be painful for Setty. But, he thought that the bankruptcy status should stand because Setty being in business might not be beneficial to the business community and so it was a wise precaution not to discharge him. His brother, David, was only discharged from the bankruptcy notice served on him in 1922 after thirty-seven years.[16]

Max, however, was doing well for himself, unlike his older brother. His car business now dealt with repairs, hiring cars out and buying and selling second-hand cars. In 1939 he was described as a garage proprietor and lived at 5 Queen Anne's Mews in Marylebone, north-west London. Setty, described as a motor car salesman, lived with him. Max, however, had numerous motoring offences (driving without a licence or insurance, speeding and so forth) to his name and as he did not keep accounts or register returns was often in trouble with the law.[17]

It is not known what Setty did during the Second World War. However, judging by what his brother Max did and how his firm was employed, we can hazard a good guess. As a Turkish citizen he was not eligible to be conscripted in the armed services and so seems to have avoided active service. The firm, with its numerous hire cars was employed in evacuating Londoners, in helping with transporting people regarding D-Day in 1944 and providing cars for ENSA (Every Night Something Amusing) and BBC performances, and all at pre-war prices. Max married in 1941 and it is possible that the two brothers may then have begun to live apart.[18]

At some point Setty went into the car business independently, at least by 1947, and operated in both Warren Street, just south of the Euston Road in central London, and had garages at 11 Cambridge Terrace Mews (telephone Walbeck 7111), just north of the said thoroughfare. His brother, with his motor car business, a night club and a shop, was, however, doing rather better. There was no office or showroom at Warren Street; he operated from Pietro Martinelli's cafe on the corner of Fitzroy Street and Warren Street (the proprietor's son later recalled Setty as being 'a delightful, caring, generous human being' whom he served tea and coffee), and it was known he could be contacted there, either in person or by telephone (Euston 3857 or 7126). He operated on a strictly cash or cheques only basis. No records were kept, but he banked at the Westminster branch in Mornington Crescent and Barclays in Edgware Road. Personally he drove a cream Citroën, registration CJN 444, and also owned a Standard Vanguard KX 1146. Setty employed Isadore Rosenthal (who had known him for ten years) and Bert Wright (described as a 'mental case' who often required hospital treatment) to purchase cars for him, though Rosenthal also acted as a salesman. These were more or less casual employees. Charles Fryer was the only 'permanent' member of staff, and was employed at Setty's garage from September 1949, although he had worked for him in previous years. He was presumably successful in business, because apparently between 1947 and 1949 he cashed about £30,000 worth of cheques and sometimes would buy ten cars a day at £1,000 each. It was believed he had £20,000 in reserve.[19]

Setty sometimes went abroad, but only about once a year. In the summer of 1949 he had had an encounter with two youths in Warren Street. They claimed he had bought a car which belonged to them and he called them 'spivs.' He then declared, 'Well, I've just bought it. What do you want me to do?' Then one of them threatened him, 'We'll get you for this' before walking away. However, when he met them on a subsequent occasion, all three seemed to be on friendly terms.[20]

He was described in 1949 thus, 'aged 46, five feet seven inches, dark complexion, dark thin hair, dark eyes, round face, large nose, well built. There is a scar on his cheek. He is dressed in a blue suit and brown shoes.'[21]

Setty met one Connie Palfreyman (1920–2003), living at Inverness Terrace, Camden, in May 1946. Initially this was a casual encounter but by the following year they saw one another at least twice a week. She was employed as a clerk at the British Oil and Turpentine Company at 282 Earls Court Road, and possibly met Setty because the firm supplied goods to the car industry. Connie had a criminal record, with three previous convictions for larceny and receiving stolen goods. The two were on good terms and often went to the theatre or cinema and had supper at restaurants such as Folman's in Noel Street or the Paramount Inn, St Martin's Street. They were allegedly planning to marry but Setty's friends and family were unaware of this.[22]

In 1947 Setty resided at Dalmeny Court in Jermyn Street and a year later began to live in a furnished flat at 53 Maitland Court (overlooking Hyde Park, a 1939 block of flats, some costing £550 to rent per year), Lancaster Terrace, near Paddington station. His new brother-in-law, Ali Armin Ouri, and his sister, Eva, who were currently childless, had been renting this property for the past few weeks. It was an expensive flat, with cream furniture, burgundy carpets and Persian rugs. Ouri, who owned assets in Palestine, was unable to work in Britain and so they shared expenses. It was a convenient arrangement and relations were amicable between them. He often brought Connie back to the flat for dinner. She thought that Setty had mixed feelings about the arrangement he had with the Ouris, though he got on well with them: 'Since their arrival; Setty has been very worried about them as he felt that they were a drain on his finances and for this reason as well he did not want to take on further liabilities by getting married.'[23]

Setty's family thought well of him, at least in public. They described him as a man of regular habits, leaving home at 9.30 am each day and returning by 7. He often spent his Sundays and some evenings at home. When he went out, it was to the dog-racing stadium at White City, where he could be found most Thursdays and Fridays. He also went with friends to horse-racing meets on Saturdays. He once won £60 there, but was not a heavy better. Connie said, 'He hated going to clubs . . . liked a quiet life' and though she liked dancing, he never did. He regularly met a couple of friends at the Goat pub near Warren Street for a brandy and a cigar after work. Rosenthal described his employer thus, 'a steady man who usually lets his family know his movements.' Sometimes he went abroad to see his Uncle Benjamin at the latter's Monte Carlo villa. He was in good health, but occasionally had flu. His sister said, 'He is of the worrying type, and is always ready to help anyone.' Sometimes he would be in debt, to the tune of £200–300, but always settled these. He may have envisaged a change of career, for he once told Connie, 'there appeared to be no future in it and was not doing very much business.'[24]

Those who knew him spoke well of him. Aaron Ellison, director of a wholesale fruit and vegetable firm on Warren Street, referred to him as 'the unofficial banker of Warren Street' and he often asked Setty to cash cheques. He thought that Setty regularly carried large sums of money about with him, £100 in Scottish notes, eighty £5 notes and several £1 notes. Max said, 'My brother was too generous. He was always willing to help a lame dog.' Bert Wright said, 'He was a straight man, better than a lot of the people one meets. He helped me out when I was in hospital, looked after my customers. And he would do the same for any of his friends.'[25]

Not all agreed with these generous assessments. Duncan Webb was virulently hostile towards him. Although he had the appearance as 'Honest Stan', who would help anyone, who was abstemious, meek and moderate, Webb described Setty in unflattering terms, 'an inscrutable moneylender, the life of a gambler, the life of a hard headed financier who exacted his pound of flesh at all costs.' Apparently he dealt directly with Jewish terrorists; according to his brother-in-law, he was part of a Jewish organisation during the Arab-Israeli War and involved in the sale of aircraft to Israel. He was alleged to have double-crossed some of the smugglers and had one of them killed and dumped in the Channel. He had several girlfriends, one a waitress at Southend and another who lived in Leigh-on-Sea. Apparently, 'He liked liquor and drank it. He was fond of women and used them and abused them. He took money under false pretences. He lent money and got it back. He sold motor cars at extortionate profits. He dodged income tax. He dodged military service. He lied and deceived his way through life.'[26] One newspaper report alleged he was friendly with a blonde woman in Southend, a former bus conductress who was now a hairdresser's model.[27]

Setty was a pivotal figure in Hume's life, but their relationship was not known to Setty's family and friends and they were only business acquaintances for most of 1947–9. This suggests that Hume was but one of many men who Setty dealt with. According to Hume, and we have no other source, he met Setty in Warren Street in December 1947. Hume had initially approached Mansfield, wanting to sell him a Pontiac car, but this was rejected. Seeing Setty outside in the street, Mansfield introduced the two men. Hume later recalled:

> I was introduced to a car dealer who seemed to be a man of mystery. I caught my first sight of him standing outside a café (probably Martinelli's at 47 Fitzroy Street) in Warren Street, a drab street with a medley of shining second hand cars of all makes parked in a line. This man was big boned, fourteen stone, with dark eyes, swarthy, foreign looking and aged about 42. I was told that his name was Setty, and that he had changed it from Sulman Seti when he came

from Baghdad years ago. We haggled over a car. He had a voice like broken bottles, and pockets stuffed with cash.

Mansfield later stated that Hume and Setty set off in a car, presumably the Pontiac, which Setty eventually bought. Hume bought a Lanchester car from Setty at a later date.[28]

It is worth considering Warren Street for a moment. It is a street just south of Warren Street Tube station and in part runs parallel with the much larger Euston Road, which is to its north. In 1949 there were at least nine car dealers and five car agents operating officially on that little road, but it was estimated that there were far more. Webb gave a lurid assessment of the business which went on there and those who were involved in it: 'a veritable warren of crooks, spivs, wasters waiting for the fool to turn up to part with his money easily. It is a warren of cafes, motor-car garages and sales rooms, strange places inhabited by strange people speaking in strange tongues.'[29]

However, journalists from the *Picture Post* in 1949 came away with a rather more complex view. The car market had been established in the street since about 1912 when Friswell's show room for second-hand cars on Euston Road was moved away due to the heavy volume of road traffic. It was one of the oldest second-hand car markets in the country. Cars arrived at the street, some were bought by dealers, cleaned up and then sold. Much business was done in the pubs and cafes of the street. The journalist noted, 'Like most streets, there are two sides to Warren Street . . . but in this case the sunnyside and the shady side refer to human behaviour not the position of the sun.' On one hand, at a time when cars were expensive and scarce, and in a neighbourhood bordering Soho, the street 'attracts a fair amount of gutter garbage from the hinterland' where touts would offer a low price to unsuspecting punters and pocket the difference that the former would receive from a dealer. On the other hand, there were firms who had operated there for decades and who kept proper accounts and had income-tax receipts; one even had a certificate from Scotland Yard thanking them for assistance in locating car thieves.[30]

Setty did not encounter Hume again until June 1948 when they were seen together at the Cambridge Terrace Mews garage. They then met again in the summer of 1949 when Hume's finances were low. Hume recalled: 'On the creep for a shady deal, I drifted into the Hollywood Club, near Marble Arch. Propped up against the bar was the sinister, bear-like figure of the unofficial banker of Warren Street – Stanley Setty. I was struck by his dazzling tie and flamboyance generally.'

They had a guarded conversation, sizing each other up. Setty took some cash from his pocket and said to Hume, 'Have a drink.' Setty told him that he was part of a syndicate who supplied war surplus to the Iraqi army. Hume was not in the same class, but sold him a gross (144) of American nylons at £1 per pair. The two arranged to meet again.[31]

Two weeks later, they met at Setty's garage on Cambridge Terrace Mews, where Setty sold Hume forged petrol coupons at 2s. 6d each. The deal made Hume £40 after he sold them on. Later Hume introduced his wife to Setty in a club (or so Hume said; in 1959 she denied ever meeting him). He recalled, 'He appeared most impressed with her.' The two men discussed business, too. Setty asked Hume to buy wrecked cars so they could be resprayed and sold again, and to take the cars' log books. Apparently, Hume stole six cars for Setty, including two Jaguars and received £300 each for them. Hume later stated, 'Soon Setty was meeting Cynthia and me socially. He often came home with me for a chat.'[32]

Yet, Hume was beginning to hate Setty for two reasons. Firstly, in August 1949 Hume and his dog Tony were at Setty's garage. Hume recounted what happened: 'I quite liked Setty until that afternoon. But he kicked Tony, who had climbed into a car and scratched the paint work. Tony yelped with pain. It was the worst thing Setty could have done. For Tony meant more to me than did my wife, or even our baby daughter.' How long this anger festered within Hume is uncertain. That was not all that annoyed Hume about Setty: 'I heard stories that he had claimed he was having secret meetings with my wife. I heard Setty had taken my wife out drinking a couple of times in the afternoon. I was fast getting the needle with Setty.'

As with much of what Hume said, there is no confirmation of any of this, and his wife flatly denied any association with Setty; her daily routine centred around home and baby Alison. However, Hume was building up resentment against Setty on these two grounds, yet he initially avoided any open confrontation with Setty, who had no idea Hume harboured such hatred towards him.[33]

Leonard Baker recalled seeing Setty and Hume together in Warren Street at this time, dealing with cars, and on one occasion Hume walked in on a deal between Baker and Setty and the latter said to Hume, 'I'll see you later.' Hume went with Setty thereafter.[34]

On 1 October Setty had been at the White City stadium, betting on the dog races and met his 39-year-old cousin, Jack Samuel Shashoua, whose father had once employed Setty in the textile trade. On 3 October (his 46th birthday), Setty and Connie went to see *The Third Visitor* (a play by Gerald Anstruther about a detective investigating a murder and then discovering that the man he thought was the victim was not dead at all) at the Duke of York's Theatre, after having supper at her house at 5.45 pm. They returned to her house afterwards and he left at 10. He told her, 'I may not be able to see you tomorrow evening as I have to go to Watford to see/sell a car. You go down to Eva's and I will see you later.' Others knew of this plan, apparently the car in question was a 3½-litre Jaguar. She recalled that occasionally he did business in the evenings and that two or three months earlier he had been to Watford to sell a Bentley to a farmer there. It was to be the last time that they ever saw one another. Setty clearly had no premonition of his imminent fate, for he was planning to go to Paris for a holiday.[35]

Chapter 4

Exit Stanley Setty

The 4 October 1949, a Tuesday, was the day after Setty's 46th birthday and it was to be his last. That morning, though, no one had any reason to believe that it would be anything out of the ordinary. He left home as usual, wearing a blue double-breasted pinstripe suit, made a year ago by Levine Brothers, a blue silk tie, Egyptian made brogues, a gold Swiss-made wrist watch and carried an Everhip fountain pen. The very epitome of the well-heeled businessman. At 9.30 am he was at his garages at Cambridge Terrace Mews.[1]

Setty was busy with monetary transactions that day, though he left the physical work to his underlings. At lunch time he ate a melon in a cafe. At midday he asked Fryer to cash a cheque for £450 at the Westminster Bank branch at Mornington Crescent. He did so and on his return to Warren Street, he gave £400 to the secretary employed by Setty's brother and the remaining £50 to Setty himself. It was now a quarter to 2.[2]

Setty then asked Rosenthal, 'Will you do something for me?' He agreed and then went with Laurence Lewis, a car dealer, at about 2.30 pm, to a branch of the Penny Yorkshire Bank on 97/99 Cheapside in the City of London. Lewis was buying a car – a Wolseley 12 saloon – from Setty and had a cheque for £1,005 cashed and received 201 mostly new £5 notes from Stanley Layton, a cashier; the money was numbered M41 039801–040000. Lewis gave the cash to Rosenthal. The latter then returned to Warren Street just after 3 and found Setty in his favourite cafe and handed over the money to him. Two lads, Eddie Noble and Eddie Ellison, saw the money change hands and they cried out to Setty, 'We'll be the bodyguard' in jest. Setty gave Rosenthal a £5 note. The latter chatted with Setty about meeting a man in Rushton Street, Islington and arranging that he should go there about a van the next morning.[3]

At 3.30 pm Setty rang Connie at her place of work, which was an unprecedented action to her knowledge.

> 'Don't get alarmed', he told her.
> 'What is it?'
> 'I have to go to Watford before six.'
> 'You won't be at Watford all night; I will see you when you get back.'

'If there's time I will ring you when I get back and if not will see you tomorrow at the same time.'[4]

Setty went to and from Warren Street several times that day (having run up 15 miles on the meter prior to 4.10 pm). At about 5 he was at the garage. Setty and Fryer talked to a potential customer, a man in his thirties, 5ft 8in tall with dark hair and a foreign accent. Fryer recalled, 'The man's behaviour was somewhat unusual as he did not know exactly what sort of car he wanted.' Setty was also negotiating a Jaguar sale that day, but Fryer knew no more. Just after 5 he called around to see his sister, who was at David Setty's house on Osnaburgh Street. She said to him, 'I have prepared dinner and perhaps you would like to come early and discuss it with David.' The 'it' referred to was a business discussion that Setty said he wanted to have with his brother. He replied, with a similar, but less exact answer, that he had given to Connie, 'I have to see some man tonight. I won't be in. Leave it for later.'[5]

At about 5.15 pm Setty was in Warren Street, where one Harry Edwin Hey, who worked for Mansfield, asked if he could garage a car with Setty, who agreed. The two went to the garage and left soon after, returning to Warren Street at about 5.30 pm. Setty gave both him and Fryer a lift from Cambridge Mews to the Fitzroy cafe in his Citroën. Ellison asked Setty that evening if he could give cash for an £80 cheque but, oddly enough, Setty said no, he had no money on his person, but could give it to him the next day. It is not obvious why Setty refused this request for money; perhaps he thought that he needed all his cash for a rather bigger transaction later that day. Setty did not stay long.[6]

He was last seen in his Citroën travelling near Osnaburgh Street towards the Euston Road. The time was 5.50 pm. Jack Samuel Shashoua told the police in a statement that he saw him on Great Portland Road South. He was travelling with one John Cheshire, alias Captain Leslie St Clair McKay, a man with a criminal record. Jack later said that Setty 'appeared to be very serious and was looking straight ahead of him.' He described Setty's passenger as 'The other man was aged between 45 and 55 years. He looked older than Setty. I had the impression that he had black hair and possibly a black moustache. He was wearing a trilby hat, the colour of which I forget.'[7] It is not known if Cheshire had anything to do with Setty's subsequent disappearance, but despite an intensive search by the police he was never located. His record suggests he would not voluntarily have come forward to make a statement. He may well have been one of several petty villains that Setty dealt with.

The next question must be where did Setty go after this? There were two possible sightings. One was of him having a drink in a hotel on the Hampstead

Road at about 6.40 pm. Secondly, William Lee, a news vendor, claimed to have seen him at that time waiting outside the Fitzroy cafe. Apart from that, no one ever came forward to make a statement and so we are in the realm of doubt. Did he go to Watford as mentioned to Connie? Rosenthal had no knowledge of this arrangement and he claimed that he knew most of Setty's business deals. However, no one in Watford reported seeing him, but arguably if a man had arranged to sell a car to Setty he might be reluctant to come forward to the police on the grounds that he might face a murder charge as being the last man known to have seen Setty; and after the discovery of the body several weeks later might not want to come forward then for fear of being charged with withholding key information. All that can be said for certain is that, as Setty had had a large sum of money withdrawn on that very afternoon, he wanted to make an immediate purchase. Possibly the Watford story was a blind to conceal a more illicit deal, but he never used that sum.

Some people who vanish are not missed or if they are, are not reported to the police. Such was the case with Haigh's first five victims and Christie's last three. Unlike these unfortunate people, Setty had regular routines and a functioning social network of people, both family, friends and work acquaintances, who missed him as soon as he disappeared. When Fryer turned up for work at Cambridge Terrace Mews at 9 on the morning of 5 October, he saw Setty's Citroën some way from the garage. Looking inside, he noted that the ignition key was missing. Having missed her brother's return the previous night, Eva rang the garage at 9.30 am. Fryer informed her that her brother was not there.[8]

Meanwhile, Eva's husband was at the Cumberland Hotel on Marble Arch, drinking coffee whilst awaiting a business meeting. Clearly he was uneasy about his brother-in-law's whereabouts, for he also rang Fryer and received the same message. He took a taxi to the garage, where he saw Rosenthal and Wright there, too. Fryer told him about the car. Ouri was also told about the £1,005 Setty had in his possession. Eva was now very concerned. She went to the police station on Albany Street (just a few minutes' walk from Cambridge Terrace Mews), one of those serving D (Marylebone) division. The police could not give her any information about her brother. Ouri stated, 'The disappearance of Setty is a complete mystery to me and I cannot find the solution to it. So far as I know he had no reason to disappear. I think his financial position is quite good and I fear that some harm has come to him.' The police took it seriously and issued a description of Setty which was to appear in nationwide police information journal the *Police Gazette*, on 8 October, which included details of those the police should look for either as suspects or as missing people.[9]

Friends and family were puzzled about the disappearance. Wright stated, 'Setty never worked in the evenings, so it must have been a wonderful deal to make him go to Watford.' Ellison thought that Setty rarely entered a stranger's car, or would leave Warren Street to see a car, always insisting that would-be sellers came to him in Warren Street. His brother David returned to London from Paris on hearing the news and remarked, 'Stanley didn't have an enemy in the world as far as I know. He did not talk to me about his car business.' Rosenthal, who had known him for nine years, later said his death was a 'terrible blow.'[10]

One reason why this missing person's enquiry was taken so seriously by the police was, according to Superintendent Peter Beveridge, because information was received in a very short time. Bert Tansill, a police officer and later a superintendent, reported to Beveridge:

> 'Guv'nor, you've heard that Setty is missing. I've had a tip that he may have been murdered.'
> 'How do you know, Bert?'
> 'A snout [police informer] has told me that Setty was carrying a lot of cash.'[11]

In the days that followed, police activity was intense. There were numerous leads to follow up. Setty had been seen, apparently, leaving London in a westward direction. Others said he was in Biggleswade, Bedfordshire. One account was that he might have gone to Malta or even Palestine. Interpol was notified. David Setty's trip to Paris on 18 October was noted, as was his niece's visit there two days later. There was even a bizarre idea that Setty might have been killed and dissolved in acid, as had Mrs Durand Deacon on 18 February earlier that year by John Haigh, and so suppliers of industrial acid were contacted. There were searches near Bedford and Luton.[12]

There were also enquiries more locally; in the West End, north London and Watford, for any sign of Setty, alive or dead. Garage proprietors and second-hand car dealers were questioned. Searches were made in lonely woods and spots on the roads between London and Watford. A watch was kept on dog tracks and bookies were asked to keep a look out for £5 notes with the numbers on that Setty had received on 4 October. In London open spaces, bombed out buildings, of which there were still many in the capital, and old air raid shelters were all investigated. Gladys Langford, an Islington teacher, noted in her diary on 27 October that a police fiancé of a friend of hers 'also said that he had had to explore all the bombed houses on his beat for traces of Setty's body.' It was assumed that Setty had been kidnapped or killed for his money and had not disappeared voluntarily (his money and passport remained in his flat). The Ouris announced a reward of £1,000 for anyone who found Setty and Mrs Ouri gave the police a little black notebook of addresses of her brother's business contacts. Setty's car was dusted for fingerprints but none were found except his own and nor were there any bloodstains. The police questioned the Ouris, Setty's employees, friends and some business colleagues to ascertain his movements. They made statements, but no answers were forthcoming.[13]

One oddity about the case is that on Thursday, 6 October someone rang Setty's flat and his brother-in-law answered. The caller identified herself as 'Mrs Rosenberg of Tel Aviv' and arranged to meet him at the Grosvenor Hotel the next day; apparently she was staying in room 461. She had a Polish or possibly German accent. Ouri went to see her at the allotted time but found no one of that name there. His wife and Connie had been in the flat until 4 pm. The three returned 2 hours later to find the door of the flat open. Nothing was apparently missing but the only way in would have been by using a key. The Ouris had one each and the only other one was held by Setty. Presumably his key had been used by the killer/kidnapper looking for any documents there which might have incriminated him (and was clearly someone who knew where Setty lived), but the question then is who was the woman who rang as a decoy? Could the killer's wife or girlfriend have been persuaded/coerced to do so?[14] This episode is usually marginalised in accounts of the case but in this author's mind it has a greater significance and will be referred to later in the narrative.

After a while, though, the hectic activity died down. If there was no body, there could still be a conviction for murder, as James Camb found in 1948 when he killed a woman by tipping her out of a porthole in a ship. Yet, there seemed nothing so far to have connected anyone to Setty's disappearance/murder. It is worth noting that none of the witnesses questioned by the police, the car dealers and employees at Warren Street, nor Setty's family and friends, made any reference to Hume, presumably because they were unaware of the business relationship between the two men or chose not to inform the police of it.

We now turn from the mysterious disappearance and return to Hume. We know very little of Hume's movements on the critical day of 4 October. His own account, as we shall note, was fictional (drinking with a friend). One Eli Smith said he was in Birmingham, early that day and travelled back to London by train, leaving at 3.30 pm and reaching London by 6.30 pm. Alfred Goldman, Hume's solicitor, later thought Hume was with him in a car showroom in London that afternoon. Either is certainly possible. Yet, we do have a fair idea as to where Mrs Hume was, by her own admission. By 5.45 pm she was at their flat; at 6 pm she was in a room on the flat's second floor, feeding Alison and between 8 and 9 she was listening to a play on the wireless, *Justice in Other Lands*, before giving Alison a final feed at 10 pm. It is useful to remember these details as they will be deemed important later on.[15]

In contrast, on the days following there is a surfeit of reliable information regarding Hume's activities. On the morning after Setty's disappearance, Wednesday, 5 October, he certainly seemed flush with money after having stared penury in the face a couple of days before. At some point that morning he went to the Golders Green branch of the Midland Bank. He paid in £90 and restored his balance to £11 19s. He also gave his wife £80, mainly in £5 notes but there were some £1 notes, too. On the following day she paid £23 into her post office savings account and another £50 into the Midland Bank account. The hairdresser and newsagent to whom Hume owed money were repaid, too.[16]

He paid his rent; a few days late. Collins recalled, 'I remember this last occasion very well.' This was because it was the first time that Hume had paid with a £5 note. Apparently, 'I saw him take a roll of £5 notes from his pocket book, two inches in diameter.' He said to Hume, 'You've done alright Bill', but there was no reply. Then Hume asked if he could rent the cellar of the building for a week or two, but Collins could not do so as it would mean giving Hume access to the shop. 'He did not say anymore about it.' Hume later made other purchases with his rapidly diminishing roll of fivers. He bought some scissors from a shop in the Burlington Arcade and an address and telephone book from Fortnum & Mason's. Both purchases were made on 22 October and both were paid for with £5 notes.[17]

At 9.45 am on the 5 October, Hume went to H.A. Saunders Ltd, a hire-car company, on St Albans Lane, Golders Green. He paid £11 5s. (including a £10 deposit) to hire a Singer 10 mc black car with a gold stripe on the body. It was full of petrol (9 gallons) and he now had it for 48 hours. It was parked outside the flat ready for use.[18]

Secondly, he had the carpet in the living room cleaned. He went to Burtol Cleaners Ltd next door at 618 Finchley Road. It was about midday when Mrs Frances Hearnden, the manageress, received him. Hume declared that he wanted it dyed and asked how long it would take. Mrs Hearnden told him it would be two weeks. Hume asked if it could be done any quicker. She said that it might be possible. She said that a man could collect it from the flat but Hume told her that he would bring it himself. Hume brought the rolled up carpet (it might have been safer to have disposed of it completely) to the shop 10 minutes later.[19]

Mrs Hearnden asked that it be unrolled so she could see its size in order to give him an estimate of the price. She later recalled, 'he did not appear anxious for it to be undone.' Hume asked the cost and was given an estimate of £2. He then left the shop. He had another task to attend to.[20]

The next port of call was back to the garage, to see Maurice Edwards, a panel beater. Edwards recalled, 'On the 5th October 1949, just after 1pm, Mr Hume met me . . . He had something wrapped in a sheet of newspaper. He took a knife out of the paper and asked me if I could put an edge on it as he wanted to sharpen it to cut his joint.' The knife was 16in long and the blade an inch wide. It was rounded at the end, though not sharp. Edwards sharpened it on the grindstone. The edges were still rough and so he offered to finish the job but Hume said he was in a hurry and so refused.[21]

Henry Simpson, an engineer and director of the flying club Hume was a member of, at Elstree aerodrome, later claimed that Hume arrived there at noon and hired an aeroplane for the afternoon. He could have used his hire car to get there and back. If he did, it was clearly a very busy time for him.[22]

Dr Blatchley came to the flat just before lunch time to see to the baby. He also gave Hume a prescription for sleeping tablets. Mrs Hume fed Alison at 10 am and at 2 pm and then left the flat shortly afterwards.[23]

That afternoon the Humes' cleaning woman, Mrs Ethel Stride, came to the flat as she did every Wednesday afternoon. She normally cleaned all the rooms in the 3 hours that she was there. She arrived at about 1 pm. Hume asked her to go out and buy a floorcloth as he had used the one he had to wash a stained carpet (she did so). She noticed that the sitting room carpet and the hall rug were missing; Hume explained he had taken the former for cleaning. She later explained what happened next:

> He [Hume] said he was tidying up a cupboard in the kitchen to make room for coal to be stored for the winter, and he said he did not want to be disturbed . . . even to answer the telephone, and if it rang I was to say he was not at home. Mr Hume was in the kitchen about an hour and then he went out. He took two parcels with him, carrying one under each arm. They were roughly round parcels.[24]

Hume then left the flat and was seen by Mrs Stride, perhaps at 3.30 pm. Under his left arm he carried a parcel and under the right was another. He put them in the back of the hire car and then drove towards Elstree aerodrome. He drove cautiously, creeping up to each set of traffic lights and carefully signalling for each turn. It would not do for the police to stop him on a minor motoring charge and then make a more serious discovery. Tony, the dog, travelled with him.[25]

Turning down Dagger Lane, Hume arrived at Elstree aerodrome to use the Auster G-A-GXT light aircraft he had hired for 24 hours. It was allegedly 4.30 pm, which was a long time to have taken to have driven a few miles, even if the journey was slow. He had used this plane before. As a member of the flying club there, and as one who had learnt to fly there, he was a well-known figure and as he walked confidently over to see the airfield controller, no one thought anything of it. He paid with four £5 notes. Fred Peters asked him, 'What's happened to your car [meaning Hume's Cadillac]?' Hume replied, 'Don't you ever read the papers? The police confiscated it.' This was spoken in jest for as stated he had sold it to Salvadori. Peters noted that Hume opened his car boot:

> and took out a heavy parcel in what appeared to be a dark Army blanket which was tied with a cord or a piece of string. It was a large bundle which he carried in front of him against his body with his arms encircling it and his hands clasped in front. It covered the whole of his body. It appeared very heavy.

Hume took it to the plane. He then returned to the car and removed a second, smaller, parcel, wrapped in thick paper and tied with string. Once again he needed both hands to carry it across to the plane. One was put in the back of the plane and the other in the co-pilot's seat. He also removed his raincoat and put that on the seat next to his. Tony was left in the car, for Hume did not expect to be gone for long.[26]

Hume flew off between 4.30 and 5.30 pm; probably at the earlier time due to fading light, and stated he was flying to Southend Municipal Aerodrome near the Essex coastline. As Hume was landing at Southend, two red Very lights whizzed up at him. Only when he had landed did he realise that this had been to warn him that he was in the direct flight path of a four-engine plane. He had violated the circuit drill and could not have arrived in a less conspicuous manner. Yet, he had hardly any petrol left in the tank so could not have done otherwise. The time was variously estimated at between 5.30 and 6.25 pm; probably the latter.[27]

Once he had left the plane on the grass strip that comprised the runway, James Small, who knew him, was asked to fly him back to Elstree that same evening. Small said that bad weather made that impossible, but he parked the plane in the hangar for Hume and had it refuelled. It was now about 6.30 pm. Hume went to the airport restaurant and found Percy Rawlings, a taxi driver, eating his dinner. Hume asked him, 'Are you the taxi bloke, will you take me to Golders Green?' Rawlings thought Hume had either a Canadian or an American accent and said that he would have to wait 15 minutes for him to finish his meal. Rawlings recalled, 'He said he was in a hurry and asked me to leave my meal.' Hume had tea and they left at 6.45 pm.[28]

When they reached the arterial road, Rawlings was concerned that a light on his car was faulty. He told Hume he wanted to stop at a garage to have it dealt with. Hume was not happy at this suggestion and again told the man he was in a hurry. Rawlings clearly took Hume's heeding to heart and they carried on, but were stopped by the police on the North Circular Road because of the rear light. Hume had originally asked to be dropped off by Hendon greyhound stadium. The fare was £4 5s. and Rawlings was given a £5 note and told to keep the change. Rawlings remembered, 'he took a roll of notes from his pocket.' It is worth noting that a £5 note was a very high denomination note at this time; so anyone being given one would remember it. Then Hume remembered Tony and rang the Elstree aerodrome from his flat, asking that someone let the dog out for a run and that he would be back tomorrow to collect car and dog. He was home by 8.45 pm.[29]

On the next day he had to collect his beloved Tony from Elstree. This time he travelled by taxi, an Austin 12, departing at 9 am. Godfrey Marsh, a taxi driver for the Golders Green taxi firm, recalled, 'He told me to hurry, as he wanted to be back at Golders Green as soon as possible as he had to take his wife and baby to Great Ormond Street Hospital by 10 o'clock.' Hume took two parcels with him; one was oblong and looked like a carpet tied at the end and the middle with string, the other was smaller and covered with brown paper. Once at the airport, at about 9.30 am, he paid off the taxi driver and went to his temporarily abandoned Singer car, with his two parcels (it was never ascertained what was in these parcels; clearly something important to Hume that he dared not leave in the flat unattended). He drove back to Golders Green, arriving at 11 am and parking the car outside his flat.[30]

Meanwhile, Hume had work to do in the flat. He asked Joseph Staddon, a painter, to do a staining job there for him. He arrived at noon. Hume explained, 'Here you are then. I've got some Dankaline Stain and I will show you what I want you to do.' Staddon was required to stain the surrounds in the living room and the kitchen. 'He was most anxious', Staddon recalled. He worked from 12 to 12.30 pm and rushed because Hume emphasised the urgency. The floor boards were worn and scratched, but 'I did not see anything unusual on any of the boards before I stained them.'[31]

There was more work to come for Staddon. At 12.30 pm, Hume said, 'I want you to help me down the stairs into the car with a parcel.' Staddon had not previously noted a very large parcel at the top of the stairs which had not been there when he entered the flat. Staddon described it, 'It was a very large parcel.

I would say about three feet long, about two feet wide and about fifteen inches thick. It was wrapped in what looked to me like carpet felt', and was tied with rope. Hume wanted Staddon to help him take it to his car. Staddon was about to put his hands underneath it and then Hume cried:

> 'Don't put your hands underneath. Hold it by the rope' [Hume later stated that he had noted that the bottom of the parcel was bloody]
> 'Where are you going to take this?'
> 'The car is by the UD Milk shop.'
> 'You'll never get it across there. It's too heavy. You'd better bring the car outside the front door and then we'll put it in.'
> 'Come along for the car. I'll give you a ride round the houses.'

They began to take the package downstairs between them. Hume told Staddon that the contents were very valuable so they must treat it with care, but, presumably because of its bulk and weight, it slipped from their hands and slid down the stairs.[32]

Hume then left the parcel with Staddon as he fetched the car from Rodborough Road. Staddon left it as well, and for 2 minutes it was unattended in the doorway. The two of them then carried the parcel with difficulty to the back seat of the car and put it into a small black case in the car. Hume was nonchalant throughout and Staddon recalled, 'All the time I was with Mr Hume that day, he was just his natural self, like I have always known him.'[33]

Hume then drove to Southend aerodrome, arriving at about 4 pm. Peter Yeoman, chief inspector there, saw him arrive and take a large parcel to the Auster aircraft. He offered to help but Hume declined. A mechanic asked what was in the parcel and Hume smiled and said 'Fish.' It was a struggle to carry the parcel to the plane, but somehow he managed it. Hume explained that he landed the aircraft at Southend, and that he was to go there and fly it back to Elstree.[34]

Hume actually landed at Gravesend airport, arriving there at 5.45 pm, and Reginald Cross of Essex Aero Ltd gave him permission to do so. James Rayfield, a metal worker employed there, saw Hume carrying a green canvas bag and a raincoat. He told the authorities that he had come from Southend. Hume could not fly back that day and so, once again, sought a taxi to get home. Charles Butcher drove him back. He recalled that Hume seemed very anxious to return home, smoked throughout the trip, and though quiet, 'he appeared to be nervous and tensed up.' He did mention that he had been flying an Auster but was forced down at Gravesend due to poor visibility. The fare was £3 10s. but unlike the previous day, Hume asked for £1 change out of the £5 he gave Butcher.[35]

On the 7th Hume went to Southend to collect the car and then arranged for the plane to be flown back to Elstree. That afternoon he took the car back to the hire firm, at 4.30 pm.[36]

In the meantime, the carpet had been sent to Hardings Dyeworks in Kingston upon Thames. The manager, Cecil Allport, noted that it was 12 by 9ft, a pale green Axminster, which was faded and stained. However, as he and his staff dealt with between twenty-five and thirty carpets a day, he could not recall any specific detail about this one. It left the works on 13 October. Ironically on the same day, Hume asked the cleaning company in Golders Green how long the job would take and the manageress recalled, 'from that day he was worrying me almost hourly every day until the carpet finally came.' Hume even rang the factory twice to ask the state of play and emphasised to them how important the work was. It was returned on 19 October and Hume paid the fee, £2 14s., by cheque. He said he was very pleased with the work and explained that it had become stained because there had been a party at his flat and drinks had been spilt upon it.[37]

Life resumed on an even keel for Hume after these trips to the aerodromes. Douglas Muirhead, a 33-year-old assistant advertising manager and a friend of Hume, visited the flat, even recalling them having a conversation on the 16th about the Setty case and commenting on Hume, 'although joining in the general conversation he made no special point about Setty . . . Hume was his usual boisterous self.' They talked about a scheme to produce bag fasteners in the west of England. With Collins, Hume told of a scheme to go to Ireland.[38]

However, just over two weeks after Setty had disappeared, he reappeared – or rather part of him did – and this very important discovery regalvanised the whole case and it took a different direction. Sydney Tiffin, a 47-year-old resident at 10 St Nicholas Road, Tillingham, Essex, was employed as a farm labourer but had been a wild fowler, who often went to the Dengie Marshes. This was a large expanse of watery land between the rivers Crouch and Blackwater on the Essex coastline, sparsely populated but a haven for wildlife; a deserted spot. He was there to look for wild ducks, and described what happened:

> On Friday the 21st of October, 1949, round about half past 12 midday I was in my punt on the flats when I saw a grey bundle floating in the sea water. I went past it, after some ducks. I returned a few minutes later and had a look at it. I took it to be a bundle of bedding. I cut the string with which it was tied with my pocket knife and part of a body floated out. I noticed there were braces on the body and I took it to be that of a man.
>
> The covering sank to the bottom in about a foot and a half of water. The tide was fairly high and a strongish breeze was blowing

from the west. I noticed that the hands were tied behind the back with something that looked to me like a piece of leather or brown webbing. As the body was floating away with the tide I took a piece of cord I had in the past tied round one of the arms, pushed a piece of wooden stake into the mud and tied the body to it. While I was tying the cord round the arm the leather or webbing, which was tied round the hands gave way and disappeared.[39]

The killer had been unlucky in two respects. Firstly, Tiffin was enjoying leave from work and liked spending time out on his punt with his gun, shooting duck to eat or sell. Secondly, the killer must have thought that he had disposed of the body out at sea. He did not know that the water was merely tidal and then only twice a month; when it ran away it was merely only a foot or two at most and so the body would inevitably be seen resting on the mud. Tiffin remarked to a journalist, 'he must be an unnoticing man.'[40]

Tiffin returned to Tillingham and then went to Bradwell-on-Sea, to report what he had found to PC Furnell of the Essex County Constabulary. Furnell and fellow constable Sewell called on Tiffin at 4.15 pm and together they all went to the spot where the body had been seen, and they decided that it had not been there on the previous day. They made a cursory examination but did not move it. According to Rebecca West who interviewed Tiffin, the dialogue between Tiffin and one of the constables went as follows:

'There's something wrong here.'
'Yes, I think there's something wrong here.'
'It's my opinion this is a murdered body.'
'Yes, I do think it's a murdered body.'

Tiffin ensured that the body was secured and would not be taken by the tide out to sea. On 22 October, Detective Sergeant William Jackson of the Essex force at Chelmsford accompanied PC Sewell there. He took photographs of the bundle in situ and then had it transferred to St John's Mortuary at Chelmsford hospital.[41]

Detective Superintendent George Henry Totterdell (1892–1976) was now in charge of the case and was present at the examination. He was a detective of long experience, having joined the Essex force in 1912. In 1921 he became a detective constable, in 1926 a detective sergeant, in 1929 a detective inspector and in 1932, his present rank. Dr Francis Edward Camps (1905–72) referred to this 'neat, grey haired man' as follows, 'No flash stuff, no short cuts, but a philosophy based upon solid thorough police investigation, to be carried out as soon as possible.'[42]

What he saw was horrific. Although here was the body of a well-fed man, the head and legs were missing; having been cut off by a sharp instrument, the bones having been sawn through. Photographs were also taken at the mortuary. It was concluded that the body could have been put where it was found by a motor boat but not by a car, or that it could have been thrown from the nearby River Blackwater and the current had washed it into the marshes. Initially the real method of disposal was not suspected. Bodies are sometimes dismembered by their killers for sake of ease of disposal and thus lack of detection; Dr Buck Ruxton had done so in 1936 and Denis Nilsen was to do so on a large scale in 1977–83.[43]

That afternoon, Dr Camps was summoned. Camps had followed in his father's footsteps and had qualified as a doctor in 1928. He then worked as a junior partner in a rural Essex practice. From 1935 he was employed at Chelmsford hospital where he became increasingly involved in the work of the coroner. He did not become a full-time forensic pathologist until 1945 when he secured a post of lecturer at the University of London. Thereafter, he became one of the three main pathologists who dealt with forensics in and around London in the post-war decades (the others being Dr Robert Donald Teare and Dr Keith Simpson). In 1949 he had conducted a post-mortem on Miss Daisy Wallis, who had been stabbed to death in her office in London. He was a hard-working and enthusiastic man; the Setty case was his first to hit the headlines.[44]

At 10.45 pm Camps was conducting the post-mortem on the torso. It was of a 'well developed, somewhat fat man' and measured 31in by 17in, making the deceased about 5ft 7in and 188lb. He found five stab wounds to the chest and concluded:

> One was situated just below the collar bone, below the middle of the collar bone, the direction being outwards and slightly downwards, into the soft tissues here, but not penetrating the chest cavity at all. Then there was a second wound, internal to that, cutting the rib and penetrating the upper lobe of the lung. There was a third wound below that, going through the second space between the ribs and penetrating the lung in a rather vital space, because it is recognised that the closer to the central part of the lung, the higher the mortality and the more rapidly death occurs.
>
> This was just inside the nipple, going laterally downwards and outwards – in fact, they all went downwards and outwards – again penetrating the lung. Finally, and lower still, there was a wound

which went into the belly cavity between the muscle dividing it and the chest.

He added that the limbs and head had been severed with a saw, with 'technical skill, although there was nothing to suggest medical knowledge.' Death had been due to shock and haemorrhage following the stab wounds. Camps thought that the body was that of Setty because of the dark skin and said, 'I think we've got Setty's torso here.'[45]

There were a few deductions that could be drawn from the body. It had been dead less than 48 hours before being immersed in the sea. The weapon used to inflict the wounds would have been sharp and two-edged, measuring 1in wide and 4in long. This was ascertained because of the depth of the stab wounds. The ribs had been fractured following death, and there would have been a massive blood spillage. Camps reasoned that the post-mortem bruising on the body was an indication that the body had been dropped from height into the sea; he had seen similar injuries from the corpses of airmen who had been killed in the recent conflict. Specimens of the torso were sent to the laboratory at New Scotland Yard. Camps made an incision on the wrists and peeled back the skin as if removing gloves, and sent it in a jar to Superintendent Frederick Cherrill, the fingerprint expert, at Scotland Yard. Because Setty had been convicted at Manchester Quarter Sessions in 1928 his fingerprints were on file and so Cherrill could make a positive identification of the corpse, declaring, 'Its Setty alright.' The clothing was removed and sent to Dr Henry Holden (1889–1963), Director of the Metropolitan Police Laboratory at Scotland Yard since 1946.[46]

What was not subsequently stated at the trial was the corpse's alcohol content. The urine sample taken indicated that the deceased had drunk eight double whiskies or eight double brandies shortly before his death. Since the cuts in the torso were neat it suggested that the man had been stabbed whilst immobile and unable to struggle; with that amount of drink inside him he may well have been unconscious. One double measure of spirits would equate to 63mg per 100ml of blood; eight times this (nearly 500mg per 100ml of blood) would be highly dangerous and could result in the death of the drinker.[47] However, more recent scientific research has shown that the conclusions reached in 1949 were probably a great over-estimation and so although they indicated that Setty had been drinking prior to death, he was not drunk.[48] Regrettably neither Cherrill nor Camps detailed this case in their memoirs.

After the discovery of the body, the police search extended to Essex, especially the district around Southend. Boat owners and others were interviewed. Setty was known in a club in Southend and acquainted with people involved in the motor trade there. There was suspicion that he had been killed by members of a black-market gang or by an assassin employed by them. Possibly he had fallen out with them or perhaps threatened to inform on them.[49]

Another theory expounded in the press was thus:

> It is also now regarded as certain in the Yard that he was tortured by members of a rival gang who were either jealous of the power he wielded or were trying to extract from him some secret about the car gang operations which he alone knew. Setty, victim of the Marsh murder, was kept a prisoner – perhaps in a lonely barn or rented garage – or at least four days before he was stabbed to death and his body dismembered.[50]

Apparently Camps remarked to Detective Superintendent Colin MacDougall (1906–85) that Setty was probably dropped from an aeroplane to sustain the broken bones that he had suffered after death. MacDougall informed Superintendent Peter Beveridge and he sent enquiries to numerous airports and aerodromes to ask if anything suspicious had been seen there. This led to Simpson informing the police on 24 October that Hume had flown from Elstree on 5 October (bizarrely, Percy Hoskins, crime reporter for the Express newspapers, thought that Hume himself contacted the police to tell them this due to an attack of jitters). Doubtless he had read about the discovery of the torso in the press, where it was widely reported on the front pages; other instances of publicity given to a murder case facilitating an arrest were the case of the 'Brides in the Bath' killer in 1915 and that of the acid bath murderer in 1949. And then it was found that one of the £5 notes taken from Setty had been used by Hume. Armed with this information, and other statements from aerodrome employees, Hume's arrest was imminent. He was now the obvious suspect and so the police naturally thought he was the killer; a tail was put on him that same day.[51]

Chapter 5

Hume Arrested

At 7.45 am on Wednesday, 26 October, just three weeks after Setty had disappeared and five days after part of him had been found, the police, in three black cars, swooped on 620b Finchley Road. It was teeming with rain. In a scene reminiscent of the pilot episode of *The Sweeney*, Hume was woken that morning. Plain clothes men from Scotland Yard and from the Albany Street police station entered his bedroom. Other detectives were posted at the front and back of the flat. There was no escape.[1]

Detective Chief Inspector John Pretsell Jamieson (1898–1976), once of the Flying Squad, said:

> 'We are police officers enquiring into certain serious matters in connection with what I think you can help.'
> 'What is it all about?' replied Hume, trying to play the innocent.
> 'I don't think this is a convenient place to discuss the subject. It would be better if we went to the Police Station.'

This was because Mrs Hume was, naturally, in the flat.

> 'All right, I will come with you.'[2]

Hume dressed. He wore dark-grey flannel trousers, a grey tweed jacket with large check squares, brown shoes and green socks. As with many young men of the time, he was hatless. The police noted that he 'keeps twitching his eyes and blinking', has a soft voice, good teeth and well-cared for hands.[3]

The men entered the police car outside the flat. Hume was impatient and asked:

> 'Can't you tell me more about it now?'
> 'Our enquiries are in connection with the murder of Stanley Setty, who disappeared on 4th October 1949.'
> 'Oh, I can't help you about that. I know nothing about it.'[4]

At Albany Street police station, Hume was offered cigarettes and cups of tea, part of the softening up process, he later remarked. He was also searched; on his person were found two pawn tickets for a suit he had pledged on 26 September and a three-stone ring pledged five days later. Jamieson began with:

'Do you own a motor car?'

Hume then gave a truthful answer:

'No.'
'When did you last drive a car?'

Hume now began to lie again:

'About three or four months ago.'
'I have good reason to believe that on the afternoon of the 5th October 1949, you drove a car to Elstree aerodrome and there took parcels from the car and put them into a plane which you had hired.'

Hume replied, with a half-truth:

'I hired a plane that day to go to Southend, but I had no parcels with me; I only had my coat. I hired a car that day and drove myself to the aerodrome.'[5]

MacDougall, an officer of twenty-four years' experience, now took over the questioning:

'I am making enquiries about the murder of Stanley Setty who was reported missing on 4th October 1949 and part of whose body was found on the shore of Essex on 21st October 1949.'
'I can't help you. I can't see it has anything to do with me. Setty has not been to my place.'
'I understand you took off for Southend from Elstree airport in a hired plane into which you loaded two parcels on 5th October 1949.'
'It's a lie. I put no parcels in the plane, all I had with me was my overcoat.'
'I can prove you put two parcels in the aeroplane that day and the next day you put a large parcel in the same plane at Southend.'
'I am several kinds of bastard, aren't I?'[6]

Beveridge observed Hume at this time and later stated:

Donald Hume was a good looking young man, and cool. He had a natural ebullience and the most extraordinary self confidence. It is a frightening thing to be taken to a police station when arrested for a major crime, but Hume seemed to be singularly unworried. He sat in his chair, smoking, and then made a long, rambling statement.[7]

MacDougall, Jamieson and Detective Sergeant Sutherland were present when Hume made a lengthy statement. Apart from some brief introductory remarks about himself, it ran as follows:

As a result of selling the cars I became friendly with Roy Salvadori, his brother Oswald, and Mr Mansfield. The B.M.T.A. [British Motor Traders Association] took civil action against several motor traders for buying motor cars sold on this understanding that they would be retained twelve months by the purchaser. During these proceedings I got to know several of the dealers in Warren Street. Since then I have visited Warren Street several times and always called in Salvadori's office. I told the Salvadoris and Mr Mansfield and several other motor traders that I could fly a plane. I did romance to them as to my capabilities as a pilot.

About six weeks to two months ago Mr Salvadori asked me if I could fly a plane to Italy to take some spares back for one of his cars. Round about this time he also asked me if I could fly him to Belgium to some place where a motor race was to be held. He said he would get in touch with me later about this but he did not do so.

While going to Salvadori's office in Warren Street I saw a man I know as Mac or Max. He is about 35 years of age, 5ft 10in or 11ins, in height, heavily built, clean shaven, fresh complexion, fair hair parted in the centre and brushed right back. He wears a large stone ring, I believe on his right hand. He usually wears suede brogue shoes.

On Friday the 30th September 1949 I was in Salvadori's offices, in the afternoon. I am definite about this date because it was the Friday before the man Setty disappeared.

Salvadori's office is in the basement, and on leaving the office and getting to the top of the stairs I met the man Mac. He was alone. He asked me if I had any cars to sell. I told him I had not. He then said, 'Are you the flying smuggler.' I said 'Yes.' He asked me how the business was going and I told him not so well. He then asked me if I had any dollars or any thing else for sale and I had 90 dollars but he would not give me enough for them and I would not sell them. This man then invited me to have a cup of tea with him. We went to the café on the corner and he led me to the far part of the room where the man Gree or Green was sitting at a table. We sat down and ordered a cup of tea. Mac said to Green, 'This is him.'

The man I have referred to as Gree or Greeny is also known as 'G.' He is about 31/32 years of age, about 5 ft. 7 ins. In height, dark complexion, thin black moustache, broken in the middle, black hair (Boston cut), wearing wide green coloured trousers, heavy light brown belted overcoat, plain suede shoes, no hat. He spoke like a Cypriot does. I should take him for a Cypriot.

The man Mac said to his companion that my business was not very good and Gree said to me 'You would like to make some money. I can put you on a deal if you can keep your mouth shut.' Mac said to me 'How can we get hold of you.' I gave them my name, address and telephone number which is Speedwell 7302. Mac said 'They tell me you can get hold of an aeroplane.' I said this was correct. Mac continued 'How about getting hold of a plane that will carry five or six people without worrying the customs.' I said I could, because I did not think he was really serious. Green then said 'How about one for Monday.' I said it might be arranged but that it would cost a lot of money. Gree then asked what type of plane it would be, because he had been in a plane to Cyprus. Mac asked me if I knew Roy Salvadori well, and I told him that I did. After some general conversation about motor cars, Mac said he had a deal on and would be getting in touch with me. I then left them.

The following Sunday, the 2nd October 1949, Mac telephoned me at home during the forenoon. My wife answered the phone and told me I was wanted. Mac said to me, 'You are not fucking us about over these aeroplanes?' I said to him, 'If you want an aeroplane you will have to find some money first.' I then told him that if I got a plane it would have to be a single-engined one and he said it would be alright if they could come. I then said, to put him off, that I did not think it would be easy to go abroad because of the necessity of obtaining trip tickets and other formalities. Mac said 'I don't care how many engines it's got as long as it is a three seater.' Mac then said 'I don't care how many engines it's got as long as we can come.' I said 'I can only take one passenger although it is a three seater.' Mac then said, 'So you are fucking us about after all.' He asked me how long it would take to get a single engine plane and I told him that before I could get the plane I would have to have some money. He then said, 'If we don't want to go abroad will it be necessary to get these papers?' I told him it would not if flying within England. He then said he would speak to his mates about it and rang off.

On Monday morning, the 3rd October 1949, Mac rang up again about 9.30 pm. He said 'I can do with the single-engine plane.' I again told him I would have to have some money and he said, 'I will fix all that, I want it for today. I will ring you back in a short while and tell you what I want.' Soon after this he rang again and said 'I don't want a plane for today.' I said to him 'You are the one that's fucking about.' He then said 'Have you got a motor car?' I said 'What type do you want to buy?' He said 'I don't want to buy one but you can drive.' He said 'I'm not messing you about, I'll fix you up with a deal.'

On the morning of the 5th October 1949, about 10 am Mac phoned me again saying 'We will call around and see you. We want that plane.' I should have said that during the morning I telephoned the United Services Flying Club and booked a single-engined aircraft for that afternoon. I am fairly well known at the Elstree Aerodrome. Either before or after booking the plane I went to Saunders Garage, Golders Green, and hired a car, self drive, for 24 hours.

Between 2 p.m. and 3 p.m. that afternoon (5th October 1949), Mac, Gree and another man they called 'The Boy' called at my address.

'Boy' is aged about 35, 5 ft. 9 or 10 ins., medium build, clean shaven, brown hair, receding from the forehead. He sometimes wore steel rimmed glasses. I believe he wore a raincoat.

Green and the 'Boy' were each carrying a parcel. I believe they arrived by motor car. I went to the door to their ring and they came upstairs to the flat. I do not know whether or not my wife saw them.

On arriving upstairs Mac said 'As you know we wanted to go abroad. It will be good for you now we have started doing deals with you if you can keep your mouth shut.' I told them I could do that alright. Mac spoke about forged petrol coupons and said he had been making them and wanted to get rid of the plates or presses. He said he wanted them dumped in the water and added that the plates or presses were hot. The three men inferred that the plates or presses were in the parcels they brought to my home. I said that this was an expensive way of getting rid of the plates or presses and offered to hide or bury them for them. They then discussed among themselves the necessity of one of them coming with me. Then Gree said to Mac 'I'll go with him.' I said 'No, I'll do it.' Gree then said 'You're getting paid for what you're doing, you're not dealing with poofs from Hyde Park.' As he said this he put one of his hands into his coat pocket and showed me a pistol or revolver. During this conversation the Boy said 'I'll fix this now', put his glasses on and pulled out a roll of notes out of his pocket. Gree said 'I'll pay him' and pulled a bigger bundle still out of his inside jacket pocket. 'Boy' handed me ten five pound notes.

It was impressed by the three men that I was to take the two parcels up in the plane and throw them into the English Channel. They explained that they had done the parcels up properly and that it would be unwise for me to interfere with them.

Before leaving my flat, Mac said 'We will call round about 8 o'clock to a quarter past tonight and pay you another fifty pounds.' They then went away.

I would describe the parcels. The one 'Boy' brought me was a Heinz Baked Beans Cardboard box, about 15 ins. by 15 ins. and was completely covered with cardboard and securely roped. I pushed my foot hard against it and it was firm. The other parcel was about two feet six in length about two feet thick and round. The outer cover was corrugated paper and the whole parcel securely tied with thick cord. It was heavy and when I squeezed it with my fingers it had a soft feeling and when I lifted the parcel it did not bend or sag. It was fairly heavy. I did not see any dry or wet stains or moisture on either of these packages. Neither was there any writing or printing on the larger parcel. Whilst the parcels were in my house and after the men had left I put them in a cupboard in the kitchen of my flat. I don't think my wife knew these men had been to the house and I cannot be sure whether or not I told her. I certainly did not tell her of the arrangements I had made with the men regarding the disposal of the parcels.

At about 3.30 p.m. that same day (5th October 1949) I placed the parcels in the back seat of the car I had hired from Saunders which was then standing opposite my flat. I drove the car alone, with my dog and the packages in the back, to Elstree airport. On arrival there I took the parcels from the car and went to the Airport offices where I saw Mr Keats who told me the aircraft was ready.

I had a cup of tea in the canteen and afterwards put the dog in the motor car and left it there outside the Airport Office expecting to be back that day. One of the ground staff, I don't know who, carried one of the parcels and I carried the other to the aeroplane and placed them both in the seat beside the pilot's seat. I should mention that before I left the airport I paid the cashier the sum of £20 in four five pound notes to settle an outstanding amount. I cannot be sure whether or not any of the £5 notes were those I got from the men I've earlier mentioned.

I took off from Elstree Airport about 4.30 p.m. and there were about twelve or thirteen gallons of petrol in the tank. I flew towards Southend, reached the pier and straight out to sea and continued on out for a quarter of an hour towards the Kent coast and just before I turned to the right I opened the door on the pilot's side of the plane and held the controls with my knees. After I got the door open I was able to hold it open against the air resistance and throw both parcels out of the plane into the sea. I was then flying about one thousand feet and would estimate that I was about four or five miles from the end of Southend pier. I then flew back to Southend Airport and landed about 6.20 p.m. When landing at Southend I obstructed a large freight plane, a Halifax, I believe, which was landed about the same time and the officials at the Airport spoke to me about my flying. I left my plane on the air field outside the Club House. I entered the Club House and saw Mr Small whom I knew and spoke to him. I asked him if he would fly me back to Elstree as he knew the way and he declined as he was on holiday. He appeared to taxi the plane up to Hanger and in fact did so. When I left the plane there was nothing in it.

I am convinced that I carried one of the parcels, the long one, I think, in the back of the plane.

After the plane was put in the hanger I made enquiries about getting a car to take me back to Golders Green by 8.15 p.m. to meet the three men as arranged. I was able to hire a car at the Airport. I remember asking the driver to leave the meal he was eating in order to get me away quickly on the arrangement I would buy him a meal in town. I had a quick cup of tea and we left the aerodrome about a quarter to seven. On the way to London the driver had trouble with his car-lights and called at three garages to try and get them put right. He still had trouble and was pulled up by the police at Southgate. We eventually arrived at Golders Green at about a quarter to nine. The driver put me down within a second or so of my flat. I then settled with him. The cost of the hire car was about £4 and I paid the driver with a £5 note inviting him to keep the change.

After leaving the car I went towards my flat and when I got to my door, Mac came up and said, 'You are really late.' I told him I had dumped the parcels in the Channel, I did not admit to him that it was between Southend and the Kent coast I had done this. I told him about leaving the plane at Southend and of the troubles I had had. Before this conversation took place Mac asked me to walk across the road with him and took me to a stationary motor car, a Humber I believe, in which were seated Gree in the front near side and Boy in the back of the near side. I noticed that in the back besides Boy there was a bulky package on the floor and leaning against the seat.

I told Mac that I had already spent about £30 and that because of this I would only have about £70 for myself. He said, 'We are going to give you a chance to earn another £50 tonight.' I asked how and said 'How about the other fifty first.' Mac said 'We will give you the hundred tonight. We want you to drop another parcel in the sea tonight.' I said 'The aeroplane is at Southend, I haven't done any night flying and I can't do it.' Green said 'We can take you to Southend it will be on our way.' I again told them I could not fly at night. They then showed me the big parcel in the back of the car. I said 'I don't think it will fit in an aeroplane.' Boy then said, 'You have started the job, you've got to finish it.' Boy said, 'You won't get any more unless you do finish it.' I then said 'If you take me out to Elstree I can put it in the back of my car, bring it back here and take it to Southend tomorrow.' They refused to go to Elstree. 'Boy' took some money out of his pocket and said, 'Here is the other hundred, I'll give it to you now and you can arrange to keep the bundle upstairs until tomorrow when you can take it down at your own convenience.' I had another look at it and said 'I still don't think it will go into the plane.' However, I agreed to take it to Southend the following day and dump it into the sea. 'Boy' gave me £90 in £5 notes and ten £1 notes. Mac and Boy then took the package and carried it into my flat. We put it into the far cupboard in the kitchen. I said 'One of you must come out tomorrow and give me a hand to get it into the car.' One of them said 'We will be away tomorrow and cannot do it, you will be able to get someone to help you.' They then left the flat.

By this time I was afraid of the three men and because of this I carried out their instructions.

The following morning, the 6th October 1949, I got to Elstree about 9.30 a.m. I had hired a car from Saunders garage. I had left the other car at Elstree and I collected it and my dog. Before leaving the airfield in the car, I said to one of the mechanics 'I will bring the plane back from Southend tonight.' I drove straight home.

During that morning, I think about 11 o'clock I drove the car outside my flat. I cannot remember the index number of it and with the employee from Saunders I placed it in the car. While I was taking it downstairs it made a gurgling noise. I thought it was a human body, that of a small or a young person. It crossed my mind that the package may have contained Setty's body, as I had read in the papers that he was missing.

I knew Stanley Setty because I sold him a Pontiac some two years ago for £200. I was introduced to him by Mr Roy Salvadori and I think he had something out of the deal.

The package the three men took to Golders Green and which I kept in my flat I would describe as follows:

It was about 4 feet tall and about 2 feet six inches across, and 2 feet deep. It was wrapped up in what I think was an Army blanket, browny grey in colour. There was I think cord or rope round it to make it secure. It was not a solid hard parcel, but had a give in it. The end of the blanket must have been folded over and sealed by sewing as there were no loose ends protruding. I remember now it was roped round and cross ways, end to end. I would recognise the type of blanket again. It was very heavy and took me all my time to lift it.

The bundle was put into the back of the car and I drove myself to Southend. It was a ginger car. I arrived at Southend at about 5 p.m. I cannot be sure of the time, it may have been later.

When I got to the airfield at Southend the plane had already been taken out of the hangar and was near the petrol pumps. I had two gallons of petrol put in the tank and I think I had then about ten. I drove the car up close to the plane and moved the package into the seat beside the side of the pilot's. I then took off and went out off Southend about the same distance as on the previous occasion. I should have mentioned that after getting the package into the plane I asked one of the ground staff to give me a hand to put it in an upright position.

When I tried to drop the parcel from the plane I had difficulty but by pushing the package against the door I managed to get the door open. I let go of the controls and the plane went into a vertical turn and the parcel fell out into the sea. I then lost my way and landed in a ploughed field in Faversham, Kent. Someone gave the propeller a swing for me and I took off and landed at Gravesend Airport. I left the plane there because it was too dark, hired a taxi and came back home arriving about 8 p.m. I paid the driver and as far as I can remember about £3.10.0. in notes of small denomination.

The next morning, on the Thursday, I went over, I think by bus to Elstree and tried to get a plane to Southend. I was unsuccessful and one of the mechanics working on the airfield volunteered to take me to Southend on the back of his motor bike. I think it was between 12 noon and 1 p.m. when we set off and we arrived at Southend airport at about 2 p.m. to 3 p.m. I picked up the Singer car and drove back to Golders Green and took the Singer car back to Saunders. It would then be about 4 30 p.m. to 5 p.m.

As far as I can remember, on the Friday morning, the 7th October 1949 having seen in the newspapers the numbers of the £5 notes that were reported to have been in Setty's possession when he disappeared, I checked the numbers with those on the notes given to me by 'The Boy.' I found that four of the notes I had received were identical with four of the thousand pounds reported to have been obtained by Setty from his bank.

I disposed of the £150 I obtained in the following manner: I gave £80 in £5 notes to my wife, forty of which she put into our baby's Post office Savings Bank Account; forty pounds she put into her own bank, Martins, Edgware Road branch, and I cannot remember how I disposed of all the other notes but the four I have mentioned I can remember. One I paid at Fortnum & Masons, Piccadilly, for a telephone address pad; one I paid at a shop in Burlington arcade where trinkets are sold, in payment for a set of scissors in a red leather case. I paid the other two at a tobacconists and confectioners in Edgware road, next to a Cinema and I believe the owner's names are Cohen.

On Sunday the 23rd October 1949 I read in the newspapers that part of Setty's body had been found in Essex tied up in a blanket about 11 o'clock that same morning my telephone rang and I think my wife answered it. The call was for me and I spoke. The man 'The Boy' spoke to me and asked me if I had read the Sunday newspapers. He said 'I hope you are not getting any views about getting squeamish and claiming any reward. You have a wife and baby.' I said 'I am in it I presume as deep as you are, for a hundred and fifty pounds at that.' There was a lot more said which I cannot remember.

The aircraft I flew was an Auster the registration number of which was A.G.X.T. I do know XT were the last two letters.

I have been asked what clothes I was wearing on the two occasions I flew the plane out to sea from Southend, the trousers were brown worsted, a zip fastening gabardine golfing jacket, and brown shoes.

I have not seen any of the three men since the night of the 6th October 1949 and I have not heard from any of them since last Sunday.

As far as I can remember approximately at 6 o'clock on Tuesday the 4th October 1949 I met by appointment made in the morning Mr Douglas Muirhead who lives somewhere in Belsize Park area and whose telephone number is Primrose 1295. Mr Muirhead works at Thomas Tillings near Shepherds Market and I was interested in a zip fastener invention he is also interested in. We had arranged to meet outside the 'Shepherd' Public House, Shepherds Market. He did meet me and we went into the public house not later than 6 p.m. and went into the Saloon Bar. I stayed with him about three hours drinking and then went home arriving there about 10 o'clock.

I was paid approximately £1,200, indirectly, in respect of a fire which occurred at a factory which is owned by a Company named 'Little Atom Electrical Products Limited' and of which I am a director.

I bank at Midland Bank Limited, Golders Green and as far as I can recall I have about £10 standing to my credit there.

This statement has been read over to me and it is true.

(signed) B.D. Hume.[8]

The police did not seem to press Hume about his actual whereabouts on the critical day of 4 October and the only logical inference was that he was rather more heavily involved in Setty's disappearance/murder than he was willing to admit. It could also be doubted whether he had the flying skills to fly from Hendon as far south as the English Channel; he may have merely flown eastwards and thrown out the parcels into the North Sea. That would have been easier and there was no reason why Hume should take a longer and more difficult route. In fact, as the body was found in the outer Essex marshes this would tie in with it having been dropped from a plane flying eastwards. The other point is that Hume said he was not given any money before the afternoon of 5 October, yet as noted he had been spending money profusely in the morning of that day (after being in a penurious state). These were three major flaws which gave a lie to his story, and others will appear, but did not seem to have been picked up on.

He also told the police, 'I would like it known that my parents always treated me badly in my youth' (it was rare for him to even allude to his father). Whether they did or not, this was clearly an attempt to try and create some sympathy for himself. It is not known if it worked, but it was a tactic he later employed with the press, who were uncritical.[9]

That night Hume slept in a cell in the police station. According to him, 'The cell I was put into was the one used by Mrs Nora Tierney (she had recently killed a neighbour's child and was at Albany Street police station on 15 August; she was found guilty and sent to Broadmoor) and the blanket I shivered under was the one they had given to her.'[10]

Next day, at 2.30 pm, MacDougall asked Hume:

> 'Have you remembered anything more about the three men as I have had enquiries made and cannot identify them.'
> 'No, I have been thinking hard. I can tell you nothing further about them. You should be able to pick them up in Warren Street.'
> 'I understand you had a knife sharpened at lunch time on Wednesday 5th October 1949 at Saunders Garage, Golders Green.'
> 'I got it sharpened for the joint.'

Hume was also asked to look through the police collection of photographs of known criminals but presumably could not pick out the three men he referred to in his statement.[11] He was then asked about two motor vans he had allegedly offered for sale to Salvadori on 30 September. Hume replied thus to this question: 'I did not have two motor-vans for sale. I was only romancing to get Salvadori to take an interest in me.'

He made an additional statement to the effect that the wrapping and rope found around Setty's torso was similar to that he had used, but owing to it being wet he could not be absolutely certain.[12]

Evidence mounted up against Hume in the next few days. The rope (similar to a clothes line) and felt wrapping were shown to aerodrome workers Davey and Peters and they identified them as those that Hume had carried. Yet, the origin of the felt wrapping could not be identified, though it had possibly been made in Lancashire. The clothes on the torso were identified by Mrs Ouri as having belonged to her brother. The flat was investigated, with the carpet and some floor boards being removed to be examined by Dr Holden. The carving knife sharpened by Edwards was examined by Camps and he said that it could have been used to dismember the corpse. One of Setty's £5 notes was handed into the police, having been obtained at a Romford dog track.[13]

Dr Walter Montgomery examined the hire car and the aircraft that Hume had used to transport the parcels. The car had been used by several people since Hume had returned it on 7 October. He found no bloodstains there. Dr Holden carried out various examinations. He found traces of blood on the floor of the aeroplane that Hume had flown, immediately behind the pilot's seat. More significantly, he examined items taken from the Humes' flat. There was human blood on the underside of the carpet in the living room. There was blood in the linoleum in the hallway. There were traces of blood in the crevices between the floorboards of the living room and on the underlying plaster between the boards. The edges of the hall between the living room and dining room yielded blood as did the handrail of the stairs and the wall of the staircase. There were bloodstains on the bathroom floor and on the bath, too. It was all blood group O, the same as that of Setty; but it also matched about 42 per cent of the population, so was hardly conclusive; though who else's could it have been? These items were taken from the flat and Montgomery stated that there was a 'fairly extensive stain on the underside of this carpet' which was a 'human bloodstain but process of dying and cleaning obscures the group.' Camps estimated that about three pints of blood had been shed but most had been quickly cleared up. Murder had been evidently carried out at the flat; the police naturally assumed that Hume, as the disposer of the body, was the guilty man.[14]

Yet, the scene of the crime had been altered considerably since the murder nearly three weeks previously. Much of the traces of the killing from both the rooms and the killer's body and clothes were now no more. There were none of the footprints or fingerprints that the police would normally have hoped to have found; nor were there any fibre traces. The weapon had been disposed of successfully as had some of the victim. That which remained was less useful than it might have been because its immersion in water for a fortnight had removed some of the potential traces it might have otherwise yielded. Forensic evidence was thus limited as the killer/s had covered some of their tracks effectively, making a successful prosecution less likely.

Other aspects of the police's wider investigations were unproductive. Despite intensive searches of the Dengie Marshes for the remainder of the body, nothing more of Setty's mortal remains was ever found and the search was called off by 25 October. Appeals were made to anyone, especially furniture dealers and shop assistants in north London and adjoining districts, who had sold the brown dyed grey wool and felt, machine stitched, prior to 5 October. Again, nothing positive was found.[15]

Many witnesses gave statements about Hume's activities in early October 1949. It would seem worthwhile to give that of the person closest to him – his wife – in full, taken on 27 October:

> Cynthia Mary Hume. Age 28, Housewife, of 620b Finchley Road, Golders Green, London, NW11, who saieth:
>
> I am married and live at 620b Finchley Road with my husband DONALD BRIAN HUME and my baby daughter.
>
> I have been asked if I can remember three men calling to see my husband at our address between 2 pm and 3 pm on Wednesday, 5th October 1949. The men may have called, but if they did I cannot remember seeing or hearing them.
>
> My baby is only 3½ months old and I may have been attending to the child or I may have been out.

Our flat at 620B Finchley Road is situated on the 2nd and 3rd floors.

I have also been asked if I can remember my husband and two men coming into our flat after 8.30 pm on the evening of the 5th October 1949, carrying a large heavy package and put it into the far kitchen cupboard.

I cannot remember anything like this happening. I would almost certainly be somewhere in the flat at that time in the evening.

I have no knowledge of my husband and a man from Saunders Garage taking the large package from the kitchen cupboard the following morning, the 6th of October and carrying it downstairs.

I remember my husband giving me in money, principally £80 0s 0d in £5 notes and the remainder in £1 notes.

I think he gave me this sum on 4th October 1949, some time in the evening. There is a possibility it may have been the following morning he gave me the money.

On the 5th October, 1949, I cannot remember the time, I paid £23 into my Post Office Savings Bank Account, at Golders Green Post Office, Finchley Road. My Post office account is 28144. The transaction is shown in my Savings Bank Book.

The same day I paid £50 of the money given me by my husband into the Midland Bank Ltd., Cross Roads Branch, Golders Green, to the credit of my account at Martins Bank, 79 Edgware Road W2. I paid this money into the Bank before 3.30 pm and I may have paid the other sums into my Post Office account about the same time.

I am in possession of a paying in slip counterfoil showing the transaction with the Midland Bank.

My husband has never told me that he was threatened by any man or men or that any threat had been made regarding myself.

Sometime recently, last night I think, my husband had told me he had bought his Christmas presents.

Some time I mentioned to him that I needed scissors and he said he thought of getting me some for Christmas. He may have bought scissors for me but he has not given them to me yet.

I have not received a telephone pad from my husband recently. He did give me a pair of nylons about a week ago.

My husband has not taken any carpet felt from the flat and we do not possess any Army or Air Force type blankets.

He has been indoors a lot more than he used to be. I cannot remember whether he was at home or out on the afternoon or evening on 4th October 1949.

I know a Mr Muirhead who works for Thomas Tillings, contractors and I know my husband has been in touch with him about a zip fastener.

I believe my husband has been earning his living recently by flying aeroplanes, because he has told me this.

I have read this statement.

(signed) CYNTHIA MARY HUME

Statement taken down in writing and signature witnessed by me C. MacDougall, Detective Superintendent.

The key sentence may be 'I would almost certainly be somewhere in the flat at that time in the evening.' This shows where she was that evening, and probably other evenings, and the reader needs to anchor that in their mind.[16]

Hume was first charged with the murder at Bow Street Magistrates' Court on 29 October and each of his subsequent public appearances were covered by most newspapers. He was the only and the obvious suspect. Hume arrived at 8.45 am and had long conferences with his solicitor, Alfred Goldman of Isidore Goldman and Son, of 125 High Holborn. Though it was sixty-five years old, this legal firm had never handled a murder case previously. Goldman was also in the moneylending business, had had dealings with Hume in the previous year and the latter had paid him at least £675 when he acted as his solicitor when Hume had been in business. He appeared before Mr John Francis Eastwood (1887–1952), KC, OBE, a Metropolitan Police magistrate. Hume just answered 'yes' to the question as to whether he understood that he would be remanded and that he would appear in a week's time. Hume stated that he was 'absolutely not guilty.'[17]

He was described as Brian Donald Hume, being 'a company director', doubtless at his own request in an attempt to beef up his status (Haigh had also used that appellation). The only information given was the details of the arrest, as supplied by MacDougall. The court was packed with spectators, including the Burnley football team, vegetable porters, flower girls, businessmen and women in fur and jewels, and also Mr Ouri. Hume recalled, after his first court appearance, 'After the strain of those days . . . the actual charge – of murdering Stanley Setty – was a relief. I had not had a shave for five days.' The solicitors for Tiffin claimed the £1,000 reward for their client on this day and he received this sum later that year.[18]

There were various descriptions of Hume written by journalists at this time. Webb wrote: 'I found it difficult to think of him as a killer. His dark, rugged looking face was unshaven. His clothes were untidy, as though it had been a

Saturday morning he was spending in his suburban garden instead of in the dock.' He added that 'Somewhere in that broad head must have been a kindly thought . . . somewhere in that demented and warped mind.'[19]

Given Webb's animosity towards Hume, his words here are surprisingly sympathetic. Another journalist wrote that Hume was 'unshaven, and wore a crumpled red checked sports coat and flannels, an RAF tie and shirt.'[20]

Those who knew Hume socially made statements to the police. Thomas Lee Barry recalled that Hume was 'very boastful . . . most of his conversations when we were together would be about flying. . . . a very likeable chap and not a person to do anything criminally wrong.' An unidentified man was reported as saying, 'I am a relative of Hume's and I can't imagine him doing a thing like that [murder] although I knew he was desperately short of money.'[21]

On 28 October Hume applied for legal aid as he lacked the money to pay for his own defence. Most criminals find themselves in this position and so are defended by a barrister who is generally youthful (Timothy Evans was defended by Mr Malcolm Morris, not yet a KC, when on trial for murder in 1950), chosen by the Clerk of the Court. However, those charged with infamous crimes, such as Heath and Haigh, were approached by the popular press which paid for their defence in exchange for an exclusive series of interviews to be published in the newspaper – the *Sunday Pictorial* and the *News of the World* (two best-selling Sunday tabloids) often indulged in this practice. And this case was unusual, with not only murder but one in which the corpse had been dismembered and disposed of from an aeroplane.

Hume was almost immediately contacted by Fred Redman, crime reporter of the *Sunday Pictorial*, when he was awaiting trial, and it was in this paper that his story appeared immediately after his trial, in three instalments. Redman recalled some extracts from Hume's letters; Hume writing, 'I have not yet played out my ace' whatever that meant. He naturally protested his innocence in another letter, 'I haven't led a particularly good life. I've broken man-made laws but I have not broken the law of God about killing a man.'[22]

Webb approached Goldman about Hume on 29 October, wanting information about his life. Initially Goldman gave him a blank refusal, 'No time now. I'm a busy man', but two days later, Goldman was positive but wanted £600 and declared, 'I'm his mouthpiece, ain't I?' Mr Claude Duveen (1903–76) was also employed in Hume's defence. He had been called to the Bar in 1927 and had chiefly dealt with bankruptcy cases up to that point.[23]

At some stage, Goldman contacted Hume's doctor, Dr Cyril Way of 923 Finchley Road, to ask whether his patient often suffered from nose bleeds (presumably to try and account for the blood found in the flat). Hume was asked by Goldman to have his blood tested but he refused. Curiously, Dr Way stated that he had also been Setty's doctor.[24]

The second court hearing was on 5 November and lasted only 2 minutes. Robert Henderson Blundell (1901–67), a Metropolitan magistrate and barrister, was told by Duveen that contrary to what Goldman had announced two days ago, there would be no need for legal aid. Hume wore a light-grey jacket and dark trousers, with his RAF tie. His hair was ruffled and unstyled.[25]

On 15 November, the case for the prosecution was opened, once again before Blundell. Maurice Crump (1909–96) appeared as the representative of the Department of the Public Prosecutor. He outlined the evidence against Hume. Jamieson and MacDougall gave statements and were cross examined by Duveen, who asked, 'Would it be right to say that Hume was under remorseless pressure from October 26 to 29?' 'No sir, he was not under any pressure at all.' Staddon and Bailey also gave evidence. Hume was remanded in custody until 25 November.[26]

On the 25th the court appearance was delayed because Duveen had been slow arriving. A journalist noted, 'Hume pulled a thick black notebook from his left hand jacket pocket, and put his legs through the grill of the dock to rest his feet on a bench in front.'[27] His final court appearance was on 6 December, when he was officially committed to the Old Bailey for trial for murder.[28]

Meanwhile, on 7 November the inquest on Setty was opened at Chelmsford before Dr Louis Francis Beccle (1904–64), a barrister and Coroner for South East Essex since 1936. Tiffin was the first witness, followed by the police officers and Dr Camps. It was explained how the body was found and how it was identified as the missing car dealer. Victor Durand (1907–94), a barrister, gave a statement from the family about Setty, stating that his reputation had been unfairly and inaccurately attacked in various newspapers because of his fraud offence in 1928:

> It may well be if you look back into the past as certain papers have apparently done, digging deep enough, you may find something against this unfortunate man . . . But it is a thousand pities that a man who has lived honestly and respectably for well over 20 years . . . should form the subject matter of articles written purely for profit and of no benefit to the public. It has hurt the relatives deeply.

Durand looked forward to the day when to slander and libel the deceased would be an offence under law. The inquest was adjourned until 7 January.[29]

Once Hume had been charged with the murder he was sent to Brixton prison in south London, a prison where men awaiting trial are held. He arrived on

29 October. Hume later recalled, 'A closed van took me to Brixton Prison. I had been there before, but this time it was different. The great black gates looked bigger and grimmer than I remembered. But everyone there was very kind to me. The first night I was there I went to bed at night and slept like a log.'[30]

Hume was sent to the hospital block, as are all new inmates. There were at least twelve, perhaps up to eighteen men, there in total. They were allowed to wear their ordinary clothes (after all they are innocent until proven guilty) and spent their days chatting, smoking, reading books and newspapers and playing games. Each man was allowed a daily ration of beer and cigarettes. The room was like an ordinary hospital ward, with a long table in the middle for meals. There were proper beds with mattresses, clean sheets, green covers, but with hard pillows. Lights went out at 9 pm and there were screams and mutterings at night time.[31]

Again, as with all prisoners, Hume had to be examined and interviewed by Dr Matheson, who had great experience of dealing with prisoners, and who had seen Haigh earlier that year. It is important for prisoners to be interviewed so that their mental health can be assessed. Those who are deemed insane and unfit to plead and thus cannot be put on trial, will usually be sent to Broadmoor instead. Matheson had the advantage of being able to see Hume's medical reports taken in 1941 and 1942, but also made his own assessments.[32]

Matheson made his report on 9 January 1950. Hume had been examined on reception and had been under medical observation in the hospital. He had been seen daily by Matheson or a colleague, and had been interviewed often. He had learnt of Hume's early life, as told by Hume, his working and RAF career and his previous offence. If Hume's version of his early life was true, then his upbringing might lead to mental instability and neurosis:

> It would tend to give him a feeling of inferiority and explain his reputation of being very boastful and imaginative. This imaginative boasting could be considered as an over compensation for his feeling of inferiority and failure in the RAF. The alleged cruelties inflicted on him as a boy could account for his readiness to believe that people are against him – anxious to trap him.[33]

Hume told the doctor that he thought that the police were attempting to frame him. Matheson thought that Hume's past history:

> does not divulge any evidence of insanity or other mental disease beyond a mild psycho-neurotic condition which might be more accurately described by saying that through lack of good training in his early life he had developed bad habits of conduct.

Dr Matheson considered that 'The attack of meningitis may have caused some personality change by making him less stable mentally.' He did not find Hume to exhibit signs of insanity, and thought:

> He is of average intelligence and is not feeble minded . . . he speaks rationally and coherently. He is always anxious to impress the interviewer how much he has suffered at the hands of his 'Aunt' and how, with reference to the present charge, everybody seems to be against him. He would weep readily when he thought tears might impress me.

Therefore, he was 'an unreliable informant who would readily imagine or relate any story which he thought might elicit sympathy and help him.'[34]

In conclusion, though there was no evidence of insanity or feeblemindedness, he thought that Hume was a psychopath, for he was deemed 'emotionally unstable, tends to be rebellious, who cannot readily adapt himself to reality and fails to profit from experience . . . a psychopathic personality due to environmental faults in his early life and probably constitutional factors as well . . . lacks judgement and seldom displays foresight and ordinary providence.' Hume had, on his solicitors' advice, refused any electro-encephalographic examination. He was fit to plead and to stand trial.[35]

Hume mixed with a variety of murderers. These included Daniel Raven, who had recently killed his in-laws, and Dennis Barrett, who had killed Kathleen Rosam. Hume said he did not trust the former, though apparently he treated Hume with consideration by tearing out all references to the Setty case from the newspapers before showing them to him. He preferred Barrett's company. 'They were a very queer crowd, and some of the things they told me were hair raising', he recalled. Hume was keen to impress the other prisoners with his own exploits as Dr Matheson noted, 'inclined to be boastful and tried to impress other inmates with stories of past exploits in the air.' They often talked to one another about their chances at their impending trials and what sentences they would receive. Hume seemed confident, writing to a friend thus, 'You would be surprised if I told you how much I have settled down here. I don't think I am liable to have my chips next February or so. However they tell me it [hanging] is pretty quick.'[36]

Hume also claimed that he had been involved in an escape attempt, along with Barrett. The plan was to overpower the prison officer in the ward and tie up the other inmates. They would then break off the table legs and use them to lever open the bars of the windows. After that knotted blankets with hooks would be used to scale the prison walls. Hume thought, 'It was all beautifully simple, and I am convinced we would have got away with it.'[37]

Yet, someone gave them away; apparently it was Ernest Couzins, accused of the murder of Victor Ellis in Canterbury. Prison officers searched the rooms and took away one man. Later Hume confessed to the governor and was put into solitary confinement, where he read his Bible, or so he said.[38] A prison officer later claimed that Hume was 'the most egotistical person he had ever met.'[39]

When Hume was in prison his wife came to visit him. She had not seen him since his arrest on 26 October. Her first visit was on 30 October. They had to sit at opposite ends of a long table and there was a piece of glass a foot high between them, with a prison officer listening to their conversation, 'all very cheerless.' However, she recalled him laughing and joking in the belief that everything would be fine. He claimed, 'I remained calm and collected.' Apparently he spent most of his time writing.[40]

Mrs Hume was seemingly very supportive of her husband. She was interviewed in the press and stressed her confidence in him, 'I am standing by my husband with all the power I've got . . . Nothing will convince me he did what he is accused of.' She was involved in defending him, but did not know where the money would come from as she had little and knew Hume had none. Yet, she did not want to have to depend on others.[41]

Whilst he was at Brixton, Hume met Timothy John Evans (1924–50), who had been charged with the murder of his wife, Beryl, and baby daughter, Geraldine, at 10 Rillington Place in Notting Hill in early November 1949. Although there seems no doubt that they met, it is unclear how accurate Hume's recollections are. Evans said of Hume, 'I'd never thought I would be in the same hospital as Hume when I used to talk about the case' (when Evans' rented rooms were searched, the police found news cuttings of Hume's case and whilst some writers have alleged (with no evidence) these were planted on Evans, Evans' statement suggests otherwise). Evans later said, 'we play dominoes and games of all kinds all day, but you have to watch Hume.'[42]

As noted, Hume did not refer to Evans in his statement about prison life made in 1950, possibly because Evans was not a newsworthy topic then – just a common or garden wife and baby murderer – whereas in 1958 and 1965 when Hume made his additional statements he was, because it was now claimed by some that Evans had been hanged in error. Judge Daniel Brabin, investigating this alleged miscarriage of justice, stated, 'I place no reliance on what Hume has written.'[43]

In 1958 Hume claimed he convinced Evans, who had confessed to the police to murder, that he should alter his plea to one of not guilty. He suggested to him, 'Don't put your head in a noose. Make up a new story and stick to it.' Hume asked Evans whether he murdered his daughter. Evans claimed, 'No, but I was there while it was done.' Hume related, 'He told me that he and Christie had gone into the bedroom together, that Christie had strangled the kid with a bit of rag while he stood and watched.' He also told Hume that 'Christie came to an arrangement with his wife and that Christie had murdered her.'[44] John Reginald Halliday Christie (1899–1953) was Evans' fellow tenant at 10 Rillington Place. Whilst he was a serial killer, the popular assumption that he killed Beryl and Geraldine Evans is highly questionable.

Seven years later, Hume gave another version of events. In this he alleged that Evans opened up to him and declared, 'In the presence of several prisoners Evans admitted to killing the baby because it kept crying. So in the presence of these lags and a guard, I hooked him and was booked for it. I have no scruples about adults killing each other, but I dislike people who hurt kids and animals.' There is a reference to a prison officer having to separate Hume and Evans, so this story may be true and it certainly fits in with Hume's violent nature. The reference to the baby crying being his motivation for murder is corroborated independently by PS Trevallian, who also reported that Evans told him the same.[45]

In John Eddowes' rigorous revisionist study of the Evans/Christie case he lays much stress on Evans being a psychopath, but much of what he says applies to Hume, too. Psychopathic behaviour has its causes in the lack of a loving family background and heredity insanity and comes to the surface when the subject has had some drinks. Violence as a means to an end, an erratic working career, inability to have realistic long-term goals, promiscuity, grandiose lying and fantasy are all part of the psychopath's make-up. These apply to Evans but, the mental instability apart, also to Hume.[46]

Whilst Hume was in prison, Setty's torso and arms were buried in that part of Golders Green Jewish Cemetery (row 57, no. 11) that was reserved for Sephardi Jews; so graves were placed horizontally rather than upright. The burial took place on 6 November 1949 and the inscription read:

IN
LOVING MEMORY
OF
STANLEY SETTY
WHO DIED
4TH OCTOBER 1949
DEEPLY MOURNED BY HIS SISTER, BROTHERS,
RELATIVES AND FRIENDS

Ironically, the cemetery, on Hoop Lane, just off the Finchley Road, is little more than half a mile north of where Hume had lived and about the same distance from the house where Hume briefly lived with his grandmother.

Chapter 6

The Crown Against Donald Hume, 1950

The trial of Hume was widely reported in the press, which is no surprise given all the attention he had garnered in the previous year. A great deal of column space was accorded to him, as was usually the case with sensational crimes, such as that of John George Haigh in the previous year. The disappearance of Setty, the finding of his dismembered corpse, the unusual method of disposal and the sudden arrest of Hume all served to make this a far from the run-of-the-mill murder case that, for example, a domestic murder would be. Webb wrote that the press were convinced that they would have a 'colourful and probably sensational murder', and he agreed. 'It has all the pathos, drama and excitement of one of the most sensational trials ever to be held.' Gladys Langford noted in her diary, 'The Setty murder case occupies much of the newspapers.' On one of the trial days queuing for the limited number of public places in court began at 3 in the morning. One of the people in the queue was a Mrs Gordon from Eastbourne, who had likewise queued for the Haigh trial; another was Mrs Shine of Euston who had petitioned for clemency for the killer Daniel Raven. The court room was crowded and even Chief Inspector Jamieson had to stand; to this, Hume joked to him in a whisper, 'Anyone can have my place.'[1]

The trial began at number one court of the Central Criminal Court, popularly known as the Old Bailey, in London where murder cases in the capital are held (other courts hear lesser offences), as it was the equivalent of an assize court in the counties outside London and Middlesex. The first day was Wednesday, 18 January 1950. Unlike many notable trials, no complete transcript for the trial exists; none was written up for the *Notable British Trials* series, which published the transcripts of many key trials up to 1953. Therefore, evidence for this trial is in part taken from the truncated version published in the *Celebrated British Trials* series in 1976 and the reports published in the contemporary press; neither of these is complete.

However, the truncated version of the trial is limited at best. Firstly, the editor's transcription is frequently at fault. He often excises quite important exchanges and nowhere explains why he selects, and rejects, information. Fortunately, a little of the trial transcript does still exist at The National

Archives; the opening speech for the prosecution and the crucial examination and cross-examination of Drs Holden and Camps concerning the key forensic evidence. This hitherto unexamined material has been used in this chapter and sheds fresh light on the case as well as providing a little light relief in an otherwise dark case.

A few words should be said about the physical setting in which the trial took place. The dock, where the accused stood, is, appropriately, in the centre of the court, and is a small square enclosure in panelling, 4ft high, with steps leading to the cells below. This is where the defendant stands. On his right is his counsel for the defence; on his left are the jury sitting in two rows. Below them are the newspaper reporters. Behind the dock are the public galleries where about thirty people may sit. Dominating the whole scene is the judicial bench of six chairs. There is the judge's clerk and the presiding judge, as well as chairs for the Lord Mayor, sheriff and aldermen, though these latter are not obliged to attend. Above all is the sword of justice.[2]

There was quite an array of legal luminaries in court that day. The judge was Mr Justice Lewis; Sir Wilfrid Hubert Poyer Lewis (1881–1950). He had been called to the Bar in 1908 and after serving as a staff officer in the First World War continued to scale the heights of the legal profession. He was Junior Counsel to the Treasury in 1930 and was made a judge of the King's Bench in 1935. He was courteous, patient and detached on the Bench and was described as 'a fine judge.'[3]

The prosecution team was Mr Travers Christmas Humphreys (1901–83) and Mr Henry Havelock Elam (1903–93), instructed by the Director of Public Prosecutions for the Crown. Humphreys was the son of the famous judge Sir Travers Humphreys (1867–1956). He had been called to the Bar in 1924 and was a Junior Treasury Counsel at the Old Bailey in 1934. He became the Recorder of Deal in 1942 and Deputy Chairman of the East Kent Quarter Sessions in 1947. In 1946 he had been Junior Counsel in the Japanese War Crimes Trials. He was also a practising Buddhist and writer on Buddhism. As noted, he had encountered Hume in 1942, though probably had forgotten all about it. Elam had been called the Bar in 1927, was Junior Prosecuting Counsel by 1945, Recorder of Exeter in 1947 and Deputy Chairman of the West Kent Quarter Sessions in the same year.[4]

Humphreys, in retrospect, thought that this was a trial of particular interest. In his memoirs he wrote that it was one of only a dozen trials in the nine years when he had been senior prosecuting counsel that he thought it worth keeping cuttings of. He wrote, 'The trial of Donald Hume . . . was made the more dramatic still by events which happened daily during its course.'[5]

Defending Hume were Mr Richard Francis Levy (1892–1968) and the aforementioned Duveen, instructed by Isadore Goldman and Son, solicitors.[6] Levy had been called to the Bar in 1918 and became a KC in 1937. In that same year he had unsuccessfully defended the Revd Harold Davidson, rector of Stiffkey, on a charge of indecency.[7]

Ironically, in the same court on the previous week, there had been a trial where Lewis had been judge and Humphreys and Elam were the counsel for the Crown. It had lasted from 11–13 January and Timothy Evans, whom Hume had met in the previous month, was on trial for the murder of his child. Evans pleaded not guilty, but was found otherwise and sentenced to death. Lewis was later unfairly presented by Ludovic Kennedy in *Ten Rillington Place* as being unnecessarily hostile towards the defendant in giving a damning and misleading summing up to the jury, though the Appeal Court exonerated Lewis.

William Duke Coleridge, the Clerk of the Court (an important administrative official who makes all the trial arrangements including ensuring that all who need them have a copy of the depositions made), read out the indictment: 'Brian Donald Hume, you are charged that on 4 October last you murdered Stanley Setty. How say you, are you guilty or not guilty?' Hume simply replied, as almost all defendants do: 'Not guilty.'

The jury of ten men and two women was then empanelled and sworn. They were then told: 'Members of the jury, the prisoner at the Bar, Brian Donald Hume, is charged with the murder of Stanley Setty on 4 October last. To this indictment he has pleaded not guilty, and it is your charge to say, having heard the evidence, whether he be guilty or not.'[8]

Rebecca West was covering the trial for the *Evening Standard* and later described how Hume struck her:

> He was a middle sized young man with an abundance of black hair, a face much fatter than his body, a mouth like a woman's, and deep set dark eyes burning with eagerness . . . He looked foreign, he might have been a Turk or an Arab . . . The first sight of him suggested a spiv. He wore the checked sports jacket, the pullover, the flannel trousers, all chosen to look raffish, which was then the uniform of the spiv and he had the air of self-conscious impudence, which is the spiv's hallmark.

Hume sat throughout the day and passed occasional notes to Levy.[9]

Humphreys then opened the case on the Crown's behalf:

> The charge is one of Wilful murder. That being the charge, it is the duty of the Prosecution to prove it, and if when you have heard the whole of the evidence you are left in any reasonable doubt as to whether or not the Prosecution have proved their case, you will acquit. Only if you are satisfied that that charge has been proved will you convict.
>
> The evidence in this case will be almost entirely circumstantial . . . No person will be called to say he saw Hume murder the dead man, Mr Setty; there is no suggestion of any confession by the accused man that he murdered Setty, but you will be asked to consider a great mass of detailed evidence, and to put together those items of evidence in such a way that they prove, perhaps more cogently even that direct evidence, the charge brought against this man. Direct evidence can sometimes lie; people may, with the best will in the world, say they saw a certain thing happen; they may be wrong; but when you get a vast quantity of detailed evidence all adding up to one inevitable conclusion, you may regard that as proof.[10]

Humphreys then went through the case as he saw it. He argued that Hume and Setty knew each other through their acquaintanceship in the car markets near Warren Street. Hume was short of money and Setty had withdrawn £1,005 in £5 notes on 4 October. That night Setty was killed and Hume was in the possession of £5 notes; four of them being part of those belonging to Setty. Hume confessed that he had dropped parts of the dismembered Setty over the sea from an aeroplane. Bloodstains were found in Hume's flat. 'You may agree with the proposition that he who cuts up the dead body of a recently murdered man is very probably the murderer', yet Hume had not confessed to dismemberment, only disposal.[11]

Hume's statement was partially correct, argued Humphreys, but only that part which could be proved to be true. 'It is part provable lies . . . a murderer must lie. He must give some explanation to account for his movements . . . he must romance in order to avoid the consequences of his act.' Humphreys then discussed the case. Setty was last seen at 5.50 pm on 4 October. His car was later found outside his garage. Only the killer would know where it was and Hume possessed that information. Hume was desperate for money, but on 5 October, following the murder, was able to pay off bills. 'I repeat, men have been murdered for much less than £1,005.'[12]

The parcel containing part of Setty's corpse was duly found and the latter identified. Camps said that the corpse had been put in the water two days after death. The murder occurred on the 4th and Hume's disposal of it being on the 6th, as he said. Camps had been remarkably accurate. Hume was questioned by the police on the 26th and denied all knowledge of the case, 'I know nothing about it.' Humphreys asserted, 'That, of course, was a lie.' There followed other lies. Humphreys then outlined Hume's statement about Max, Greeny and the Boy. He completely ridiculed the story: 'It is complete fantasy, say the prosecution, about three men, whose very existence he had to invent, and who, the prosecution say, do not exist outside the fertile and romancing imagination of the accused.'[13] He then wound up his speech:

> What happened in the flat on the night of the 4th of October I do not know, members of the jury, and it is no part of the case for the Prosecution to speculate. What does matter is this: Setty was there murdered and cut up . . . I rely on no medical theory . . . it may be that Setty was stabbed in the sitting room near the door. He would immediately cough, and the blood would dribble out pretty fast from those wounds. That may account for the blood on the carpet near the door and the bloodstains . . . You may think then he had to face one of the most difficult problems facing any murderer; the disposal of the body. He has cut it up and has got it into parcels; he has got almost unique opportunities because he can fly, and he flies, and drops those parcels, as he thinks, in the sea forever, and he must have hoped against hope as the days went by that they would never return. But they did return. Members of the jury, or part of them, on the returning tide, and that is why you are trying Brian Donald Hume for murder.

He had spoken for 50 minutes.[14]

The witnesses were then called. PC Thomas Macindoe showed the jury a plan of the flat at Finchley Road. Chief Inspector Percy Law of the Photographic Department showed photographs he had taken at the flat. Mrs Ouri testified to last seeing her brother alive on the evening of 4 October and that the clothing found on the corpse was his. Witnesses testified to the fact that Setty had had £1,005 in £5 notes withdrawn for him, in exchange for a car, but disagreed whether it was on 4 October or the following day. Isadore Rosenthal, who had handed them to Setty and gave the latter date, was cross-examined by Levy:

> 'Are you sure the sale was 5 October?'
> 'Yes. It was a Tuesday.'

Lewis intervened to point out that the Tuesday that week was 4 October.
Levy continued:

> 'Is Warren Street a place where deals are made in cars which have
> something possibly tainted about them?'
> 'Well, there are rumours, but we usually get to know which cars are
> tainted and which are not.'
> 'It is the recognised centre for illicit car deals?'
> 'Well . . .'

Levy had made his point that Setty was involved in less than legitimate dealing
and so would have come into contact with criminals, some of whom might
be violent.[15]

Mansfield was the next to step up to the witness box. He stated that he had
introduced Hume to Setty in 1947 but when he read the descriptions of Max,
Greeny and the Boy declared that he did not know anyone who resembled
them. Given that these three were absolutely integral to his client's story, Levy
had to do his best to cast doubt on the witness' reliability and proceeded in
this attempt:

> 'Suppose you were asked to help the police in identifying a gang of
> men who you knew would not stop short of murder if they found
> that you had given them away, would you be very anxious to help
> the police?'
> 'I think so, yes.'
> 'Were you warned to keep quiet about these things because the men
> that they were seeking might be violent?'
> 'No, I don't think I was. No, I was not. Not by the police.'
> 'Were you warned by anyone else?'
> 'No, I don't think so.'[16]

Salvadori was the next witness and, as with Mansfield, testified that he knew
Setty and Hume but did not know the trio Hume claimed existed. Collins was
next and he said that Hume paid him his rent with a £5 note. He was asked by
Levy if he had seen the three men go into Hume's flat and he said he had not,
but he had seen one foreign looking man enter; perhaps this was Setty, though
he was never pressed on this point. Muirhead was next and he said he had not
seen Hume on the evening of the 4th, though Hume had earlier sworn they
had spent the evening drinking together.[17] This told against Hume but was not
exploited, for it showed Hume had lied about his whereabouts on the night
Setty disappeared and the question must be why he had done so.

More witnesses gave their testimonies. These showed that Hume was awash with money on the day after the murder, that he had sent his carpet to be cleaned on that day and had asked that a carving knife be sharpened on the 5th, too (the jury asked if the knife could have been sharpened in order to conceal any damage that might have been caused to it by cutting up a body but it is not known if this query was resolved). Mrs Stride then told the court that Hume told her on the 5th to go out and buy a floor cloth as he had used it to clean a stained carpet; both of which were no longer in the flat. She had not seen any men enter the flat that afternoon and no one brought any parcels in. She did remember that Hume told her he wanted to be undisturbed in the kitchen for an hour, and that when he left he did so carrying two parcels with him.[18]

Humphreys also asked whether she had seen a joint of meat that day and she replied not. Levy cross-examined her by suggesting that this was because she had not looked for one and she rebutted this by stating, 'No, it would be most noticeable in these days [food was scarce due to rationing].' There was laughter at this point in the court and Hume joined in. But Levy was able to make her admit some negative points in Hume's favour; that she had seen no sign of anything associated with death in the flat; nor did she hear 'any noise like the sawing up of bones.' Lewis had her clarify that Mrs Hume was absent from the flat for much of the afternoon.[19]

According to West, 'She [Mrs Stride] had, on the first day of the trial, wholly destroyed both the case for the prosecution and the case for the defence.' She had witnessed nothing that pointed to murder and dismemberment having occurred in the flat. Nor did she provide any evidence to suggest that anyone brought the parcels to Hume.[20]

The next two witnesses gave evidence that on the 5th Hume arrived at Elstree aerodrome with two parcels, took an Auster aeroplane up and arrived at Southend airport later that day without any parcels. Staddon was the final witness for the day and he told the court that he helped Hume down the stairs with a heavy parcel on the following day. At the conclusion of this, the jury was taken to Hume's flat, which they examined for 15 minutes. West later described the flat thus:

> A dark steep and narrow staircase with a murderous turn to it led past the front door of the lower maisonette, which was inhabited by a schoolmaster and his wife, up to Hume's own front door, which opened on a slit of a lobby. To the left was a living room, looking over the street; to the right was a smaller dining room, long and narrow, with beyond it a pantry, and beyond that again an attic kitchenette with the slant of a roof coming fairly low. None of these rooms was

large. The living room was, perhaps, fifteen feet by eleven and the dining-room fifteen feet by eight. Another steep and narrow and perilous stairway led up to a bedroom, a nursery and a bathroom.[21]

The second day of the trial began on Thursday, 19 January. But there was no Justice Lewis at the Old Bailey. He had been taken ill in the night at his Kensington home, possibly this being brought on by the strain of his Home Guard work in London during the Second World War. This had been his last trial and he died on 15 March 1950 (not just a few days after the end of the Evans trial of the previous week, as stated by Ludovic Kennedy). His replacement was another able member of the Bench, Mr Justice Sellers. Sir Frederick Aked Sellers (1893–1979) had been an army officer in the First World War, winning the Military Cross. He was called to the Bar in 1919, was made a KC in 1935 and in 1946 became a judge of the King's Bench Division. He had been Recorder of Bolton, 1938–46 and had stood twice as a prospective Liberal MP (unsuccessfully). The jury was discharged and a new one sworn in. Humphreys said that the jury should try the case on the evidence of the witnesses, not speeches of counsel, so he did not subject the jury to a repeat of his speech of yesterday. He briefly outlined it, however, before all of yesterday's witnesses were recalled, perhaps diluting the prosecution's case.[22]

These proceedings were interrupted when a telegram was handed to Levy, who then went into a consultation with Humphreys. Levy stated that this was a matter for the judge to decide. The jury retired and the telegram was passed to Sellers, who was then also handed a letter. Apparently these had been sent to Mrs Hume by Webb, the top crime journalist on the Sunday tabloid the *People*. He was instrumental in the destruction of the Messina gangsters who ran a vice racket in Soho and the West End in the 1950s. Mrs Hume's solicitors had opened the letters and were concerned about their content, considering that Mrs Hume was a key witness for the defence.[23] Levy commented: 'It appears that a national newspaper is bringing pressure to bear on Mrs Hume not to give evidence. Your lordship may think that this is a most unwarrantable and improper attempt to affect the course of justice.'

For once in the trial Humphreys agreed with Levy about this 'outrageous conduct' and suggested that Mrs Hume be provided with protection until she had given her evidence. Webb then arrived in the court room and admitted he sent the letter and telegram.[24] He was interrogated by Sellers:

'Have you any explanation to give the court?'
'My Lord, I have an explanation. Since this case has been on – that is, since Mr Hume had been arrested – I have been in constant

touch with Mrs Hume, and the last time I saw her was as recently as last Friday.'

'How long have you known Mrs Hume?'

'I met her once about a year ago.'

'When did you next see her?'

'Two weeks after Hume was arrested.'

'In what circumstances? – What was your association with her?'

'Purely social.'

'Would it be right to say your association with her was as a newspaper man?'

'Not quite correct.'

'Tell me what is correct?'

'Mrs Hume told me several newspapers were asking her to write an article under her own name. I advised her not to do so.'

'Why did you act as you have? I have read the telegram and I have read the letter.'

'Yesterday I was talking to Mrs Hume's mother and she told me her daughter had been spirited away.'

'What has that got to do with you?'

'Mrs Hume had asked me to see her about the trial or at the end of the trial. I gather that she is involved in the case.'

'What has that got to do with you? What interest is it of yours?'

'I was asked by her mother and her to be her escort.'

'What have you got to say about this interference?'

'I was acting as a friend.'

'Do you know that in Common Law it is a misdemeanour to interfere with a witness?'

'I humbly apologise. I did not understand she was a witness in this trial.'

Webb concluded that Mrs Hume's mother had asked him to ask her daughter not to write the article, but he had not tried to stop her attending court as a witness. He did not know that she was being called by the defence to do so and if he had known that he would never have written to her in the way he had done as he knew too much of the law to do that. Sellers accepted the explanation but warned that interfering with witnesses was a very serious issue.[25]

Webb's exact relationship with Cynthia at this point is unclear. He knew her as a friend and was clearly trusted by her and her mother, but whether they were on more intimate terms at this stage is unknown. His behaviour was questionable to say the least. As an experienced crime reporter he must have known that it was highly likely that as the wife of the defendant she would be called by the defence as a witness, yet he claimed to be innocent of such knowledge. It is possible that he may have surmised that the story she had told the police and would tell in court might be inaccurate and so he had to help assist and advise her at this time, with his superior knowledge and experience of police and court procedure.

The case for the prosecution then continued. Dr Montgomery explained how he had examined the cars used by Hume in transporting the parcels (three weeks later) but stated he found no evidence of bloodstains in them. Tiffin told the court how he had discovered the bundle in the marshes. Marsh stated how he had driven Hume to Elstree aerodrome on the 6th and that Hume had two parcels with him. Levy cross-examined him, by suggesting that he was wrong about the parcels and that Hume only had an overcoat with him, but Marsh stuck to his guns, 'He had two parcels with him' (it was never ascertained what was in these or when or where they were disposed of, but clearly for him to carry them with him suggested they were important). Another witness confirmed Hume had a parcel with him on arrival at Southend airport later that day, where he took an aeroplane. Finally, the court was told by the last witness of the day that Hume had arrived by aeroplane at Gravesend airport later that day but without any parcels.[26]

Friday, 20 January was the third day of the trial. Dr Holden was the next witness for the prosecution. He stated that he had examined the aeroplane used by Hume and the surfaces of several rooms in his flat. Here he had found many traces of blood belonging to Setty's blood group. No bloodstains had been found in the coal cupboard, however. Levy cast as much doubt on this evidence as possible, by having Holden admit that bloodstains can remain in place for a long time and that some of the blood might have come from Tony the dog.

He then turned to the carpet and asked Holden why he had been unable to find blood on the underfelt but had found it on the carpet. Holden answered thus:

> 'I think it highly probable that the pile would clean more easily than the binding material which forms the under surface of the carpet.'
> 'If blood was spilt upon the carpet whilst it was laid upon underfelt, would it be inevitable, that some would get onto the underfelt?'
> 'I should have expected it.'

Levy suggested that as the carpet, when sent to the cleaners, was wrapped with the underfelt on the outside, that it might have come into contact with an item or a person with blood on them and that this might have been transferred to the underfelt, but Holden thought that this was not likely. Levy also tried to suggest that the stains found might be of other human substances such as excrement or pus or even nasal slime.

He was also asked about various boards in the coal cupboard and the coal cupboard itself. There had been, perhaps, some blood on one of the boards but none on the others. Levy also indulged in a little humour. During Holden's investigation in the Humes' flat he had found a spider's web in the coal cupboard in which the parcels had allegedly been temporarily stored, and which Holden suggested had not been disturbed for some time. Levy asked, 'Perhaps you were unwilling to brave the spider's web?' In itself, the web was an irrelevance for webs can grow quickly and it was several weeks between the alleged storage of the parcels there and Holden's investigation there.

Humphreys then re-examined Holden. He stressed that blood was more likely to have remained in the underfelt rather than on the surface. He also stated that the carpet was highly unlikely to have picked up so much blood to create a stain of 14 by 9in by being in transit with other soiled garments, carpets or heavily injured employees.[27]

Mansfield was recalled and asked about a court case in which Hume had been a witness against him; did this make him resent Hume, but he answered that it did not.

Perhaps the most important witness for the prosecution was Dr Camps, who was called next. His exchanges with Levy are very important because they reveal his analysis of how the murder was carried out. Nowhere else is this available.

Dr Camps began conventionally enough with a description of the injuries inflicted on Setty's torso; five major stab wounds, caused by a two-edged dagger and all inflicted prior to death. Apparently 'I think he could have died in a matter of minutes.' Then the flesh had been cut and the bones sawn through for dismemberment purposes. There had been injuries post-mortem due to the body being dropped from height and then immersed in the sea. Very little blood remained in the body by the time it was found.[28]

Levy then cross-examined the doctor, beginning with a discussion as to how much blood would have been in Setty's body and how much blood could have been expected to have been found in the flat depending on whether the body was in parts in parcels, as Hume alleged, or had been killed there, as the prosecution suggested. Camps believed that the latter was more probable 'taking into consideration the other evidence I have heard.' But, Levy asked, looking for a loophole, could it have seeped from the parcels? It was possible, Camps admitted, 'but it would be accompanied by a considerable staining of the parcel' and he repeated this statement. Much depended on how much blood had seeped out during the killing and dismemberment and this was an unknown exact quantity.

Levy stated, 'It would depend upon how rapidly the body was parcelled up.' This could not be answered, but Camps stated, 'I think this body was cut up quickly', as there were no marks on the dead white body, 'it indicates that the body has been cut up shortly after death.' The work had been neatly carried out.[29]

The next question was how rapidly had death taken place after the initial assault. Pretty quickly, Camps replied; within about 5 minutes. One blow or two might have been fatal. He had dealt with five cases of fatal stabbings that year, so his expertise and experience was considerable. The question of the lack of defence wounds on the hands was mentioned and Camps agreed this was a good point, 'One does expect to find what are known as defence wounds', adding the rider 'if his hands were free.' Levy believed the hands were held and so that would suggest a multiple-person assault that was premeditated and so Hume was innocent. Camps thought not, 'I should have thought it was more in keeping with a sudden assault' and that there were no signs of bruising as there would have been if the hands were held.[30]

Would the assailant have been bloodstained? Camps had talked in previous hearings of the case in the lower court about 'blood spurting' from the body but now he wanted to make it clear that he had been imprecise. What he had meant was that blood would have oozed and flowed from the body and that the victim's clothes would have prevented blood from 'spurting' out. Camps also told how Setty would have been able to walk a few steps into another room before falling down and dying. If this fat man had fallen bodily this would have made a noise audible downstairs, but he may well have slumped and so not made an audible noise.[31]

There then was a discussion about how long the dismemberment would have taken. Camps thought that an inexperienced cutter might take an hour, and that the sawing of bones would take the longest time, especially through the moveable neck bones. Camps then remarked:

'I could do it myself in considerably less [time] than that.' Levy's dry response was, 'Yes, no doubt you could. I am not asking you to give a demonstration.'[32]

After a short adjournment, they returned to the issue of the attack, Levy suggesting that Setty must have been killed by two or more men, one holding his arms whilst the other stabbed him, otherwise he would have expected to see wounds on Setty's hands as he tried to defend himself against being stabbed. It was also suggested that Setty's coat must have been open as the stab wounds went through his shirt and vest. Levy asked:

'You mean that they would not go through the coat?'
'They could, but I doubt it. They could go through with the coat half open. Again, his hands could be fixed by his coat, and it is a well recognised method of assault, by pulling the man's coat half off.'

'You mean the coat could be drawn over his shoulders?'
'Yes, as a means of immobilisation.'

There was then a discussion about the lack of defence wounds and what this suggested. Levy seized on this:

'That is why I am suggesting to you that the mere fact that he did not lash out makes it very probable that the attack was by a number of persons and not by one person?'
'That may well be, but there is no evidence from my findings, to support it.'
'But the evidence is consistent with that is it not?'
'No.'
'Why not?'
'In the absence of any bruising of him being held.'
'Would that cause bruising, the arms being held?'
'Yes it might well be if they were held strongly or firmly.'
'We have often, I suppose, had our arms held without seeing any bruises?'
'Yes, at the time, but I think it is recognised that we always look at bodies twenty four hours afterwards, and bruises come up later.'
'Supposing his arms had been held behind?'
'Very firm holding would show bruising.'

Levy suggested that a lot of noise would have occurred during the killing. Camps replied:

'I think it depends on what I said before. It is conjecture, because we do not know what happened, do we? I think it is quite consistent with a single assailant.'
'And you think it is equally consistent with there being a number?'
'Yes, there might have been a number.'[33]

Then Levy wanted to discuss where the dismemberment had taken place. Had it taken place in the kitchen, surely there would have been a great deal of blood spilt there? Camps replied, 'Yes, if the blood went on the floor.' He thought that a covering such as a rubber sheet or a mackintosh could have been placed on the floor to catch the blood and then disposed of. But surely traces would be found asked Levy, Camps replying, 'It depends upon the extent of the washing.'[34]

Humphreys then re-examined Camps to determine how long the assault would have taken place. Camps agreed that the blows had been 'administered pretty fast, one after another':

> 'How quickly could these blows be caused?'
> 'A matter of seconds.'

Camps demonstrated:

> 'My lord, that is but three seconds . . . do you think a man could make any effective defence?'
> 'Not in that time.'[35]

To summarise Camps' findings, therefore: Setty had been attacked by a right-handed man and had received five knife thrusts to the left side of his torso. The assault had taken a matter of seconds and he had been unable to defend himself in that time (and unstated, given his consumption of alcohol – never mentioned in court – his reactions would have been even slower). He had staggered a few steps from the sitting room to the dining room and died a few minutes later. The body had then been cut up very shortly afterwards, though when it had been parcelled up is another question. The evidence was beginning to point against the defendant.

MacDougall was then called. It was noticed, that, of Hume, 'His interest quickened when Superintendent Colin MacDougall . . . was under cross examination . . . He nodded his head vigorously when Superintendent MacDougall agreed that Hume had declared that he had been threatened.' Hume also wrote copious notes and continuously sent them to Levy. The police officer explained that a search for the three men as described by Hume (Max, Greeny and the Boy) had been made and a Mr Green had been found (not difficult for the surname is a common one). Humphreys asked him about this:

> 'Did he answer the description of any of those three men?'
> 'Absolutely dissimilar.'
> 'Did you later find some other man, not of the names given, but vaguely answering the description of one of those men?'
> 'I did, sir.'[36]

The Clerk of the Court then read out Hume's lengthy statement about the three men paying him to dispose of the three parcels, as has been related already. The police officer told how pawn tickets were found on Hume's person and that he had told him he had been threatened and asked for police protection. He was asked by Levy about Setty:

> 'Would it be right to say that Setty was a well known dealer in this black car market in Warren Street?'
> 'No. He was looked upon as quite an honest dealer.'

As before, Levy was trying to suggest that the murdered man dealt with criminals and so it was not improbable he might fall foul of a gang. He asked other questions designed to cast doubts on Hume's guilt.

> 'Has a careful and thorough examination been made for fingerprints and other marks at Hume's flat?'
> 'Yes.'
> 'Were any of the fingerprints found those of Setty?'
> 'No.'
> 'Were all Hume's clothes examined on the premises?'
> 'Yes',
> 'Was there a single sign of a bloodstain on any of them?'
> 'No.'[37]

Of course, the police examination had taken place three weeks after the murder and that clearly gave time for anyone who wanted to conceal or destroy fingerprints, or fibres and bloodstains that had been on their clothes, plenty of time to wipe away the former and have the latter cleaned, so the evidence of their lack was hardly conclusive. The relatively primitive state of forensic science at the time meant that definitive proof of guilt could not be provided. This was the end of the case for the prosecution. Levy had been able to make the evidence given by his opponent's witnesses seem less than solid, but it was unknown at this point how much this had had an effect on the jury. In any case, Levy had his own case to present. Totterdell thought, 'On the face of it the weight of the evidence appeared to weigh on the side of the prosecution.'[38] Likewise, as Humphreys wrote, 'The story, as proved in court, seemed quite deadly.'[39] Matters looked bleak for Hume. Yet, as William Bixley, a veteran court official noted, 'The prosecution had a massive array of evidence against him but it was mostly circumstantial.'[40] Circumstantial evidence can often prove lethal to the defendant, of course, so this was no consolation to Hume.

Chapter 7

The Case for Hume and Verdict, 1950

The court case was adjourned for the two days of the weekend. When it recommenced on Monday, 23 January 1950, it was the opportunity for Levy to present witnesses to support the case that he was arguing for; that the jury should find Hume not guilty of murder and thus save his life.

Levy began by reminding the jury that the prosecution's case was firstly that Setty, murdered on 4 October, and subsequently dismembered, was disposed of from an aeroplane and he did not invite them to disagree with this last part of the hypothesis. He then added, 'They invite you to say that the murder and the cutting up were carried out by Hume.' He said that they argued that the bloodstains in the flat, taken with the fact that Hume had disposed of the corpse, was proof that he was also a murderer. However, Levy suggested, 'Members of the jury, you may feel that there is rather a long road between those facts and that conclusion.'[1]

He added that the prosecution claimed that because Setty had £1,005 on his person and that Hume was financially embarrassed (with an overdraft and had been pawning his possessions), he had a strong motive for killing. Yet, Levy stated that Hume had paid a medical bill of £30 on the day before the murder, that Hume had had overdrafts before and that the prosecution had given an incomplete picture of Hume's financial situation. Levy remarked, 'Nobody has suggested before that he murdered anybody in order to reduce his overdraft.'[2] Ronald Howe (1896–1977), Assistant Commissioner for Crime, later noted likewise, 'Hume was not at that time desperate for money and he always found it easy to come by.'[3] Yet, Haigh had murdered in 1949 to pay his very pressing debts and reduce his overdraft. Monetary motivation is not an uncommon reason for murder.

Levy discussed the prosecution's dismissal of Hume's story about the three men who had approached him, which he relied on as being accurate. He cast aspersions on the denials of Mansfield and Salvadori about them. 'Are these the sort of persons on whose evidence you would hang a cat, let alone a man?' He suggested they were unreliable witnesses and had been found guilty of inducing others to commit frauds. 'Do you think men of the calibre of Mansfield and Salvadori would risk their necks by giving information to the police about people they knew to be ruthless murderers?'[4]

Instead, Levy had a witness, allegedly unbiased, who had lived near Setty's garage and would later attest to knowing about the three men whom Hume spoke of as having visited Setty. He also defended Hume's character: 'Hume does not pretend to be an angel: he is no angel. It may well be that Hume is the sort of man who goes about claiming to be more than he is. He may be an exhibitionist – but it is not every liar who is a murderer, assuming that Hume is a liar.'[5]

Levy then surveyed the evidence that his witnesses would present. He told them that Mrs Hume was in the flat on the evening that Hume was alleged to have committed the murder, but would state that she knew nothing of the murder and dismemberment. 'Setty was a strong man. Do you think a man like that could be stabbed to death five times from the front by a much smaller man (in weight though not in height), such as Hume is, without creating some commotion?'[6]

Levy added that Dr Teare would state that it was very unlikely that a man could be attacked frontally and not try and defend himself or make any noise. The former was only possible, he suggested, if Setty was held by one or more others and thus the murder could not have been committed by Hume alone. Again he ended with a rhetorical question: 'Do you think it is impossible for a man to be restrained without bruising his arms?'[7]

It was also suggested that since no one else, either neighbours or visitors, had noticed anything untoward, that nothing criminal had happened in Hume's flat. Mrs Hume, Mrs Stride, Dr Blatchley and Mr Spencer would all say that they had not seen or heard anything suspicious (not necessarily conclusive for in 1936 the neighbour of a woman murdered in her Soho flat later said that he had heard nothing suspicious and in 1953 Christie's neighbours never heard anything as he committed his last three murders; in any case, Camps' statement about the speed of the killing (a few seconds) would have ruled out any noise). The time taken to cut up a body was not short and nor was it a clean business that could be easily concealed. He stated 'that it was utterly impossible that the body could have been cut up in that flat' (again contrary to Camps' assertion, though it would be difficult if not impossible to conceal this from anyone else in the flat). He added that the provenance of various stains found in the flat could not be scientifically ascertained.[8]

Levy had spoken for 1 hour and 40 minutes and had made a good impression to observers, as was noted, 'His quiet voice and demeanour never disturbed or flurried, are perfect weapons for dealing with court opponents.'[9]

Levy had his client as his first witness, as is usual when they are called as such. Defendants were not obliged to be examined and therefore cross-examined by the prosecution in court and no adverse interpretation could be placed upon their not doing so. Heath and Haigh elected not to do so in 1946 and 1949, for instance, though since both were pleading guilty but insane, to appear sane in the dock would not have been helpful. Defendants not pleading insanity, such as Evans, tended to appear in the dock and hope that their defence counsel would show them in a sufficiently favourable light in contrast to the prosecution which would exploit any chink in the armour of their defence. Levy clearly thought that Hume would make a good impression, though it was taking a risk. In the previous week the defendant, Evans, had been ripped to shreds by Humphreys in a fatal cross-examination.

Hume left the dock and stood in the witness box, 'leaning forward, his hands gripping the ledge before him as he declared in a rising voice', and gave the court a brief precis of his life; aged 30, married with a young daughter. He told how he had served with the RAF during the war – the most prestigious and popular of the three branches of the armed forces. Afterwards he had obtained a pilot's licence and had dealings with the car trade, where he had met Mansfield and Salvadori and was also known as the 'flying smuggler', but as stated the veracity of this is not certain. He had also met 'Max' too.[10]

Levy took Hume through his descriptions of Max and Hume elaborated on that of Green, both as to his physical description and the clothing he had worn. He then went through his meetings with the three men, their payments to him and the work he had done for them in receiving three parcels and subsequently disposing of them by aeroplane over the sea. He explained why the carpet was dyed – it was dirty – and why he needed the knife sharpening – to carve a joint or to cut horsemeat for his dog. He explained his absence in the kitchen for an hour when Mrs Stride was there, having to clear up the coal cupboard, so as to be able to receive more coal and because he needed to sort some insurance policies which were, bizarrely, in a deed box there (this was never verified).[11]

Hume then explained in detail the arrangement he had made with the three men, that one had produced a revolver at some stage, that he had flown from Elstree and how he had finally suspected that the last parcel might contain human remains. He spoke about being threatened and how, after he had been arrested, he had asked for police protection for his wife and child. Finally, Levy decided to finish the examination with an assertion of Hume's innocence:

> 'Have you ever had in your possession a knife one inch wide and four inches long, which it has been suggested was used for stabbing Setty?'
> 'No.'

'Did you murder Stanley Setty?'
'No.'[12]

Now the sympathetic examination by his counsel was over, Hume faced the infinitely more difficult ordeal of a lengthy cross-examination by Humphreys, who was determined to exploit any weakness he could find in the defendant's case. In the next 60 minutes he fired 304 questions at him:

'I want the jury to understand the man they are trying. On your own confession you were prepared to assist men who told you in terms that they were forgers of petrol coupons?'
'They did mention that, yes, sir.'
'And you believed it?'
'Yes, sir.'
'You were prepared, for money, to remove the traces of that crime?'
'Yes, sir.'[13]

Having established Hume's criminal credentials, Humphreys then turned to the question of Hume's knowledge of what the parcels really contained:

'What did you think it was?'
'I thought it might have been part of a human body.'
'It was obviously part of a human body, wasn't it?'
'No sir, not obviously.'

Humphreys suggested that Hume realised the body parts were those of Setty and quoted Hume's own statement to show that he had said that he had suspected that at the time. Hume tried to deny this and said he had not properly read over the police statement that he had signed because he was tired at 10.30 pm on the day that it was made out. 'What else could they have been connected with that spurts human blood unless it is a human body?' Hume did not reply. He could hardly deny it and to agree would have been pointless.[14]

Hume continued to deny that he suspected the body parts he was throwing into the sea were those of the man whose disappearance had been heavily reported. Humphreys asked about what Hume thought about the three men:

'How do you think the three men had been connected with a human body unless they were the murderers of it?'
'I did not realise it was a human body until after they had gone.'
'What did you think the three men were who had brought you a human body?'
'They could have been murderers.'

There was some discussion about Hume selling aircraft during the recent Arab-Israeli War and that he was then known as the 'flying smuggler.' He denied being a smuggler, however. Humphreys pressed him on his own integrity:

> 'Would it be right to describe you as a romantic liar?'
> 'No, completely the opposite.'
> 'As a person prepared to lie when it suits you?'
> 'It would be completely wrong.'[15]

Humphreys also questioned Hume as to why he did not report his suspicions to the police, but he said they would not have believed him, as they did not now. Humphreys also suggested to Hume that he enjoyed the high life in the West End with a woman who was not his wife, and that he posed as a former RAF pilot but did not have the financial wherewithal to sustain such a lifestyle. Hume denied all this. Humphreys also discussed Hume's sales of aeroplanes to the Iraqi government and the fact that he had been in trouble with the law over wearing a RAF uniform to which he had not been entitled.[16]

Humphreys then decided to question Hume about the three men that he suggested did not exist:

> 'I think you agree that your wife never saw these three men and that Mrs Stride never saw them?'
> 'I admit that.'
> 'You know the police have not been able to find these men? You would have thought it would have been easy to spot them by the clothes which you have described them as wearing?'
> 'Not necessarily. They had a photograph of the Mad parson [this was John Edward Allen, found guilty of murder but insane, and escaped from Broadmoor in 1947 disguised as a vicar and was not recaptured until 1949] and did not find him, although he was living opposite Albany Street Police Station.'

Humphreys changed tack:

> 'The men who approached you were practically complete strangers. You never got to know anything more about them than that they are called Mac, Green and the Boy; and you ask the jury to believe they came to you and asked you to help them dispose of a human body?'
> 'I repeat I know nothing about a human body.'
> 'If they had come to you like that, they would have been at your mercy, would they not? You could have phoned the police and they would have had the place surrounded?'
> 'No, I was scared stiff.'
> 'Why not, if you are an honest man?'

'I am not saying I am one hundred per cent honest. I am saying
I am a semi-honest man – but I'm not a murderer. My attitude when
I saw the large parcel was, "This is something dodgy – so, out". I had
got rid of the first two parcels and I could get rid of the other in the
same way.'[17]

That was the end of the fourth day of the trial. Gladys Langford wrote in her
diary, 'Leming said he thought Hume would escape conviction for Setty's murder and it looks as tho' he may.' Humphreys' cross-examination of Hume was
not over. On the next day, Tuesday, 24 January, day five of the trial, Hume was
recalled and Humphreys proceeded to cross-examine him about the bloodstains in the flat. He admitted to cleaning up those in the coal cupboard and
dining room. He could not say how the stains in the hall or the sitting room
were made as he had said that the men with the parcels carried them into the
flat, and had not dragged them over the floor. Humphreys said Hume had
been unwilling to open the carpet up when it was taken to the cleaners, but
Hume denied this and Levy stepped in to say that Mrs Hearnden had not said
he was unwilling to do so, though in fact she had said that he was, so either
Levy erred or was deliberately stating a mistruth to his client's advantage.[18]

Humphreys went over to the attack again and levelled a direct accusation at
Hume. 'I suggest that you stabbed Setty in the sitting room and that he died in
the dining room?' 'Now you are romancing.' Humphreys went on to say that
there was only his wife's word that he was in the flat that night and that he had
plenty of time to cut up a corpse. Hume admitted that he did have a carving
knife. There was a discussion over Hume's being in debt before the murder
and that Hume had borrowed money from Setty to pay the doctor, to which
Hume replied, 'Absolute baloney.' Hume was perhaps losing his cool because
the judge had to restrain him from answering questions before Humphreys
had finished them. Hume was asked about Mansfield knowing 'Max' and he
stated that he did because of the court case that the three of them had been
involved in.[19]

There was then a series of exchanges about Hume's finances. Hume claimed
that he was solvent and had £280, some of which had been given to him by
his father-in-law. There is no evidence for this in Hume's bank account or anywhere else (he later said that his father-in-law detested him). Humphreys said
he found this difficult to believe because Hume had had cheques returned and
had had to pawn his suit for £6. Hume said that he had no explanation to give
and that he did not know the exact dates of various transactions. The sharpening of the knife was also discussed, with Hume repeating that he needed it to
cut up a joint, though Mrs Stride had seen no evidence of it.[20]

Humphreys also pressed Hume about the timings of the arrival on 5 October of the three men, whom neither Mrs Hume nor Mrs Stride had seen any sign of. Hume was adamant that they did arrive:

'I don't know about the time, but these men definitely did come on that day . . . I am the one who knows whether I killed Setty or not, other than the men who murdered him. I have a clear conscience regarding the killing of the unfortunate man.'

Sellers intervened.

'You are adopting this as a personal matter.'
'My life is a personal matter.'[21]

There was then some questioning over whether the three men could have entered the flat without anyone else knowing that they did. Hume argued that his wife might have been out and that Mrs Stride might not have heard the door bell. Sellers intervened, too, and told Hume, 'You will appreciate why all these questions are being put to you by counsel. It is suggested that this did not happen at all, and that these men never came to your flat at all?'

Hume replied that he quite understood the point and that the parcels they brought were in the coal cupboard without his wife ever being aware of them because she was frightened of the mice in there. He told how Mrs Stride was excluded from the kitchen when she arrived because 'I was wearing short white trunks. I had taken my other clothes off . . . I did not want to be seen walking round the flat in them.' Humphreys asked one final question:

'Were you cutting up portions of Setty's body and parcelling it?'
'Definitely not.'
'No further questions.'[22]

Humphreys later wrote, 'It was only because I was not quite sure that the jury accepted it that I cross-examined Hume at length to get his admission that he was at least an accessory after the fact.' Webb thought that Hume had got the better of the exchange, later writing, 'Hume's lightning retorts to Mr Humphreys verbally cut the ground from under his feet.'[23]

West believed that Humphrey's conduct of the prosecution was most curious. With reference to the barrister's emphasising Hume's associating with women in nightclubs, she wrote, 'Mr Humphrey's tone suggested that this was the kind of thing that stabbing and cutting up people led to if done too often.' She was also dismissive about the importance of Hume pawning goods, running up debts on the grounds that many people do such and referred to Humphreys as being 'a financial virgin'.[24]

Sellers also asked him to try and clarify the state of his finances. Was he or was he not hard up? Hume said that though he had an overdraft at the bank on 3 October, he also paid a doctor's bill of £30 and had £280 in hand. He denied he pawned his suit; only a ring had been taken to a pawnbrokers (the pawn tickets indicate that he had pawned both items). He was asked again about Max, Greeny and the Boy:

> 'Did you know the names of the three men or their addresses or anything about them?'
> 'No. I only knew the man Mac.'
> Did you know where to find him?'
> 'It was either taking the £50 or nothing at all.'
> 'Will you answer my question? Did you know where to find him?'
> 'No.'

There was some discussion about the amount Hume would be paid by the three. Hume said that he initially had a promise of payment, not actual cash, and that he would not have known where to find them again. Nor had he told his wife about the men or the packages arriving at the flat.[25]

Hume had finished being cross-examined. In one way he had done well; he had stuck to a consistent story throughout his time under arrest and in the court room; unlike Evans who had changed his story throughout and so was exposed as an obvious liar. Bixley thought Hume came across well, writing, 'I felt that he made a good appearance considering the terrible weight of evidence against him.' Hoskins wrote of 'Hume, a supreme liar, the biggest and best I have ever met in a lifetime.'[26] On the other hand, putting the blame on others who cannot be tracked down due to necessarily vague descriptions of names and physical appearances and who lack addresses is a very typical ploy used by criminals; one which can neither be proved nor, more importantly for them, disproved.

Mrs Hume was the next witness, described as 'a small woman, with a quiet pleasing voice . . . [who] . . . bit her lip, shook her head and answered firmly', and it was noted that she smiled across at her husband in the dock. She said that the carpet had become dirty so her husband took it to the cleaners. She fed Alison five times a day; the evening feed being at 6 pm. The two were regularly out of the flat from between 2 and 2.30 pm until about 5.45 pm per day. The doctor had visited on 3 and 5 October and she had been listening to the radio from 8–9 pm on 4 October. Her evidence was largely negative.[27] As to the 5th, she recalled Alison being ill and the doctor having to be called, and eating lunch with her husband.[28]

It is worth reproducing what we know of the further examination and cross-examination of this witness, as it provides additional information to that contained in the police statement. Levy began:

'Is there any particular play which you remember having heard about this time on the wireless?'

'I did not remember it until I was given to understand that I might remember from the Radio Times. I do remember that the play was about the French Bluebeard. I remembered the programme through a photograph of Landru, the subject of the play.'

'I think the play was called Justice in Other Lands and that this broadcast was about Landru. I shall prove by other means that this play purports to have been broadcast on 4 October between eight and nine in the evening. Do you remember whether your husband was at home or not on that particular evening?'

'No.'

'Have you ever met Setty?'

'No.'

'So far as this particular night, Tuesday, 4 October, is concerned, can you recollect one way or the other whether he actually came to bed with you or not?'

'I don't know. I imagine he did, but I cannot say for certain.'

'If he did not come to bed, say, for hours, do you think you would have known it, or remembered it?'

'I think I would be likely to remember it.'

'Would it have been possible, do you think, for your husband to bring anyone to that flat in that period, sometime between six and eleven on that night, and murder him in the flat – and murder him without you knowing anything about it?'

'Quite impossible.'

'Did you hear any sound or any commotion or anything that could possibly suggest any such happening while you were in the flat?'

'No.'

'You knew very little about your husband's life or how he earned his money?'

'Very little.'

'On the afternoon of 5 October, did you know of three men going into the flat?'

'No.'

'During the whole of that morning, from 6 am, when you fed the baby, until you had lunch, do you think it could have been possible for your husband to have been cutting up the body of a man in the flat without your knowing anything about it?'
'No.'
'Did he in fact do anything of that sort to your knowledge?'
She shook her head.
'Did you, during the whole of that period, see the slightest sign of anything unusual such as I have suggested?'
'No.'
'Did you see any signs of blood?'
'No.'
'Did you smell anything?'
'No.'
'Did you see any blood stained knives or anything?'
'I saw nothing.'

Humphreys then cross-examined her:

'You did not know much of your husband's private life, did you?'
'No.'
'He told you he was earning his living by flying planes?'
'Yes.'
'Did you know various parcels came to the flat on 5 and 6 October and were taken away by him?'
'No.'
'Did you know that three men came into the flat on 5 October?'
'No.'
'Did your husband give you any money that day?'
'He gave me £80, mostly in £5 notes.'
'Can you remember whether you had a coal fire the first week in October?'
'I don't know.'
'Do you remember what sort of a rug there was in the hall?'
'A normal rug – green, with a floral pattern.'
'Mrs Stride said that when she came to the flat it had gone. Can you remember what happened to it?'
'No.'

Donald Hume's birthplace, Ulwell Road, Swanage.

Hume's birth certificate.

Hume's grandmother's house, 8 Bigwood Road.

Herriard school.

Hume's home in Herriard.

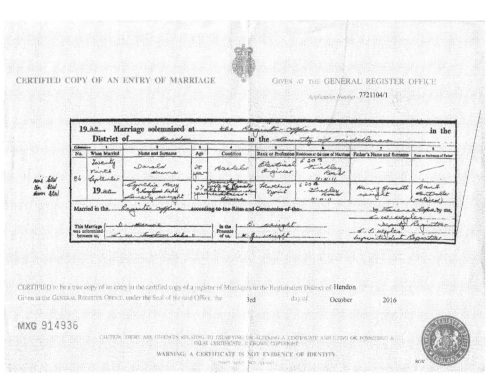

Hume's marriage certificate.

Police mugshots of Stanley Setty. (Reproduced with the permission of the Mayor's Office for Policing)

Maitland Court flats, where Stanley Setty lived with his sister and brother-in-law.

Cambridge Terrace Mews, where Setty operated a garage.

620 Finchley Road, where Hume lived in flat with his wife and baby.

Hume standing outside Fitzroy cafe.

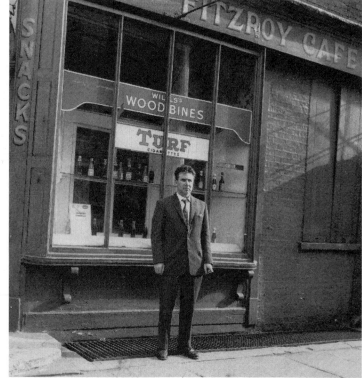

Hume seated in his flat.

Hume leaping over a brook at Dengie Marshes.

Hume with an SS dagger.

Stanley Setty's gravestone.

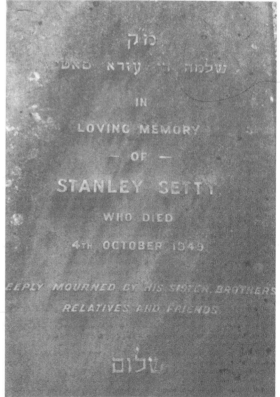

Bow Street Magistrates' Court.

Timothy Evans, whom Hume met in
Brixton prison.

The Old Bailey.

The entrance to Wormwood Scrubs prison.

Dartmoor prison.

The city of Zurich, Switzerland.

The Globe pub, Brentford, which Hume visited
before carrying out his first bank robbery.

The building housing the Midland Bank, Brentford.

Hume being escorted into the court room by a Swiss police officer.

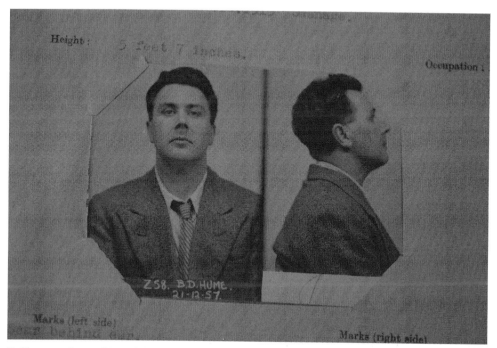

Police mugshots of Donald Hume. (Reproduced with the permission of the Mayor's Office for Policing)

13/12/2015

SALVADOR 1344 Cage CSC HMP WAKE

Jonathan

An Absolute legend "Don" (should make a movie on his life's journey)

He spent years on Cornwall Block in Broadmoor Asylum. 90% of my time was spent in Norfolk Intensive Ward in Seclusion (so I never got much chance to see the old room). The short spells I spent with him. "Down the field he was always polite, respectful and a humble man.

His eyes shine. He still had the fire going in him. He had to scheme with Allen the Asylum to crush him on one of my roof protests. He shouts up to me

"Sling some slates off for me"

He had a great sense of humour.

Yes a good sort of chap with old school morals (bare in mind its a nut house full of nutters) so its very difficult to maintain your sanity in such a place (He did) So had my respect. (Always)

He had decades of madness sucking away at him (in some crazy way it was probably easier for me being kept in seclusion)

Coz I would of got nasty and very explosive.

Yet... Don was in my book a true legend (Not for many in prison or asylum can fly a plane) And never forget the years he spent in the entire prison system. He drove them fuckers mad & they couldn't control him... they flew him about in chains...

He said something to me one day down the field.

Query: "Let em think your mad... But never let em think your silly."

Yet... A legend! And a friend Yours in the name of sanity

I could be free in 2017 come to one of my art shows.

Xmas 2015

A card sent to the author from Charles Bronson giving his impression of Donald Hume.

Hume's last-known address, Thompson House, Notting Hill.

The Copper Beeches Hotel, Basingstoke.

The site behind the hotel where Hume's body was found.

Hume's death certificate.

'Do you remember a party at the flat to celebrate the baby's arrival?'

'We did have some friends in.'

'Do you remember the carpet going to be dyed on 5 October?'

'Yes, there were stains all over it.'

'I am talking about one bad stain in the middle.'

She was shown the carpet and the stain, admitting she was short-sighted.

'You do not remember seeing that stain before 5 October?'

'Well, that is on the underside of the carpet.'

'Do you remember seeing the stain on the front of the carpet about the place where it now appears on the back?'

'I don't remember seeing it.'

'So as far as you know, when the carpet came back from the cleaners it was put down in the same position as before?'

'I don't know.'

'How many times was the floor stained between September 1948, when you moved into the flat, and September 1949?'

'I don't know how many times, but I know it was more than once. My husband did it twice.'

'Do you remember if there was a joint for lunch on 5 October?'

'No.'

'Do you remember sending your husband out that day in a hurry to get a knife sharpened?'

'No.'

'You were never to your knowledge threatened by anybody about anything, were you?'

'Not to my knowledge.'

Levy added that Mrs Hume wanted to make a statement about what happened in court on Friday, but Sellers thought it unnecessary because Webb had already given an explanation.[29]

West commented that many people were suspicious about Mrs Hume for stating that she had not noticed anything untoward in the flat on 4–6 October. She defended her by stating that she had had a difficult pregnancy and was focussed purely on her baby daughter to the complete exclusion of anything else. West thought that she, as with Mrs Stride, destroyed the cases for both defence and prosecution as she said nothing about either a murder occurring in the flat nor the arrival of the parcels as attested by Hume.[30]

The next witness for the defence was Cyril John Lee, who had served as a lieutenant in the Royal Artillery during the Second World War and had lived at 2 Cambridge Terrace Mews in 1947 and 1948. He did not know Hume but read about the trial and decided to contact the defence. He could tell that at Setty's garage there was a brisk trade in repair work and spraying motor cars. The type of people whom he recalled visiting were 'mostly local business people', but that later 'a rather different sort of people started to appear. Not the sort of people I would like to see around my doorstep ... spivs ... A very mixed bag.'[31]

Having re-established that Setty lived on the edges of criminality, Levy became more explicit:

> 'Did you hear the names Green, Mac or the Boy in connection with Setty's garage?'
> 'To be very precise about it, I did hear two of those names called out in the mews outside my flat.'
> 'Was your mews near the garage?'
> 'Yes, it is a short mews, about one hundred feet long and thirty feet wide. I did hear the names Maxie and the Boy.'
> 'In what way did you hear them?'
> 'Somebody called out to them.'
> 'So far as these two men are concerned, did you notice the persons to whom the names were addressed?'
> 'No.'
> 'So you are not able to give us a description of these two?'
> 'No.'
> 'Have you seen in the newspapers a more detailed description by which Hume has described the man Green?'
> 'I've seen it but not in the newspapers.'
> 'Did you ever see anyone of that description?'
> 'Yes, on one occasion.'
> 'Did you hear any name or address which you could attach to him?'
> 'No.'
> 'So you cannot tell us by what name he was known?'
> 'No, I cannot.'[32]

Humphreys then asked:

> 'Would it be of any use to you if I produced the Boy? There is in this court a man with that name, and his name is Baker?'
> 'I might recognise him as having been there.'

The man in question was called and stood before Sellers.

'Have you ever seen him before?'
'No.'
'Do you know that Setty's brother has another garage next door in
the same mews, and that he is called Max?'
'No.'[33]

The next witness was Spencer who stated that he had been at home in the
flat below Hume's on the 4th but had heard nothing untoward. It is worth
noting, though, that it was a noisy location. There was a bus stop just outside the flat which served three bus routes, and because of the slope each
vehicle would have been even noisier when making the necessary hill start.
In any case, given the speed of Setty's demise he could have been killed without much sound, so Spencer's evidence was null and void and having heard
Camp's evidence, the jury should have been aware of this. Humphreys, however, had him admit that if the carpet of Hume's flat was down, sound was
barely audible and that where he was sitting was partly beneath Hume's coal
cupboard. He could hear people moving about upstairs but 'not more than
usual' and did not hear anything heavy being put into the coal cellar on the
night of the 5th, as had been claimed by the defence. Stanley Hussey was the
next witness; he was shown a carving knife and said he had sharpened it for
Hume on 15 June. Dr Blatchley recalled receiving his £30 fee from Hume on
3 October and having visited the flat two days later. There he had noticed
nothing untoward and had not seen any blood in the bathroom.[34]

The last witness for the day was another important one. This was
Dr Robert Donald Teare (1911–79). He was lecturer of Forensic Medicine at
St Bartholomew's Hospital and was one of the three main pathologists who
undertook criminal cases in and around London in the 1940s–1960s. In the
previous month he had examined the strangled corpses of Beryl and Geraldine
Evans at 10 Rillington Place and in the mortuary thereafter. Dr Keith Simpson,
another key pathologist of this era, referred to him thus, 'a solid likeable man,
with a good sense of humour, competent both in the field and the witness box.'[35]

Teare was questioned about blood; that it would flow freely for about
90 minutes after death and that he would not expect much blood to have
flowed from the body immediately after it had been stabbed. Yet, it would
have seeped thereafter. 'I should expect that there would be a considerable
amount of coughing up of blood.' Levy then wanted to bring up the topic of
whether there was one assailant or, as he argued, more than one, thus letting
Hume off the hook:

'I want your views as to the probable consequences of a frontal
attack by stabbing upon a man like Setty by a single assailant. It has

been said by Dr Camps, I think, that it is conceivable that the whole thing might pass off very quietly without struggle or noise of any kind. Would you expect that?'

'No, I would not.'

'What would you expect?'

'I would expect either considerable resistance on the part of the attacked man, resulting in all probability in injuries to his body in the way of defence or protective injuries to hand or arm; or I should expect a volume of blood to be coughed up which would be distributed over the assailant and adjacent structures such as walls or furniture – and the floor, of course.'

'Would you expect a person stabbed like that to be in a condition in which he could fight back or struggle?'

'I think he would have some time and some power with which to fight back.'

Would you expect him to remain silent?'

'That I cannot answer.'

'On the other hand, if he were restrained by one or more person from behind, Dr Camps has given it as his view that it could not have been done without leaving bruise marks where the restraint has been applied. What do you say about that?'

'A man could be restrained from behind without any bruise marks developing.'

Teare was also asked about blood seeping out from packages, especially if they had been dropped as Staddon and Hume had let go of one on the stairs:

'I should expect that the impact with the floor would squeeze blood out of the folds in almost every direction.'

Finally Levy asked:

'Do you think it probable from these wounds that he was killed by one single assailant?'

Teare hesitated and the judge intervened:

'Do you regard this as a medical question?'

'I think that the absence of marks of defence upon the body renders it more likely that he was killed by more than one person.'

It was apparently a good point and Teare may well have recalled his post-mortem examination of Rachel Fennick in 1948. She had been stabbed to death in her Soho flat and there had been non-fatal injuries to her hands caused by the murder weapon as she had vainly tried to defend herself.[36]

Levy then asked him about the cutting up of the bones, which Teare stated his experience of:

'Is it a very quiet process, sawing up human bones?'
'No, it is not. It produces noise which drowns ordinary conversation. It is impossible to dictate to one's secretary while bones are being sawn.'
'Would you expect the noise to be heard in the room below in an ordinary house?'
'Yes.'
'How long do you think it would take a person inexperienced in sawing human bones to saw across the thigh of a man of Setty's size?'
'I should think it would take more than a minute.'[37]

Humphreys' turn came and he had Teare state that a stabbing results in the coughing up of blood and that bruising shows up after death. He proceeded with other questions:

'You say you usually find that a man puts his hands up to defend himself in which case he may get cut with the assailant's knife. Is that it?'
'Yes.'
'But suppose the assailant is holding him off with a pretty strong left arm, he can't do much can he?'
'No.'
'In this case there was a 13½ stone man, 5ft 6in in height, and very fat. Assuming a man in the forties, fat or very fat, is struck a violent blow in the chest, which is in fact a knife going deep into him, it is practically going to knock him out, isn't it, as far as being an assailant and fighting back is concerned?'
'No, I don't think so.'
'Do you know that his stomach was found to contain a great deal of alcohol?'
'It's the first time.'[38]

Humphreys could surely have made more of this for an even slightly inebriated man would have been more easily and quickly despatched. With that the fifth day of the trial was over.

Day six was on Wednesday, 25 January and there was a surprise witness. Levy explained that on the previous night another witness was available for the defence. This was Douglas Clay, a writer, of Gloucester Avenue, London. This time he was questioned by Duveen. Clay had been to Paris in the previous February and remained there until August. Whilst there he met a number of people 'who were part of a gang: they were engaged in smuggling of arms to Palestine and cars to this country.'[39]

> 'Were there two members of the gang who particularly attracted
> your attention?'
> 'There were two members of that gang who were employed in
> general duties, but generally strong-arm work, who were known as
> the Boy and Maxie.'

Clay later informed the authorities in France and England about these men. Clay had come across them by the fact of meeting a man in a night club in order to exchange travellers' cheques and when the man was arrested he heard about the gang members. Humphreys asked:

> 'You would agree that Maxie is a very well known name?'
> 'Yes. There was one very famous Max in Paris at that time, and
> I asked them if they meant the famous Max.'

Levy asked if another Max that Clay met looked like the Max that Hume had described, 'No, not in any way. Not even in age.' This should have been enough to render Clay's evidence useless for the defence's case.[40]

It was now time for the closing speech on behalf of each side. Levy began by stating that the verdict depended on Hume's veracity. He then went on to state that Hume's finances were, contrary to what the prosecution alleged, healthy, with nearly £2,000 passing through his account in the first nine months of 1949 (though, of course, large amounts went out, too). To be able to pay his doctor £30 was not a sign of poverty. Levy said that if Hume was guilty of murder, then the killing could only have occurred in the flat – no one could drag a 13-stone corpse up the stairs. He then spoke of the three men, who, he declared, had been identified by men other than Hume (though this was not really so). 'In the light of that sort of evidence, can you for a moment accept the fact that all these three men never existed and are a product of the fertile imagination of Mr Hume?'[41]

Levy also pointed to the fact that very little blood had been found in the flat, whereas there should have been a lot had a violent murder occurred there (it had clearly been cleaned up, so another invalid point had been made). Levy remarked, 'But there is no suggestion of that at all.' He then made much of the presence of Mrs Hume in the flat at the time of the alleged murder and dissection:

> Do you think that it would have occurred to anybody but a madman to take a man there for the purpose of murdering him and cutting him up, knowing that at any time he might be interrupted by his wife – a gentle little woman, as you could see – who like any other woman, would immediately go into hysterics and scream the place down? Mrs Hume is as honest a witness as you could ever have seen.

However, he said, it would be easy for a gang to cut up Setty elsewhere and take his remains to Hume.[42]

Levy then emphasised Teare's evidence; that a man attacked by a knife wielding assailant would instinctively put up his hands to defend himself, but he appeared not to have done so. Indeed, he argued that Hume would have attacked Setty by stabbing him in the back not in the chest. 'The chances of its having been done from the front by one man are so remote that you can dismiss them as being absurd.' Rather, the likelihood was that Setty was killed by several men not by one, 'And there you have Mac, The Boy and Green.'[43] Levy concluded by drawing on Mrs Hume's evidence to help support her husband's story:

> It is quite impossible that Mrs Hume could have been in that flat all the time she was and be entirely ignorant of the sort of goings on that the Prosecution suggest were taking place. Therefore I ask you to reject without the slightest hesitation the whole theory that this man could have been murdered by Hume in that flat in the way the Prosecution suggest.[44]

West was impressed by the speech, which put Levy in 'the first rank of criminal lawyers', focussing as it did on the vagueness of the prosecution's case, not the accuracy of Hume's statement:

> It was a superb speech, as free from humbug and tricks as Euclid, and it lived in the memory by its logic and lucidity. It showed the strength of the best sort of Jewish mind, which becomes majestic as it pursues an argument, because justice is the product of sound argument, and Jehovah is a just God.[45]

However, much of this pleading must be ruled out of court. As has been said, the absence of defence wounds and the lack of noise were not because Setty was attacked by several assailants but because he had been killed in a matter of seconds after having drunk a little. The point about Mrs Hume being unaware of murder and dismemberment is solely dependent on her word which was never proven, as she was never seriously cross-examined.

Mr Humphreys now rose to give the closing speech for the prosecution and he attempted to counter some of Levy's conclusions. To deal with the question of motive and to resolve the issue of whether Hume was in funds or not, as Levy suggested, he avoided his earlier emphasis on Hume's poverty and stated, 'it may have been a chance quarrel, it may have been a dispute arising from some contract, upon some business they were doing together; they may both have been drunk [this is the second time he mentioned alcoholic consumption. Hume later admitting visiting pubs prior to the murder and there is no doubt that Setty had had some alcohol]. I don't have to prove why that murder took place' (this was true; prosecution does not need to prove motive). Then to Levy's point that Setty was probably killed by a gang not by Hume, 'It has never been the case of the Prosecution that Hume must necessarily have alone murdered Setty. He may have brought some other man to the flat with him . . . It matters not according to the laws of England, whether or not Setty was alone.'[46]

Humphreys then cast doubt over the role of Mrs Hume and said that a married couple tend to stick together:

'I do not say that Mrs Hume had no part in this murder; I say I have no evidence whatsoever that she had no part in it. I certainly do not agree necessarily that she had no part in the cutting up of the body and the tidying up of the flat. That is entirely a matter for you to consider.'

This was speculation and what the prosecution needed was positive evidence.

Then there were three points to consider. Did Hume murder Setty? Was he killed and dissected at the flat? And then there was the disposal of the body. The answer to the third was undisputed. Hume knowingly disposed of parcels containing Setty's remains; something he admitted. So was Setty killed in the flat and cut up? If so, Hume was guilty. Then there was the question of Mac, the Boy and Greeny. Humphreys did not deny that three men of their description existed somewhere, but that Hume's story of their bringing the parcels to him for him to dispose of them was 'a complete fabrication.'[47]

If Hume's story was correct, then it 'was a most amazing series of coincidences which you think was utterly beyond belief.' Hume had the carpet cleaned, the knife was sharpened and he spent an hour undisturbed in the kitchen. He reminded the jury that Mrs Hume would not 'fail to support her husband to the hilt in the terrible crisis.' He suggested it was incredible that she never saw the three men come to the flat, never heard the doorbell, never saw the parcels and never saw any blood. He poured scorn on the absurdity of Hume telling Mrs Stride he had to be undisturbed in the kitchen for an hour merely because he was almost unclothed, 'That you may think is the lowest depths of lying.' He concluded his speech thus:

> 'If you add to the fact that Setty's body was obviously cut up in the flat, so was obviously murdered there, the fact that this self-confessed criminal, self-confessed liar admitted that he got rid of the murdered man's remains, do you want further proof that he was party to the murder? I have to prove no more.'[48]

West was unimpressed at Humphrey's apparent 'acute spiritual distress.' She thought his words about Mrs Hume were 'strange' for she thought it was insinuated that Mrs Hume was possibly guilty of murder or perjury yet was not being charged with either, though 'there was not a shadow of evidence that she had committed any offence whatsoever.'[49] Yet, she was, by her own account, in the flat on the evening of Setty's demise.

It was now time for the judge to begin his summing up, to present to the jury what seemed to him to be the salient points of the case for them to consider when they left the court to discuss their verdict. He began by pointing out the dilemma of the prosecution:

> 'The difficulty of the case is that the Prosecution are not in a position to bring before you direct evidence which proves the charge which is alleged. What they are seeking to do is to establish certain facts before you, and on those facts, if you find them proved, they ask you to say they point conclusively to the guilt of the defendant of the crime with which he is charged. But a further difficulty in the case is this: they allege that the evidence which has been given by Hume is invented and is deliberately untrue.'[50]

Hume's story was seen as crucial; was it true or 'skilful and sustained lying'? He disposed of the body, but did this mean he also killed Setty? There was no evidence of Hume's activity on the day of the murder, 4 October. Was Hume's statement to the police accurate? That was for the jury to decide. Was the fact that a knife was sharpened decisive or was it irrelevant? Was it a coincidence that the carpet had to be cleaned on that day?[51]

Was Hume an honest man? He had described himself as being 'semi-honest.' If he was a liar, was he doing so for innocent reasons or for more sinister ones? Then there were the parcels; how did they arrive? There was insufficient time for the whole of the judge's summing up that day so he finished there and then.[52]

That evening the prosecution received an anonymous telephone call from a man who had a potentially crucial piece of information. He said, 'I don't know if it's of any interest but just around that time Hume bought the rope, or some rope, from our shop.' Where was this shop, he was asked. 'Oh, just across the road from Hume's flat.' By then, though, it was too late for this information to be investigated; if true, it was a very strong point for the prosecution's case, for it was alleged that whoever tied up the parcels, post dismemberment, was the killer and it disposed of Hume's story that he merely received three parcels.[53] Humphreys also noted this fact.[54]

The seventh day of the trial was Thursday, 26 January. Sellers continued in his summing up. He again stressed the lack of evidence as to Hume's movements on the 4th, the day of Setty's disappearance. The evidence of the bloodstains had to be considered – were they the result of Setty being killed in the flat or were they from the parcels containing Setty's body brought there, and if the latter, 'how did they come about?' What about the three men, 'there is no corroboration from Mrs Hume or Mrs Stride.' What of Hume's 'improbable story (of course improbable stories do happen).'

> 'You have to consider this story, which involves three men bringing parcels along a busy road to Hume's flat. You have to consider how much they knew of Hume – how much they could trust him. All this came out of a casual meeting on 3 October. You know that Hume lived in the flat with his wife and young child. How were the three men to know his wife would not be there? Was it not a grave risk for these men to carry the parcels up to the flat to place them in the care of a man they had no reason to trust? . . . a grave risk, you may think, for them to take . . . with the possibility of Mrs Hume being there. She might have gone to the police.'[55]

Did the jury believe the story of the three men? If so, Hume must be found innocent. Or were they invented? After all, Sellers asked:

> 'Suppose he were inventing these things and these men. It is perhaps reasonable that he might choose those names. They are not unfamiliar names in a certain society. It is not difficult to invent names, neither is it difficult to invent descriptions.'

Hume did not know the names and addresses of the three yet he said they left owing him money. The judge reminded the jury that the testimony of Clay and Lee should not be forgotten.[56]

The bloodstains and the carpet were referred to; Hume had not said the parcels came into the living room, yet blood was found there. Was this crucially important? Could Hume have attacked Setty from the front without any evidence of defence wounds on Setty's body? Similarly, Hume was uninjured. Was the motive money or one that is unknown? Finally, there was another series of questions to consider:

> 'If you reject Hume's evidence entirely, or you reject it as even so doubtful that you can disregard it altogether, you will still have this question: Did all the matters the Prosecution have spoken about actually happen?'[57]

According to Bixley:

> It was one of those cases where it was anybody's guess as to what the verdict would be. The Judge's impartial summing up gave the facts, and to my mind, as I think everyone else who was an onlooker at that trial, the jury had a formidable task to sift the truth from the welter of evidence, to take an objective view of facts without being biased by the natural loathing for the callousness of the young man in the dock.

It is worth considering for a moment the role of the jury, as Bixley explained:

> A jury is not asked to convince itself of an accused person's innocence but to be certain of his guilt. It may well feel very doubtful that the prisoner they have watched in the dock is innocent, but that must not prevent them believing that the prosecution has failed to prove his guilt and that therefore he is entitled to go free.[58]

What was not commented on was that Hume's story and his explanation did not make sense. His story was that the 'three men' arrived at the flat in the early afternoon of 5 October and brought the bloody parcels with them; the bloodstains found in the flat being caused by these parcels resting on the floor at some point. He was also paid at this stage. Yet, this makes a nonsense of the known chronology; Hume was spending fivers that morning and he took the carpet to the cleaners around noon. In other words, before the alleged three killers arrived. It could also be noted that no one saw these three men with their bulky objects; not Mrs Hume, nor Mrs Stride. Finally, would three killers not dispose of a corpse that they had already cut up by themselves; burying it in a remote spot they could drive to, or weigh it down and throw it into the sea or the Thames. Entrusting it to a man barely known to them was to risk their very lives. Hume's story therefore did not stand up to close scrutiny.

Be that as it may, the jury retired at 12.30 pm, wanted to return at 2.45 and returned at 3.02 – a lengthy discussion indeed (in the recent cases of Evans and Haigh the jury had been out in both cases for less than an hour.). Hume was brought up from the cells, his face showing the strain of the two-and-a-half-hour wait. Three prison officers and a doctor stood near the door from the cells. There was the ominous black cap by the judge's elbow, for a guilty verdict could mean death by hanging for Hume (not necessarily, of course; of the thirty-one men sentenced to death for murder in the previous year, 'only' seventeen were actually hanged).

The Clerk of the Court addressed them:

> 'Members of the jury, will your foreman please stand? Mr Foreman of the jury, are you agreed upon your verdict?'
> 'My Lord, we are not agreed (at this time a jury had to reach a unanimous decision for it to be valid). I feel that it is doubtful that we shall reach a unanimous decision.'

It is not known how many jurors dissented from the guilty verdict. The judge then thanked them and dismissed them for their 'long and strenuous service.'

Humphreys had already considered the possibility of the jury being unable to reach a unanimous decision, and had discussed it with the director of public prosecutions, Sir Theobald Mathew (1898–1964). He therefore asked that a new jury be sworn in and that no evidence be offered on this indictment and that evidence be offered on another on the file. There had not been a jury in disagreement over a murder trial verdict since the case of the Peasenhall murder, Rex vs Gardiner, in 1901, and after two trials the defendant was acquitted.[59]

Therefore a new jury was sworn in and instructed by the judge to return a verdict of 'Not Guilty.' Apparently, 'Hume seemed to sag as he heard the verdict, then he lifted his head and looked across at the jury.' The Clerk then told Hume that there was a second indictment against him, that of being an accessory after the fact of murder, knowingly disposing of the body of a murdered man. To this, 'Hume swallowed hard and moistened his lips. Then in a clear voice came his answer. One word: Guilty.' Humphreys said there was nothing new to add to this and Levy said that some of the jury must have accepted Hume's version of events, to which Sellers agreed. Levy restated the story about the men bringing the parcels to Hume and concluded:

> 'He [Hume] was then, with the receiving of the third parcel, on the horns of a very grave dilemma. He knew that if he failed to carry

out the orders, he was dealing with a gang of men who would not hesitate to murder, and that his life was, to some extent, in danger. It might be said that he could and should have communicated with the police. If he had done this his life would not have been worth a moment's grace. He found himself in an appalling position and he felt he had no alternative.'[60]

The judge then addressed Hume:

'I find it hard to imagine a graver case. For no other reason than money, £150, you were prepared to take part of the body, the torso, knowing what it was, and keep it in your flat overnight. Then without any communication to the police, you took it away and flung it into the Thames estuary with the intention and belief that nothing more would be known of it, thereby obliterating all evidence of the crime of murder. The sentence of the Court upon you is twelve years' imprisonment.'[61]

Levy had done well for his client. A newspaper decreed that he was the 'Man of the Week' and that 'His defence of Hume should be worth thousands of pounds a year to him in future cases.' He had pointed to every possible chink in the armour of the prosecution and so had raised doubts in the minds of at least one of the jury.[62]

Mrs Hume had not attended the last day of the trial. She had remained at home with the curtains drawn. News of the verdict was conveyed to her by George O'Brien, a private detective. He later said, 'She took it well, but naturally she's very upset. She will see no one. Mrs Hume will not leave the flat without me.' Despite what had happened there, she remained at the flat until 1952, living there with her elder sister, Beatrice Fenwick, who had divorced her first husband.[63]

No one ever enquired how the Setty family felt with the inconclusive verdict. Although they had been able to give Setty a burial, or at least part of him, there had been no closure for them. They were left with the impression that perhaps the three mysterious men killed him, and got away with it, or that perhaps Hume had done so, but had escaped justice. It must have been an unsettling time for them. In 1961 Jack Setty told the police that his brother's murder could not be undone and that Hume was undergoing the punishment he deserved.[64]

According to Dr Camps, 'The Setty Case had in a sense been unique and Hume had no doubt been a very unusual gentleman.'[65] The truth concerning Setty's death, however, had not been unearthed and so justice had not been done as a killer had escaped his just deserts. What was clear was that the prosecution had failed to present a sufficiently convincing case against Hume that could lead the jury to finding him guilty.

West believed Hume's story was true, 'It is certain that in essence Hume's own story was true, and that Mr Setty's corpse had been left at his apartment already dismembered and packaged; and that he was not the murderer but only an accessory after the fact.' She added that 'this murder seems likely to rank as one of the greatest unsolved mysteries. The possibility that Hume murdered Mr Setty can definitely be excluded.' Indeed, 'The mystery which involved him with Mr Setty will be written about as long as there is a literature of crime.' She believed that Hume had not killed Setty in the flat because the neighbour heard nothing and no one saw any evidence of the murder having taken place there. She also believed there was no physical evidence (overlooking the bloodstains). Nor did she believe there was a financial motive for Hume to kill him, though murder is often committed for non monetary reasons. She did not believe that three men brought in the dismembered remains to the flat as neither Mrs Hume nor Mrs Stride had seen them but also thought that the real killer was the man who sent the agents along with the body parcels, though this seems contradictory and she had no explanation as to how Setty's corpse arrived at the flat.[66]

Hoskins had a rather different opinion, or so he wrote in his memoirs over two decades later. He believed that the evidence of Setty having consumed a large amount of alcohol before death would have rendered him defenceless and so he could have been killed with a minimum of sound or resistance. The prosecution case was less than what it should have been despite high-quality work by police and pathologists. According to him, 'No man in my opinion was ever luckier to draw twelve years.'[67]

Chapter 8

The Consequences, 1958

As the *Sunday Pictorial* had paid for Hume's defence, the paper wanted its quid pro quo and Hume honoured the bargain. On the Sunday after the verdict the first of three exclusive articles by him was published. The first was 'I plotted to Escape' in which Hume tells of his time in Brixton prison, the notorious killers he met and his alleged aborted escape attempt. The second, 'I was an arms smuggler', is his story about being 'a dealer in death' for foreign clients. In the third, 'The Truth about the Setty Killing: Does Hume know?', Hume repeats the story that he had told the police after his arrest. How much of all these was true is another question; some of it might well be embellishment as there is no evidence to support it from other sources.[1] Until the Coroners and Justice Act of 2009 it was perfectly legal for convicted criminals to sell their stories and many did so.

Meanwhile, initially Hume was sent to Wormwood Scrubs prison in west London, 'a huge extravagantly architected place of dingy brick and grubby stone', its exterior later made famous by countless TV and film dramas from *The Italian Job* to *The Sweeney* and *Minder*.[2] He termed his civilian occupation as 'Company Director and Pilot', making himself sound more impressive than was actually the case, but this is not uncommon amongst criminals; the equally fraudulent John Haigh termed himself 'Company Director' wherever possible. Apparently, Hume was not a happy man, weeping and storming in his cell like a caged animal. Psychiatrists examined him and found that though intelligent, he was excitable and garrulous. Major Benjamin Grew, the governor, wrote that he was 'Dishonest, not addicted to drink.' In February 1950 he asked to see Grew and was interviewed again by MacDougall.[3]

When in prison on a sentence, Hume, as with other prisoners, was forced to wear the coarse, grey prison uniform. He was given starchy, dull foods to eat. One example was fried fish, cabbage, potatoes and pudding, to be eaten out of a single, deep tin with a spoon. His life would be regimented and controlled as never before; a bath-time day, a day to return library books, a pay day and church on Sundays. Peter Wildeblood commented on his experience of life as an inmate there in the early 1950s, that it was a 'powerful shock. Suddenly in the space of a few hours, a man's whole life is changed.' He considered it to be 'the worst place to which a first offender can be sent, and that its sanitary conditions would . . . disgrace a Hottentot village.' In the prison workshops where he would be employed there was no talking amongst prisoners. At that time birching in prison was still legal, though there's no evidence that Hume was ever disciplined in such a fashion. Prison was not a pleasant experience.[4] Hume made allegations that there were others involved in the murder of Setty and he did not mean the three individuals he mentioned in court. He wrote to his wife:

> I am here because I was man enough to keep my mouth shut. I was unwise to be a stooge. If I had my chance for a trial again things would be different. Others as guilty – and more – would be in my position. If I find you are deserting me, Cynthia, mainly I know, by outside pressure, I will take immediate action which will be very unpleasant all round. I should hate to see you in my position for protecting someone like him. If the felt is wearing out in the lounge, why not use that in the nursery, or did we use it all?[5]

This seems to have been a clear indication that he was accusing her of having some part in the murder of Setty, together with a third party and the final point suggests that he and his wife used felt from the nursery to wrap up the body parts. In 1962, journalists Playfair and Sington suggest that he was paranoid about his wife's behaviour, referring to her having seen Setty, and then accused her of deserting him.[6]

Hume thought that the sentence he had been given was far too severe and briefly planned to appeal against it, but this never occurred (appeals were rarely successful). He did, however, make a dramatic revelation to Goldman, which has hitherto never been made public. It is an explanation of what happened to Setty at 620b Finchley Road on the evening of 4 October and was Hume's second known account; and unknown until now. It completely overturned the version of events that he had given to the police and which his defence had relied on in court. Hume and Goldman conferred in the prison on 31 January. Hume said:

> 'If my wife does not come and see me here I am going to send for Superintendent MacDougall and tell him the whole story. I am not going to carry the can for her she is not worth it.'
> 'Did you kill Setty?' asked the solicitor, a question surely on everyone's lips.

It was then that Hume made a shocking revelation, differing from what he had written to his wife, but in the same tenor:

'No, I came home unexpectedly and found him [Setty] with my wife. I laid him out and she stabbed him four or five times. She knew him before I did and in fact introduced us. I worked all night cutting up the body. The three men (Green, Mac and the Boy) I mentioned in my statement to the police never existed. I took the names from the book *Brighton Rock* and the third man was Mr MacDougall's description.'[7]

Brighton Rock was a novel published in 1938 about murderous gangsters in and around Brighton in the 1930s. The protagonist is the teenage sociopath Pinkie. Nine years later it was filmed, starring Richard Attenborough as Pinkie. Pinkie is known as the Boy and the author was Graham Greene. Both book and film were popular and Hume clearly was cognisant with the story.

Goldman pressed his client for further details, which Hume was ready to supply and gave full vent to his feelings:

'My wife is a bitch. I know of five different men who have been associating with her since we married. I am not even sure that the child is mine. She will not stand by me as she has promised. She and her father have had all my money.'

Goldman soon told MacDougall about this conversation. Hume's allegations about his wife's adultery and the murder seem nonsensical as she was pregnant and then looking after a newborn baby for most of 1949. It seems fantastic that she would have had the inclination or the capacity for such behaviour.[8]

Meanwhile, searches were still being made in Paris and elsewhere for the three men mentioned in Hume's statement. MacDougall was sceptical about this, stating, 'I am of opinion that these men . . . do not exist.' He was aware that two of the names were from the novel *Brighton Rock* and that the name of Mac and his description was one of himself.[9]

On 13 February, MacDougall and DS Neil Sutherland arrived at Wormwood Scrubs and at 11 am were seated opposite Hume. MacDougall spoke first:

'I have been told by Mr Goldman that you want to see us.'

Sutherland then took down the following statement by Hume:

'Yes, I want to tell you some more facts, but I want a little further time to think things over, I will write out my story myself and send it to you. I mentioned this to Mr Goldman when he was here about my appeal. You need not waste any more of your time looking for the three men I told you about, that was just a story we made up. I didn't actually do the knifing. I have been shielding Cynthia, my wife, and she hasn't played the game. I did the cutting up of Setty's body in the flat and worked all night at it [dismembering the corpse for subsequent disposal as already inferred by witnesses]. I came home unexpectedly. Setty was a bastard with women [Webb later made a very similar remark, as already noted in Chapter 3]. I hope you do not hold it against me for telling lies, but you understand I was fighting for my life. I think the Judge saw through me from the start but my wife seemed so nice, coy and demure in the box that they all fell for her. She is a wicked woman. I will write out my story and you shall hear it later.'[10]

If this version of facts – where Cynthia Hume was the killer of Setty – is true it begs additional questions. Had he gone there as the result of an appointment or by chance? When did he drink – at the flat or earlier? She certainly stated that she was at the flat on the evening of 4 October. Yet, she had denied all knowledge of anything untoward taking place in the flat on that evening. The question is, to what extent was Hume lying? Or could he have pressurised her into lying to support him?[11]

Could Cynthia have possibly committed the murder? Women rarely kill, but some do; Ruth Ellis in 1955 is an obvious example. It seems highly unlikely, if not impossible, in this case for Setty was a hefty man and although he had been drinking, he was far from paralytic. The question is, though, why should she do so? There was no known animosity between her and Setty and she vehemently denied ever meeting him when Hume suggested she had been having an affair with him. Yet, why should Hume have shielded his allegedly adulterous wife? Were the impoverished couple acting together in a conspiracy against the wealthy Setty, luring him the their flat to kill him for his money and then, two days later, decoying his brother-in-law away from his flat to search it for any evidence connecting Setty to Hume? This is a possibility and fits the facts but the evidence for supporting it is thin indeed. It could have happened but we are far from certain that it did, and Hume's account is probably the outpourings of an angry man who knows he has lost his liberty for the next few years and wants to hit back at his wife, perhaps out of paranoia.

Relations between Hume and his wife certainly had quickly broken down after her glowing testimony to him in the press in January; and after his sentence, though this is not to say that they were as poor as that in October 1949. It seems, though, that Mrs Hume had been a regular visitor to her husband in prison and often wrote to him. There was no lack of outward affection on her part, but this was not enough for her husband as the veiled threat in the above letter notes. He may have felt angry because he was now behind bars for the next few years and he blamed her for it. One newspaper claimed that Hume's actions were 'in order to influence her concerning the child's future.' Hume was certainly known to blame others. But she did not appreciate being implicated in the murder as he was strongly suggesting. She decided to divorce her husband on the grounds of cruelty, and to have custody of Alison. As has been stated, she told the divorce court that he had knocked her about during her pregnancy and afterwards. He wrote her abusive letters from prison, telling her not to divorce him or he would implicate her in Setty's murder. Webb wrote of these 'outrageous allegations.' In the end, Hume did not contest the divorce case. Mrs Hume's demands were granted. Seven years later, Webb married Mrs Hume, but their married life was brief as he died two weeks later.[12]

The police do not seem to have taken any further action after Hume's sensational statement. They probably did not believe it. Hume could have been charged with perverting the course of justice and then his wife charged with murder. Neither charge was proceeded with, presumably because neither they nor the public prosecutor thought there was sufficient evidence to pursue them. Yet, Hume alluded to it again in 1959, as we shall see.

There is, however, a letter written by Hume to MacDougall shortly after their meeting in prison. This was in response to the detective's suggestion that he write down what happened. Hume claimed that he was happy to do so. He wrote that 'A full and comprehensive statement will be made by me, as far as is possible from 8.40 onwards on the night of the 4th October.' Yet, this would not be made until he had completed his sentence. He claimed that his diary and other documents would:

> Prove movements conclusively on the 4th October 1949 from 1800 hours until 2000 hours and that my subsequent arrival at the flat could not have been before 2040 hours. I should also be able to prove that I was not expected back at the flat until Friday night as I was due in Birmingham on the Wednesday morning having been wired by the accountants.

He then said he had to cancel the meeting 'to settle more pressing issues at Golders Green of which you are aware.' He would also produce documents to state that his financial affairs were in good health, contrary to what was suggested at the trial. He also said he hoped that ninety-six of the missing £5 notes would be found and he had not told all before because he had complete faith in Mr Goldman and that he was not a brave man.[13]

Needless to say, Hume never did produce any evidence about his movements on the night in question. His letter is clearly meant to absolve himself of guilt and suggest that his wife was entertaining Setty in the flat that night and did not expect to be interrupted by her husband, but Hume returned, and, it implied, he caught them in flagrante delicto. This seems nonsensical behaviour on the part of a new mother preoccupied with her young baby.

Unaware of all this, journalists were still interested in Hume. Fred Redman of the *Sunday Pictorial* believed that Hume might well have more to tell. He thought that now the high drama of the trial was over, Hume would have time to reflect and to seize any possibility of an early release. He had written to Redman to tell him, 'I have not yet played my ace.' This might have been a reference to making an escape attempt or to trying to commit suicide, but Redman believed that both possibilities were closed to him now.[14]

Redman thought that Hume's articles in the *Sunday Pictorial* were not the whole story. For instance, Hume had said nothing about his movements on the crucial day of 4 October. He did not explain how there came to be a bloodstain on the living room carpet after he had said that the parcels went straight to the kitchen coal cupboard and nowhere near the other room (a good point). How could the three men he claimed brought the remains of Setty to his flat arrive and leave on two occasions unseen by everyone? Not such a good point; no one saw any of five of Christie's victims enter 10 Rillington Place. The Crown case was not complete, either, but Redman concluded, 'I was left with the impression that for some reason . . . Hume was leaving gaps in his tale which might one day be cleared up.'[15]

The question was, who killed Setty? There seemed to have been some doubt and Hume seems to have been given the benefit of it. Sir Harold Scott (1887–1968), Commissioner of Scotland Yard from 1945–53, wrote in 1955, 'the question of who killed Setty, and how and where, remains unsolved.' Rebecca West was convinced of Hume's innocence, writing that 'the features of the murderer behind Hume are so mysterious' and 'The mystery which involved him and Setty will be written about as long as there is an interest in crime, but it will be only on the printed page . . . its practical effects will have been quietly smoothed away.' Earlier, she had written, 'Hume did not murder Setty' but in no way was sympathetic towards him, 'many murderers have shown more respect to their victims than he showed to this corpse which he agreed to dispose of for money. It was as if he had contracted out of humanity. Humane instinct withered within him . . . a poor wretch who . . .had gone past his humanity, not to animalism but to callousness.' Rebecca West told Ivan Butler in 1976 the following:

> I knew that Hume had confessed to the murder of Setty . . . He started confessing very soon after he got into prison, and continued

to produce confessions at intervals for years, but I think there was a good reason not to take them seriously, as I learned on good authority. They always showed ignorance of a detail known to the police which had never been published.[16]

Webb thought likewise, that Hume had told several stories, all involving others. He also stated that the case was far from over and in 1953 wrote that he was keeping an open file on the 'Setty Case' in his filing cabinet. In his opinion the killer was the man who bought the rope to bind the parcels containing Setty:

> The man who bought that felt and rope murdered Stanley Setty. Scotland Yard know who that man is. So do I [neither ever named him, so may have been bluffing]. He is still alive, but I do not think he will ever be brought to trial. I therefore propose keeping my dossier on the Setty case unclosed, since the murderer of Stanley Setty has not be been brought to book.

He added that the police claimed, 'we know who did it, but we haven't a ghost's chance of proving it', though as we will see, some officers were convinced of Hume's guilt, as was Webb himself. Quite why the man who bought the rope that bound the parcels was necessarily the killer is another question; he could well have been an accomplice.[17]

Camps lectured on the subject on 23 November 1950 before the Medico-Legal Society. He stated, 'From the medical point of view the case is unique, I believe as the first case of disposal of the body by dropping it into the sea from an aeroplane.' He thought that this method 'offers great possibilities of the perfect crime.' Fellow pathologist, Dr Simpson, wondered at the nerve that Hume must have possessed to have taken out the parcels containing body parts in daylight and in full view of onlookers. Camps could not, however, offer a solution to the mystery, 'Who killed Setty and the circumstances under which it occurred must remain a mystery.'[18]

Bixley, writing his memoirs in 1957, concurred with the then general view that Hume was innocent, writing that it was 'one of those comparatively rare instances of a still unsolved murder mystery where clues to the crimes were sufficient to warrant a charge . . . It contained and still contains elements of mystery which are intriguing.' He concluded, 'The law had ordained that Hume did not kill Setty, and I believe that the law was right.' He thought there had never been a wrongful acquittal.[19]

These writers were constrained in publishing their views; anyone suggesting Hume's guilt could have faced legal action for libel against a man deemed 'not guilty' by the court. After Hume's confession of 1958 (see later in this chapter), though, all writers on the topic have accepted his guilt.

Discoveries concerning the case, none conclusive, were still being made after Hume was imprisoned. One was the black trunk in which Setty's corpse was initially placed which was smeared with blood. The police never found it where Hume had placed it at Golders Green Tube station. It was never retrieved by him, of course, and so four months after its deposit, in February 1950, it was transferred to the railway's lost property office at Baker Street. On 14 March 1950 it was examined by Dr Holden and he found human bloodstains and two dog hairs in it. Because of this, MacDougall went to visit Hume four days later; the latter ensuring that his wife and Goldman were also present. Hume asked if he would be charged as being an accessory before the fact, but was reassured that he could not be retried for murder. MacDougall told Hume he wanted to interview him and Hume told him he would write it all down. The story would be told when he was released and when his diary and other documents were to hand. Goldman told MacDougall Hume that would give him a statement but this was never delivered.[20]

Elsewhere, a skull was discovered at Saltings, St Osyth in Essex on 22 April 1951, only a few miles from the Dengie Marshes. It was of a man aged 35–45. Some teeth were missing. Dr Camps examined it on 3 July. He concluded that this was not that of Setty for it had been exposed for longer than that of Setty had. Mrs Ouri said that her brother had all his teeth. None of this prevented it being placed in Scotland Yard's Black Museum and being identified as such; an Anglo-Saxon expert who visited the museum identified it as being over a millennium old. Other relics to end up in the museum were the bloodstained floorboards which had been prised from Hume's flat; though these have been disposed of long ago. An SS dagger belonging to Hume was also exhibited there.[21]

Another mystery that was never settled was Setty's wealth – he never made a will nor did the courts decide how to apportion his goods in what is known as a Grant. The Official Receiver at Manchester had taken all the money from his safe, however, by 1951, as he was an undischarged bankrupt. According to Max Setty, he had given his brother £6,000 in £5 notes to keep there.[22] On 8 August 1950, however, solicitors found that he was bankrupt but looked for any personal belongings he might have owned. They found a radiogram, worth £80, he had been given as part of a debt repayment, two motor cars (the Citroën and a Standard Vanguard) and a deposit account at Selfridges. The two cars were sold for £1,611, more than what they were worth new.[23]

Hume was sent to Wakefield prison on 10 October 1950, and described as 5ft 6in tall (the same height as Setty), with brown hair. He was listed as a director and of Anglican faith, but the latter must have been purely nominal as at this point in his life he was not noted as having any religious faith whatsoever, and had not even been married in church, though later he seemed to turn to Catholicism. He hoped that at Wakefield there would be 'scope for intellectual and academic attainments.' In 1951 he told the governor he had information for the government about Soviet agents operating in the United Kingdom. He claimed he knew that Soviet agents had information about transmitters such as ASDIC and frequency modulators. He would give up this information if he could have a guarantee that his sentence would be cut. Generally, though, there was a policy of not making bargains with prisoners, but this might be relaxed if the information was of great value. Yet, the governor commented, 'by virtue of his knowledge of the underworld, [Hume] is one of the most unscrupulous scoundrels he has had in his hands.' No deals, then, because Hume was not trusted to be able to supply accurate information.[24]

At Wakefield, it was noted that his behaviour was generally good:

> Hume's conduct . . . was variable. None of the assistant governors charged with his oversight seems to have thought him in any way trustworthy, though one records liking him. But he was never in serious trouble there, and indeed was only twice on report and then for comparatively minor offences. He forfeited three days remission on each occasion.[25]

Whilst in Wakefield Hume met Klaus Fuchs (1911–88), a German born scientist who had lived in England and, as a Communist, betrayed nuclear secrets to the Soviet Union before being gaoled for his crimes. They talked for hours each day, Hume giving Fuchs cigarettes, chocolates, newspapers and even books. One of the latter was a title forbidden to Fuchs as it dealt in part with him (Alan Moorehead's *The Traitors*). Fuchs told Hume about science and played chess with him. They had a master and servant relationship with Hume as servant. He claimed Fuchs rekindled his adolescent interest in Communism. Fuchs later admitted that he had known Hume but had not liked him. Hume also claimed to have met Dr Allan Nunn May (1911–2003), another scientist who had spied for the Soviet Union.[26]

On 6 June 1952 Hume was returned to Wormwood Scrubs for medical treatment (unstated) and sent back to Wakefield on 4 November of that year. He did not remain there long for on 30 July 1953, Hume was moved to Dartmoor prison, seen as offering a more austere regime compared with the relatively liberal Wakefield. This could have been because he misbehaved and so this switch was a punishment. His conduct there was noted as follows:

> He had some difficulty in settling down. In October of that year he had 14 days' remission for a moderately serious act of indiscipline

and the following month he was in trouble again, though for a lesser offence, which cost him two days' remission (he also lost another six days' remission). Thereafter he seems to have settled down. He was twice more on report, but on neither occasion was the offence serious enough to attract more than a caution.[27]

In February 1954, reports were also good, 'Hume has evidently attained a degree of superficial conformity, though it is noteworthy that all three reporting officers remarked on his extreme conceit . . . Later reports all show Hume as a reasonably well behaved, industrious and apparently co-operative prisoner.'[28]

Little else is known about Hume's time in Dartmoor. When he had just arrived, he wrote to MacDougall, asking him for the birth certificate and passport he claimed had been taken from him on his arrest. He was told that the certificate was not taken from him and that the passport would expire before he was released.[29]

According to Hume, he had become a memorable character whilst in Dartmoor. The other convicts named him 'The Fuse' because of his skill with electrics. He showed them how to make radio sets from smuggled parts of bits of GPO equipment sent to the prison to be dismantled by the prisoners. As has already been inferred, Hume was a well-behaved prisoner. On the final night of his stay in prison he was given a send-off, 'Many of the men whose crimes had made headlines gathered together.' They ate a special pre-release feast spread out on a table-tennis table. In the centre was a huge cake on which was iced a monoplane like the one he had used to dispose of Setty, with a bundle being dropped and a message, 'A Fuse will be blowing shortly.'[30]

Yet, although Hume wanted to be admired by his fellows as one of the boys and as a Number One, those who knew him at this time gave a different account of him. They did not like him nor did they accept him. He was seen as being self-centred and a liar, as a man who boasted of RAF service and who was resented due to this. He was a neurotically bad loser and would go into tantrums when he lost at darts and so others let him win. Although he was quarrelsome and quick to take offence, this was only a pose of toughness. He would often back down when it came to a possible fight and if it did he would fight like a woman; scratching his opponent and screaming. Nor did he have the will to try and defy authority. He was deferential to staff and 'crawled' to them to try and win favours. He was not interested in escape attempts and was rarely on charge for any infractions of prison regulations. Ronald Howe later wrote, 'He was extremely unpopular being regarded both as a homosexual and as an informer.' Yet, at a Christmas party he adapted the words of the war-time song 'Bless 'em all, Bless 'em all, The Long and the short and the tall' into 'F——'em all . . . .' Whilst in Dartmoor, Hume let Brian Pearsall, a budding artist, paint his portrait; dressed in an open necked white shirt with a moor in the background.[31]

Hume met one Thomas Arthur Crocker whilst in prison. He told Crocker that he would be receiving a large amount of money from newspaper articles published about him when he left prison. He asked if he could use Crocker's address as somewhere to which his post could be sent, in return for a fee. He had letters sent to 5 Provost Road, Hampstead, but Mrs Crocker recalled that he never gave her any money.[32]

Hume was released from Dartmoor prison on 1 February 1958, after serving just over eight years of a twelve-year sentence. Apparently, 'Hume has not in fact come to notice very much in prison.' He was eager to make money from the newspapers when he left. The governor thought, however, that Hume might be able to earn a legitimate living on leaving prison.[33]

Hume was emerging into a far different world to the one he had previously known. In 1949 Britain had a Labour government whose austerity policies continued rationing, high taxes and shortages of consumer goods. In 1958 the Conservatives had been in office for seven years and Britain had now abandoned austerity and was very much a consumer society, enjoying cars, televisions, foreign holidays and refrigerators – people 'never had it so good', as Prime Minister Harold Macmillan boasted.

It was not so good for Hume, of course. He did not seem a contented man. As a journalist wrote on his release, 'Donald Hume has emerged from jail as a hopeless example of society's failure to use prison to rehabilitate a man . . . I grew to know that after eight years in jail he had emerged as a nervous, rebellious, fantastically touchy wreck of a man.'[34]

One man who had a great interest in Hume and had often visited him and corresponded with him was Webb. He hoped to write the first book on the case. With the connivance of the prison authorities, Hume was smuggled out of the prison at midnight in order to avoid other journalists. Webb and Hume went to an Exeter hotel and registered under assumed names. They were met by one John Potter, a colleague of Webb's, in a bedroom there. Potter wrote, 'I have never met a man whom I disliked more at first sight. He was small and slight with dark, snake like eyes. His whole demeanour was reptilian.'[35]

Webb asked Hume point blank, 'I have come for one story only – your story of how you killed Setty.' Hume may have been unaware of the double-jeopardy protection he enjoyed. He replied, 'I swear I never killed the old geezer.'

Webb stated that Hume might be paid £10,000 for an exclusive story, or perhaps half that amount if Webb published a story accusing Hume of the murder and then Hume rebutted it. Hume thought it over for an hour or two, but even after a drink in a Dorset pub, refused to sign any confession because he was still fearful that Superintendent MacDougall would have him back in prison.[36]

The trio arrived at the offices of the *People* newspaper, but the editor, Stuart Campbell, was busy with other work and could only give them the briefest of attention. This upset Hume and he began to become suspicious and surly. Accusing Webb of potential treachery, he left the place and Webb told Potter, 'He is a maniacal killer. He will murder somebody else within the year.'[37]

Yet, Webb's version was different to Potter's. According to him:

> I drove him to London. I wanted to ask him certain questions, but Hume was too anxious to talk about himself. He began boasting right away that he killed Setty and began telling me the gruesome details. He was sure that he could get at least £3000 from a news-paper. When I told him that the People was not prepared to buy he became violently angry.[38]

Yet, Hume was happy to talk to others. They represented money, of course. Another journalist who met him that evening was veteran crime correspond-ent of the *News of the World*, Norman Rae. Hume talked to him about the amount of money in banks. He added, 'At any rate, Norman, I will never go back to Stir [prison]. I'd rather be hanged next time than face another eight years inside. But I'll take care they don't catch me again.' He also told how he killed Setty, 'he seemed to take delight in describing how he killed Setty, cut up the body' and disposed of the remains. He added, 'It was sheer bad luck, old man, that they were ever found.'[39]

Hume spent his first evening as a free man in the cocktail bar of a West End hotel. He sipped champagne and spoke with journalists. Victor Sims of the *Sunday Pictorial* reported: 'One moment he was a gay, cheerful, even likea-ble fellow, chatting optimistically about the new life that lay ahead for him in Canada or Australia. But the next he would be a snarling, growling lone wolf with a grudge against society – like an animal that has escaped from its cage.'[40]

Hume had plenty of conversation. Some of it was about notorious fellow prisoners that he had met whilst in prison, such as Fuchs and Evans. But he would not talk to Sims about Setty. Hume replied to him, 'If I opened my mouth about that', he said, 'the police would have to get busy, I can tell you, and that would worry some people.' This appears to be an allusion to the allegations he had made to MacDougall and Goldman at Wormwood Scrubs about his wife's involvement in the Setty murder.[41] He talked of meeting Fuchs. Hume admired the man and apparently he had 'given him a fanatical new interest in Communist politics.'[42]

An *Empire News* journalist also talked to Hume that night. They were in an espresso bar in Old Compton Street, Soho. Hume told the man:

> 'If the world doesn't let me get a decent living I'll take what I want. I'll get myself a gun and I wouldn't be afraid to use it, you know.'
> 'Don't be a fool.'
> 'Yeah, you think I'm a fool, too.'

Hume tried to look tough. He added,

> 'I've got a charmed life.'
> 'What's charmed about it?'
> 'Well, they didn't top me. I did Albert Pierrepoint [principal hangman in Britain at that time; hanged Evans, Haigh, Christie, Ruth Ellis and many others] out of hanging me.'
> 'So you did murder Setty as I always thought?'[43]

Hume did not reply. The journalist described the situation:

> He looked at me and said nothing for what seemed like an eternity. As we sat in the room almost not staring at each other, I mentally recalled how and when we first met. I had thought that he was an intelligent man although there was something about those eyes which disturbed me. His eyes were those of a killer. It's a vague look – most people would not recognise it – because they have not looked very closely into the eyes of a gun man.

'Setty deserved to die. They can't try a man twice for the same murder', Hume said, adding that he would tell his story and it would be popular. Then he would go abroad, Canada, Australia or Eastern Europe and work as an electrical engineer.[44]

The only snag to his release was the news that sent:

> a jolt that hurt as much as those years inside. I found that my pet dog Tony, the only real pal I ever had, had been put to sleep. Now I'm on my own. I feel I have taken my punishment for the crime I was found guilty of –and I'm in the clear. Now I'm going abroad under a new name.

Hume made no attempt to contact either his former wife or his daughter, who was now aged 9. Whilst it should be no surprise that he would never want to see Mrs Hume, not to want to make contact with his only daughter is more surprising and is perhaps evidence of a cold-hearted nature. Yet, his formative experience of family life was hardly a positive one. Or did he believe his earlier comment, doubting he was her father? Or was this merely a convenient excuse?[45]

Hume appeared, for a time, to want to make a fresh start in life. He contacted, on his own initiative, the New Bridge organisation, founded in 1956, which seeks to help newly released prisoners. Through them he obtained a job as an electrician. This suggests that he had an awareness he needed help. The organisation investigated the possibility of psychiatric help for him, but none could be found and it is unlikely that he could have been treated except as an inpatient.[46]

Hume settled down in a room in a lodging house in London, location unknown. He explained to the landlady that he was Johnny Lea, from Canada, and that he worked as an engineer in Weybridge. He seemed ordinary enough and well mannered. He did his own cooking and carried out odd jobs around the house, even helping with any unruly fellow tenants. He gave helpful advice and little gifts. His room was kept unlocked and when his landlady once looked inside she saw books about flight including Dietrich's *My Flights with the Fuehrer*. Her daughter once briefly suspected his true identity, stating that his eyes looked 'most peculiar.'[47]

Hoskins, who had reported the 1950 trial for his newspaper, recalled in his memoirs that on 6 February Hume arrived at the newspaper offices and offered to sell him the true story of the murder of Setty. Hoskins was convinced of his guilt and thought, of all the killers he had seen, 'Hume was the one who most disgusted me.' This was because Hume showed no remorse and his eyes were alight at the joy of cashing in on his crime. Hoskins refused to pay for the story and gave his opinion on Hume:

> He was something to look at. Brilliantined black hair curled untidily over his prison white face. His eyes glowed in his head as he spoke about the 'perfect murder.' He wriggled and fidgeted in his chair, and kept swinging around as though to make sure no one eavesdropped on our conversation. He looked what he was: an evil, sly and highly dangerous animal.[48]

Yet, Hoskins was interested in one story Hume had to tell and this was published in the *Sunday Express* a week after his release. This described Hume's meetings with Timothy Evans. This was now a very controversial – and thus newsworthy – subject because some believed that Evans had been hanged in error for the murder that had been committed by his neighbour,

John Christie. There is no doubt that Hume met Evans, but whether his story of their meetings is correct is another matter.

Hume related how he told Evans, 'Don't stick your neck in a noose.' He thought that he was stupid to have confessed to murder. 'He's a bit of an idiot, this boy. He needs some advice', thought Hume. Hume's words of wisdom were to 'Blame everyone but yourself.' Evans said that he didn't murder either his wife or daughter, though Hume was sceptical about the claim. He said that his baby had to die because 'the kid kept on crying' (Evans also gave this as his reason for murder to PS Leonard Trevallian) and that 'I was there while it [the murder] was done.' He also advised Evans to appear to be more dense than he was during his court appearances, and that he should have said that he was illiterate so that the statements the police took from him were untrue.[49]

Another journal interested in Hume was the German current affairs weekly *Der Spiegel*. Its London correspondent, a Mr H.G. Alexander, met him in a Lyons cafe in Knightsbridge. Hume offered them an article about Fuchs. Alexander recalled that Hume was modestly dressed and they ate a simple snack. The manuscript he was given seemed accurate and interesting. Hume seemed engaging, intelligent and trustworthy. He said he wanted a quiet life, working as an electrician and playing bridge rather than womanising. He was critical of the press for hounding him, wanting a 'confession' that he murdered Setty. Alexander thought that Hume planned to confess to that crime, one he was certain Hume did not commit. The article was accepted and later published (it also appeared in the *Daily Express*) and the two men went to the Ideal Home Exhibition to view electrical appliances. Alexander concluded, 'I was sorry for the little man in the shabby suit who had wished – genuinely, I think, at that stage – to sell electric fires and play bridge.'[50]

Yet, the story that the newspapers really wanted from him was his version of the reality of what had happened to Setty. Newspapers were the main medium of news at this time. The *Sunday Pictorial* had a circulation of 6 million and other Sunday newspapers had millions of readers. Newspapers knew that serious crime sold – the more horrible and sensational the better (cases such as those of Haigh and Heath had done wonders for circulation figures). Stories had to have popular appeal and journalists preferred ones that were naturally intriguing or could be adapted in this way – featuring black and white characters with simple story lines and if possible ripe for moralising as well as being shocking and entertaining. The truth was not high on this list of priorities. They were willing to pay good money, too.

Out of gaol, Hume changed his name by deed poll in April. He knew that with the publication of any confession he might make that 'people weren't going to take to me.' He was now Donald Brown, a nondescript surname but retaining his Christian name, and obtained a passport under this name. Yet, he felt he needed another alias and another passport. So he went back to Somerset House, which he had visited in the 1930s to see his birth certificate and discovered that he was indeed born out of wedlock. This time he was looking for a birth certificate of someone whose identity he could assume, for a copy of a birth certificate is needed to obtain a passport. He chose that of John Stephen Bird (born in Axminster, Devon in 1927) on the grounds that 'bird' is another name for time spent in prison but also because the surname is indicative of freedom, 'free as a bird', and because of its connotations with flight – Hume was always fascinated with this throughout his life. His next step in obtaining a passport was to change his appearance for a photograph and he did this by donning a false moustache and glasses and altering his hair style. He used a photograph booth in Finchley.[51]

Then he needed the signature of a responsible person who had known him for ten years. But who could he ask? Not the staff of the prisons he had recently been incarcerated in. He made an office stamp out of rubber and forged a solicitor's signature. He then returned to the passport office that he had been to in the previous week, but now as John Stephen Bird, a chemical engineer. He was accepted in his new guise. Hume had made money from selling various stories to journalists and also claimed to have received an advance on a book about his life (there is no indication that this was ever written and none that it was ever published).[52]

The passport was issued on 14 May 1958. He planned to emigrate to Australia and went to Australia House in London to investigate the possibilities. However, the High Commissioner's Office there contacted the police, the connection was made and the details of Hume's criminal background revealed. There was now no way that Hume would enter Australia.[53]

After apparently working at Welwyn Garden City as an electrician, Hume contacted the offices of the *Sunday Pictorial*. Hume wanted the media's attention for that made him feel important and potentially wealthy. He may also have wanted to have some revenge on his ex-wife. He spoke to Redman again, outlining various possible stories he could relay about prison conditions and possible reform, but Redman told Hume, 'There is only one story we want from you.' Hume said nothing and walked out.[54]

Some time later he rang the newspaper offices and asked, 'What would it be worth if I told you the real truth about Setty?' Negotiations followed. They were not always easy for Hume, 'never the easiest man in the world to deal with, stormed, raved, wept in turn as the day came closer to signing the contract.' On the day before he did so, he walked all night 'deep in thought, confirming to himself his decision to confess' by speaking to them. Once at the offices he asked to see a picture of his dog. They found one and then he 'covered his face in his hands and burst into tears.'[55]

Hume made the confession; he needed the money if nothing else, and also might have wanted to make a name for himself and be the Number One that he had boasted of being when in Dartmoor. Then he and Sims worked together for the next few days and weeks. Sims wanted to verify the story and confirm every fact that Hume would relate, though much depended on Hume's word alone. Hume was secretive about where he was staying and how he could be contacted. He trusted nobody.[56] He now had the chance to play the part of the hard man, the killer and the newspaper was willing to lap this up.

The men went to a hotel in Southend. Hume signed his name Brown and scattered books about the Nuremberg trials in his hotel room. He disguised himself when he was to be seen in public, lest the police or any criminal associates saw him. When he gave his story to Sims, he was careful to lock the hotel door and as he relaxed, smoking, on the bed, he told Sims, 'You'll be able to say one day that you were locked in a room alone with a murderer.' Hume often went into fits of anger, 'Not an hour passed without Hume flying into a fit of fury. He crashed his fist angrily on to my desk . . . and threatened more than once to call the whole thing off. Then suddenly, his passion spent, he would calm down – and continue with his story.' Hume kept the journalist's typed up sheets with him and listened carefully to any footsteps outside the room. When Sims queried some of his statement he stormed and raved at him, 'you are calling me a liar!'[57]

In the evenings the two men went out. Once they went to the cinema to see a film. It concerned murder and when the killer stabbed his victim seven times, Hume laughed. He stamped his feet with joy. On another night they went to the Kursaal on Southend's sea front and he found a woman to dance with. This club was open from 7.30–11 pm on Wednesdays and 7–11.30 pm on Saturdays, with an entry fee of 2s. 6d. on Wednesdays and 3s. 6d. on Saturdays. On another night, Hume was discussing how he made electrical items in Dartmoor and went to a telephone box to rip off the handset to show Sims how he did it. At the end of a fraught week, Sims had a 22,000-word typed document with him (it no longer survives).[58]

Bill Turner, the newspaper's photographer, accompanied them in order to take photographs of Hume at the sites of the murder, where the body had been found and at other related places in Essex and London; at Warren Street, at Finchley Road and then at the aerodromes and Dengie Marshes. Hume burst out in anger when he went to the latter: 'He cursed the wild-fowler who had stumbled on the torso – and who had immediately contacted the police. "If that idiot had been minding his own business – no one would have known" he fumed.'

When Hume was to be photographed with an SS dagger he was went to the newspaper offices on 2 May, and also watched the FA Cup Final with Turner, Sims and Mike Molly, an assistant. Hume became very excited during the game between Nottingham Forest and Luton Town (the former won, 2–1). Sims had no problems in believing Hume, 'There was no doubt by now that Hume, a noted romancer, and liar, was telling the truth about the murder of Stanley Setty. No man, in his wildest imagination, could have dreamed fiction to match such facts as these.'[59] The newspaper, of course, was hardly unbiased; Hume's story was worth much to them in terms of increased circulation.

Sims agreed not to publish the story until Hume was out of the country. However, he did contact Scotland Yard without Hume's knowledge. But there was nothing that they could do. Hume could not be tried twice for the same crime, which he knew was the case. It was not for several decades that this would change.[60]

On 1 June 1958, the *Sunday Pictorial* began printing Hume's story in five parts. His first statements were startling:

> 'I DID MURDER SETTY. I chose to make my confession to the Sunday Pictorial, because I knew this newspaper would demand the real truth from me, and because it has the widest readership. I am also going to tell you how I did it. But, first, please try to understand what makes a man a killer.[61]

Hume later stated, 'I am glad to have confessed. I have made many mistakes but I am sure that confessing after all this time was not one of them.' Yet, it was relatively safe to have done so for he could not be tried again for the same offence and he was well paid for it.[62]

Hume was paid £2,000 by the newspaper. He portrayed himself as a man who had had a grudge against society which had started from his being born outside wedlock. He had been the victim of an uncaring mother and a harsh orphanage. He was bitter and had been aggrieved at Setty's behaviour towards him. He had taken upon himself a creed of violence, 'If anything gets in your way or annoys you – get rid of it.' The titles of the five-episode serialisation were melodramatic 'The Body Follows Me Home' and 'The Tale that Saved My Neck.' Some of his details differed from those of the witnesses at the trial and in their statements to the police. Naturally, the articles portrayed him in the best possible light, though not denying he had murdered Setty. He suggested that the motivation was that Setty was spending time with his wife and that

Setty had annoyed him by kicking his beloved dog, Tony; neither of which can be verified and his wife denied the former.[63]

Hume's third known account of the murder, which since he made it has been accepted by all who have written about the case, is as follows:

It was just getting dark as I arrived home at my flat in Finchley Road, Golders' Green, about 7.35 pm on October 4th 1949. I had knocked back a few drinks.

I was surprised to notice Setty's cream Citroën car CJN 444 outside. What was going on upstairs in my flat? As I climbed the stairs I could feel my temper mounting inside me.

I burst open the door and into the front room. There I saw Setty sitting on the sofa.

Something snapped inside my brain. I boiled with rage. Setty got to his feet and adjusted his flashy tie.

'What's up with you?' he asked.[64]

But, furious as I was, I did not know then that seventeen minutes later I would have his dead body – and his blood – on my hands.

I began to tremble with rage when this black marketer refused to get out.[65]

I was trembling with rage. Someone was trying to kick me around, just as I had been kicked around ever since I was a kid. I rushed out of the room to the landing, where a collection of war souvenirs hung on the wall. I jerked a German SS dagger out of its sheath, then I rushed back into the room. And I was advancing towards Setty brandishing the dagger in my right hand.[66]

The handle of the dagger glinted in the light. I could see the initials, SS.

In war they stood for Schutz Staffel, the elite army corps of Nazi Germany.

Now those SS initials stood for forty four year old Stanley Setty.

I dashed dagger in hand through the doorway of my living room towards Setty.

I planned to frighten the living daylights out of him. But I reckoned without myself – and my own mad rage.

Back in the living room, I brandished the blade. Baghdad born Setty's dusky face seemed to whiten. His forehead looked shiny. For a moment he seemed scared and then he said,

'Go away, you silly bastard. What do you think you're doing? Playing at soldiers?'

I looked him straight in the eye.

'I'm not playing' I said earnestly. I took another step forward, the dagger still in my right hand. Setty sneered, 'You can't frighten me.'

And then he took a swing at me with the flat of his hand. He towered above me [actually he was only an inch taller], tall and powerful.

We grappled. In a split second – it happened so quickly – we were rolling on the floor. I was wielding the dagger just like our Stone Age ancestors did 20,000 years ago. It seemed to come naturally to me. We rolled over and over and my sweaty hand plunged the weapon frenziedly and repeatedly into his chest and legs.

I had to hurt him.

I aimed my blows anywhere. But Setty continued to struggle. He was as strong as an ox.

The more I stuck the dagger into him the more he tried to push my head back and break my neck.

I tried to push Setty away from me to keep his blood off my clothes and force a gap between us.

I forced my knee into him. He grunted but he wouldn't release his grip. It was like a vice.

I held the knife up to strike the sixth or seventh blow. I can't remember.

I plunged the blade into his ribs. I know I heard them crack.

He sank back against the sofa and slumped on the floor. He writhed and rolled over to a spot beneath the window on his back.

Setty began to cough violently and a trickle of red came from his mouth as he heaved and panted.

I stood over him with the dagger in my hand.

And with a feeling of triumph at winning the fight, I watched the life run from him.

I looked at the clock, it was 7.52 pm. The fight had lasted less than two minutes.

Now Setty lay on his back his eyes seemed glassly fixed on the ceiling.

When I looked down at him, I thought, 'The ball has stopped bouncing for you, chum.'[67]

We should also bear in mind Hume's fascination with the Nazis, and that he was probably anti-Semitic. Anti-Semitism was on the rise in Britain at this time, with riots against Jews in several cities in 1949, partly because Jewish terrorists had hanged two British soldiers in Palestine and because they were accused of profiteering from the black market – and Hume could well have viewed Setty as being involved in the latter. Hume's prejudice against Jews was not a reason for murdering Setty but it certainly made him less likely to resist his violent tendencies towards the man.[68] Perhaps he refers to using an SS dagger to make the fight sound more dramatic but it is likely a smaller knife was used; Camps referred to a 4in blade and that of an SS dagger is a lot longer.

Hume later claimed that the sense of elation at having emerged victorious from a fight to the death soon passed. He then began to panic and rushed over to the window of the living room, which overlooked the busy thorough-fare. He was worried in case anyone had seen or heard what he had just done. Did anyone know Setty had travelled to see him? Looking behind the cur-tains, he could see nothing out of the ordinary. Couples walked arm in arm towards cinemas and everything seemed as it would have done normally. His panic ceased.[69]

Yet, a man lay dead in the living room; a man slain by himself. He wandered off to the back room and found Tony, who had slept through the whole epi-sode. Hume needed time to think what to do next. As he said, 'The thought flashed through my mind that perhaps I could get away with murder.' There were two main points he had to address. Firstly, to get rid of all traces of the murder having taken place at the flat. Secondly, he had to dispose of the body. The former was perhaps the easier of the two to deal with and one on which he could set to work immediately.[70]

Hume returned to the lounge and dragged the heavy body of Setty to the coal cupboard, no easy task, and he had to ensure the corpse remained on its back so as not to transfer blood to the floor. He finally managed to do so, by hauling him by the arms across the three rooms of that floor of the flat. Once in the coal cupboard, he covered the body with a piece of felt. He then tidied up the living room. An armchair was pulled over the pool of blood where Setty had died. Furniture knocked over was put to rights. Using a flannel and a bowl of water he wiped the blood off the settee. Fortunately, the blood loss had not been so great that it had seeped through the floor boards to the rooms below (as occurred in Thomas Hardy's novel *Tess of the D'Urbervilles*), thus alert-ing the Spencers that murder had occurred in the room above. A lampshade which had been broken was disposed of.[71]

Then there was the bloodied pale-blue-green carpet in the living room. Fortunately for Hume, it was rather dirty anyway. He did his best to wipe away the spots of blood so they would be indistinguishable from the dirt already ingrained in the fabric. He was by then beginning to regain his composure. The next task was to remove Setty's car from outside the house. He rushed downstairs and opened the car door (car doors were then not locked as a matter of course). But there was no key in the ignition. It must still be on Setty's person. So he raced back up the stairs to the flat and went to the coal cupboard. A search of Setty's pockets produced the key. Once downstairs, he donned gloves in order not to leave any fingerprints in the car. He drove off.[72]

It was now 9.30 pm as he drove down Finchley Road, to Swiss Cottage, down Avenue Road and into Regent's Park. He then drove around the park and into Cambridge Terrace Mews. Leaving the car there (neighbours later recalled the car being parked there at about 10 pm), he returned to Albany Street and hailed a taxi. He was home by 10.45 pm. He tidied up the flat all over. He was then confronted by a more difficult question: how to dispose of the body. This is not a problem for killers who slay in locations that cannot be connected with them; such as in an otherwise empty railway carriage or in a street or open ground at night-time. But to kill in premises which are intimately associated with the killer, such as their place of work or at home, presents problems, especially if they do not live alone – and even if they do, few are so lonely to lack any visitors at all. Then there is the smell of a decomposing corpse to consider.[73]

Hume was, understandably, unable to sleep. He chain-smoked as he thought how not to get caught and how to turn this unpremeditated killing into the perfect crime. He wondered if he should turn himself into the police, even after all he had done to conceal the crime. Should he go back for the car and should he haul the corpse from the coal cupboard? Setty would soon be missed. Hume had heard that he was a police informant (there is no evidence to corroborate this) and that the police would soon be asking questions as to his whereabouts.[74]

Hume ruled out going to the police. He recalled, 'Then I asked myself: Why should I tell the police? There's a fifty fifty chance of getting away with it. Anyway he deserved it.' Hume steeled himself to see the matter through to the end. As he lay smoking an idea came to him, 'I slowly convinced myself that I could dispose of a body without anyone finding out.' By dawn his fingers were stained with nicotine, but his nerve had returned and he was now certain how he could successfully dispose of the body.[75]

Self-preservation led to inspiration. His method was original; he stated, 'My plan was to drop the body into the sea from a hired plane.' Hume knew how to fly and a body ejected over the sea should never be found. His problem was how to transfer the body to an aircraft, and he had thought about how to do that, too.[76]

Hume had a busy day ahead of him on Wednesday, 5 October. He later claimed that he did not find Setty's money until later that day when he was dealing with the corpse, but it would appear that he had found it earlier. Hume thought that there was about £1,000 worth of fivers. Unfortunately for him, because these had been in Setty's jacket pocket, near to where he was stabbed, most of them were saturated in blood and had to be disposed of. Many were ripped and so were also hardly usable as legal tender. Even those which could be salvaged had some traces of blood and so Hume had to cut these pieces off carefully. He thought he only had £90 of usable notes, but clearly must have had more if his earlier statements are to be believed (almost £200). He wrote, 'It broke my heart to burn the fivers.'[77]

There were a number of other tasks Hume had to deal with. Firstly, he went over the furniture with a clothes brush to remove every possible stain. He also wiped all the surfaces to remove any fingerprints. The underfelt of the carpet was also examined and bloodstains were found there. To take these away, he cut off the bloody strips and disposed of them. He then tugged the felt at each end and stretched it a good 2ft in order to give the appearance that there never had been any staining there.[78]

To remove the body from the flat Hume would have to dismember it. The body was so heavy that it could not be moved far as it was. He dragged it out of the coal cupboard and into the kitchen. Hume described his butchery:

> I picked up the tools I thought I needed. They were a hack saw and a sharp 2s 6d lino knife. Strangely even now I felt no squeamishness or horror of what I was about to do [in this he resembled other killers who dismember their victims; such as Dr Crippen or Denis Nilsen, and who are surprised that the public thinks that chopping up a body is horrific, indicative of how killers inhabit a different sphere of reality]. Puffing and panting because the body was lying in an awkward position I heave it out. I used the lino knife to cut away some of the clothes until finally the body was clothed only in a cream, silk shirt, jacket, underpants, socks and shoes.
>
> I have no fear of the dead. It's the ones who are living you have to worry about. I knew nothing about surgery, but I worked swiftly.... I ripped off a piece of felt and put the legs – and most of the bloodstained clothes I had removed – into a heap. I wrapped them all up in Parcel No.1 .... The worst part of the job was to follow. I didn't want the staring eyes to look at me, so I covered them with a piece of

rag. Then I picked up my hack saw. What I had to do wasn't hurting him any more, but it was saving my life.

I sighed with relief when it was all done. I quickly found a cardboard box that had once contained tins of baked beans and placed the head inside.

Hume's hatred of Setty may also have helped him psychologically in his task because to dismember is not only a practical necessity for survival but is also the act of completely destroying that which he hated.[79]

Small pieces of brick and rubble which he had earlier taken from the back yard were placed around the head. This was in order to make certain that the parcel was heavy enough to sink when it was dropped out of the aircraft. Bodies naturally rise to the surface as gasses therein are released unless action is taken to prevent this. He ripped the bloodstained jacket from the body. He tied up the torso and replaced it in the coal cupboard. He put it into a large black cabin trunk, but that would not close so he had to reconsider. Thrusting the now bloodstained trunk aside, he tied the torso up in felt, wrapped it in a white blanket and then tied it up with rope. More blanket and felt was used as wrapping. It was then bundled into the coal cupboard once more. Hume surveyed the kitchen, 'Surprisingly, there wasn't much of a mess and I managed to clear up.'[80]

Hume flew off from Elstree aerodrome between 4.30 and 5.30 pm; probably at the earlier time due to fading light, and stated he was flying to Southend Municipal Aerodrome near the Essex coastline. After he had taxied out for the take-off, he could have flown towards the North Sea or to the Thames estuary to drop his parcels. However, he decided to fly in the direction of Southend in case anyone was watching, as he had stated he was to fly there anyway. He then veered the plane south-westwards and he soon reached the English Channel. He felt he had to fly out to sea so no one would see him dropping his bundles as would have happened if he had flown towards Southend pier. Visibility was good and he could fly under Visual Flight Rules, rather than rely on his navigational aids.[81]

Hume could not fly much further because the plane only had enough petrol to fly for 3½ hours. He had been flying for 90 minutes at 70mph at 2,000ft. The French coast and the Channel Islands were now visible. He later recalled, 'This was far enough. I began to throw the three weapons out, one by one ... I circled and dumped the two parcels. I looked for a sign of them in the sea. There was none. They must have sunk like stones.' It was now time for his return trip. He needed to arrive at Southend in case enquiries were made. The sun was going down and the weather was deteriorating. He could not see any landmarks and had to depend on his instruments.[82]

Next day was Thursday, 6 October. All Hume had to do now was to dispose of the torso. Once at Southend airport, with the torso in an upright position and tied to one of the plane's seats, Tony leapt onto the back seat and all was ready to go. It was 4.07 pm. Hume recalled, 'I was anxious to get off the ground quickly, but the take-off was dicey.' As the machine gathered speed down the runway, the control column became stuck and could not be pulled back. There were buildings ahead and Hume broke into a sweat as he tried to wind the tail trimmer handle in order to take off. He did so and missed the tops of the structures by a few feet.[83]

He turned out to sea over Southend pier and reflected on the mess there would have been had he crashed – and after all that work and planning! He then flew steadily south-west, as he had on the previous afternoon. After an hour and a half he had flown over Kent and was now mid-Channel. It was hazy but he could see the sea below the clouds and there were various ships visible. He kept flying to a spot where he had heard that the water was deep and would keep his secret forever. From flying at 3,000ft he descended to 2,000ft.[84]

This was where he would drop the parcel. Reducing his speed to 60mph, the plane's slowest speed, he put the flaps down. He then tried to open the door against the slipstream, hoping the weight would force it open. But it would not open. He then put his flaps up and tried to gain height for a second attempt. Once again, the control column did not have the room to do so. He banked the aircraft steeply, hoping the parcel would slip downwards and force the door open with its weight. Hume had to hold on to Tony lest he fell out if the door opened and the dog barked furiously. With the other hand he shoved, nothing happened. He pushed the parcel again with all his might.[85]

Hume later recalled, 'Suddenly there was an enormous bang as the door whipped open and then slammed shut. The torso was gone. It went spinning down – so slowly, it seemed – to the grey sea below.' But that was not the end of Hume's immediate worries. The rope which had encircled the parcel had become slack by too much handling and had become looped on a hook in the cabin. It was no longer with the parcel and the weights and outer wrapping of the parcel had also become parted from the torso.[86]

Dust and dirt – the parcel had been stored in the coal cupboard – was flying everywhere inside the plane and Hume was briefly blinded. Furthermore, the plane was diving down towards the sea, out of control. Hume managed to right it and wiped the sweat off his brow. He then had another shock, 'But as I circled and peered below my heart almost stopped. The torso was floating on the water, covered only by the inner wrapping.' He had a wild idea of ditching the aircraft and tying the bundle to it and so allowing both to sink without trace. He would then swim to the nearest land. However a second thought cancelled the first. He didn't know how far he would have to swim and he had no lifebelt. There was not much daylight left. And the bundle might not be washed up anywhere.[87] It was very unsatisfactory compared with his successful ditching of the parcels on the previous day.

Hume flew back towards England, uncertain of his position. The poor weather helped him lose what little bearings he had. He was soon somewhere over Kent and, hopelessly lost, he landed the plane in a field. A farmer told him that he was near Faversham in Kent. The man swung his propeller for him and Hume started the engine again. Tony had had a quick run before re-entering the plane with his master. It was now becoming dark and there was insufficient fuel to reach Elstree and so he landed at Gravesend airport.[88]

Meanwhile, Hume went about his business. He later wrote, 'In the days that followed I tried to carry on normally.' He avidly scanned the newspapers for any stories about the crime or the police investigation. This was partly due to wanting to know how the police investigation was progressing but also to stoke his own ego by reading about how clever he had been. He seems to have been initially pleased:

> Each day I scanned the papers anxiously for news of the search for the missing car dealer. At first the police, and the newspaper reporters trailing them around seemed to be way off the scent . . . I lay in bed not unduly fearful, although the headlines read 'All night Yard probe into Setty Mystery' or 'Unknown Visits to Fiver Man's Flat.' But when the newspapers began to ask, 'Did one man kill Setty?' I began to wonder whether I could get away with murder after all.[89]

Hume later reported about some of the newspaper accounts he had read concerning Setty's disappearance: 'Some newspapers reported that a murder hunt started in London, had switched to Paris. One even suggested that it was another acid bath murder.'[90]

Hume wrote:

> On the morning of October 23 I opened my Sunday Pictorial and saw the headline I had been dreading: 'SETTY TORSO WASHED UP.' The tides and prevailing south west wind had played a cruel trick on me . . . A million questions throbbed through my mind. Had I covered my tracks well enough? Would the police now come looking for me? What was I going to say to them if they did?[91]

Checking his newspaper the next day, Hume noted that the police knew the numbers on the bank notes that Setty had had with him when he died. He compared these with some of the fivers he had taken from Setty. Four of them matched. He recalled, 'What could I do? Go to the police? I was in it up to the neck and I don't think the police would ever help anyone like me.'[92]

For some reason, despite disposing of everything else that was obviously incriminating, Hume had forgotten the trunk in the coal cupboard, which he had initially thrust the torso into, but could not do so because it would not fit. Yet, the trunk was bloodstained on the inside. He had to get rid of it as soon as possible. Possibly he recalled that in the previous decade there had been a spate of killers putting their victims into luggage and depositing them at railway stations. Hume adopted this tactic and fortunately for him there was a left luggage section at Golders Green Tube station, only a few minutes' walk from his flat. Oddly enough, he kept the ticket he was given as a receipt for the case and hid it behind some coloured wires in the telephone junction box in his flat, when he could just have easily have discarded it so it would never be found.[93]

Hume was uncertain whether the police would find him but thought that airfields would be checked and anyone with 'a record' would be spoken to. He thought he had a fifty-fifty chance.[94]

Hume then recounted his arrest by the police and the account that he gave them, which has already been related:

> I had to be smart. I had to keep my wits about me to stay one jump ahead. Was it any use trying to deny those plane flights with the cut-up body. No, too many people could be found to rip my alibi to shreds. Too many eyes had watched me handle those parcels. So I concocted a story which I suppose was almost as fantastic as my own crime. The lies rolled off my tongue. In fact, as I underwent the most intensive questioning inside Albany Street Police Station, the biggest lie of all time began to take shape in my mind.
>
> My description of MAC was based on shrewd, straight as a die Superintendent Colin MacDougall. GREENY'S description I based on Chief Inspector John Jamieson and THE BOY'S on Detective Sergeant Sutherland. These were the three officers from the Yard who investigated Setty's disappearance and whose builds and descriptions were fresh in my mind'[95]

He said little about the trial, but added:

> The trial was an awful duel stretched over a nerve-wracking seven days. I realised that the Crown's prosecuting counsel had little on me, for the actual killing and dismemberment. So I agreed with

everything I knew they could substantiate. And I denied everything they couldn't. I believe that I impressed everybody with my apparent calmness throughout. But nobody knew what turmoil raged inside me. I'll tell you this: The hangman's rope must be very easy after the ordeal of a murder trial.[96]

How accurate was this version, Hume's third, but his second in public? Howe believed the story was 'untrue and something produced simply for the benefit of the sentimental readers of the newspapers' and that most of it was 'nothing but a pack of lies.' He did, though, believe that 'the whole truth about Setty's murder has never come to light.' Yet, he was convinced that 'I have no doubt in my own mind that he did murder Setty and indeed the police did believe this all along.'[97]

There are discrepancies with witness statements, in that Mrs Stride stated that she saw him leave the flat with parcels whereas he said he left before she arrived. The next question that was also unaddressed is what was his wife doing at the time? She said to the police, 'I would almost certainly be somewhere in the flat at that time in the evening', though was less certain at the trial, where she stated, 'I may have been upstairs attending to the child or I may have been out.' Since she recalled listening at 8–9pm to *Justice in Other Lands*, a wireless drama on the Home Service frequency about the French serial wife murderer Henri Landru, she certainly appears to have been in the flat; she later claimed to have been in the lounge – the very same room in which Setty was killed.[98] These replies do not dovetail with Hume's account. The flat was a small one. It seems highly unlikely that she would have been unaware of a third party who was downstairs, especially as he was there before her husband arrived (and she probably let him in) and that Setty and Hume had had a fight. Feeding and changing a baby requires time and effort, but even so, to be wholly unaware of Setty's presence and violent death seems improbable. Secondly, a mother with a small baby is unlikely to spend an evening out of the house for a baby needs changing and feeding on a regular basis and these are more easily done at home rather than elsewhere. The conclusion must be that Mrs Hume was possibly aware of what had happened but kept her mouth closed, whether out of love or fear. So it seems likely she let him in, though whether he was a regular visitor or not is uncertain. Probably not.

But there is more to it than this. The main thrust of the murder story must be incorrect. Dr Camps had found that Setty had been killed quickly and had been dismembered shortly afterwards. Thus the story of the fight and dismemberment are nonsense.

Yet, Hume's story in the newspaper has become the universally accepted version of what happened. We can now never be entirely certain of what happened between Setty and Hume. Despite all books that cover the crime including without any doubts Hume's version of how he killed Setty, a little-known article written by Playfair and Sington in 1962 begged to differ and suggested that the given account must be incorrect. It put forward a number of points in doing so. Hume's account, it stated, did not explain why Setty came to the flat or who admitted him or why he did not come with a minder. Then the story of the fight is deemed incredible. Why did Hume's dog, his wife or his baby not react to it at all? There could not have been a struggle because the wounds in Setty's corpse were all clean and so he could not have moved an inch during their infliction. Hume's description was a 'manifest untruth' and the article suggested that Hume might have created it, as well as to make money, to cast doubt on his wife's honesty as he did not explicitly state that she was absent from the flat at the time of the murder. As well as suggesting that she had perjured herself at the trial, the story provoked other conjectures 'less worthy and just as baseless.' They concluded that some aspects of the killing of Setty remained a mystery, but did not offer an alternative scenario.[99] We shall return to the question of the Setty killing at the end of the book.

Many were unhappy about the publication of this story (which was also published in an Italian magazine *La Europeo* under the title '*Ho ucciso un uomo*', meaning 'I killed a man'). The Press Council received numerous complaints from members of the public. The Press Council made the following statement that they strongly condemned the articles and claimed they were not in the public interest for they gave 'an atmosphere of successful crime to so sordid a story, or to allow criminals to justify or mitigate their crimes by romantic explanations which, never having been tested in a court of law, may, or may not be, true.'[100]

One newspaper commented, after the second instalment of the series had been published:

> It is no doubt that in the public interest that such 'confessions' should be made public and the Sunday Pictorial can take pride in having beaten its rivals in securing the biggest and most nauseating for some years. Whether the public interest is quite so well served in printing all the unedifying details, and by paying the confessor a large sum of money, is more open to debate. Just what he has been paid, of course, is not stated, it would be interesting to know. The market value of getting away with murder must be high, even if the social virtues in a society which exalts it are not.[101]

Even more horrified by the articles was Cynthia. It should also be noted in this account that Hume, though he did not accuse her in public of murder (as his second and private statement had), took the opportunity to attack his wife by other means; by suggesting that she took his mind off his business to the latter's detriment, that he loved his dog more than her and that Setty was seeing her behind his back. Although she was unwilling to attract more public attention, she felt that she could not allow statements to be published which alleged she had an affair with Setty and, indirectly hinted that she committed perjury at her former husband's trial. Unable to gain satisfaction from Hume, her lawyers contacted the newspaper editor, Colin Valdar. He promised not to republish the offending passage and paid damages to mark his regret at causing her distress. Yet, the public prosecutor believed that there was at least an inference that she knew of the murder and disposal of the body and so had committed perjury (after all, Hume did not explicitly state that she was absent from the flat when the murder occurred).[102]

The accuracy of Hume's confession was also doubted in some quarters, but intriguingly we do not know why. Humphreys wrote in his memoirs about Hume's writings, 'This is not, however, what the police think really happened, and the truth, I believe, is uglier still.'[103] What Humphreys believed was never known, however. Yet, there is nothing in the open files that suggests what the police really thought. Some of the contents of the police file at The National Archives which deals with Setty's murder (MEPO3/3144) are closed and will not be open until 2035; its contents date from 1949–70.

It has been alleged that Hume spent some time after his windfall in making at least one conquest. His curly black hair and the charm of his blue eyes allegedly led to a Mayfair barmaid being parted with her savings yet still claiming to love him. A pretty air hostess at London airport also fell for his apparent charms.[104]

Meanwhile, Hume wanted to start a new life abroad. Refused entry into Australia, he chose another English-speaking country, Canada, as his final destination (he knew no foreign languages). But first he wanted to travel to the Continent. On Sunday, 25 May, one week before his articles in the *Sunday Pictorial* were due for publication, he arrived at Ringway airport in Manchester in order to fly to Switzerland. He noticed the newsstands holding copies of the *Sunday Pictorial* with announcements that his story would follow in subsequent issues. He quickly boarded the aircraft, eager to escape Britain where his crimes would soon be broadcast and where he might well face hostility. With him was the £2,000 earned for his story, and that had to be smuggled out as currency restrictions decreed that only £25 could be legally taken abroad. Once aboard, he thought: 'As it soared into the skies and headed for

Zurich, a strange feeling of comfort swept over me. I felt safe – and FREE. I had no feeling of nostalgia. What had Britain done for me?' At 38 years old, this was the first time that he had been abroad. Apparently, he wished the plane could have flown over Dartmoor so that he could have thrown a toilet roll out on the governor.[105]

At Kloten airport near Zurich, Hume hailed a taxi to take him to the city, one of the world's financial centres. Knowing no one in the country, he struck up a conversation with one Robert, the driver, who proved as talkative as cabbies are traditionally supposed to be. He told Robert that he flew planes for the Canadians and gave him one of his 'business' cards, with Johnny Bird, of 1441 Queen Street, Montreal, printed on it, to shore up his bona fides. What Hume then desired most of all was 'the demanding embraces of a girl' and he thought Robert could assist him to that end.[106]

Hume was dropped at the St Gotthard Hotel, 'a fairly classy place on the main street.' It was then that Hume asked Robert to take him to a likely spot where he could find a woman. Robert replied, 'Sir, it is Sunday. And you cannot always get what you want today. Wait till tomorrow.' It was not what the frustrated Hume wanted to hear, as he recounted in the following year:

> I could hardly wait. Eight years or more without a woman for company is more than any man can stand. I longed to wrap myself around some gorgeous Swiss miss. Someone who didn't realise she was dating a killer. In one night, I felt I could rid myself of all the worries, the haunting fears, the anxieties and pent up urges that come to a man who has spent endless nights behind bars. I was still a bundle of nerves.[107]

Despite Hume's concerns, he slept soundly in the hotel bed. Next morning the sun shone and he felt good to be alive and free. He picked up the telephone and learnt that Robert was waiting for him in the hotel lobby. Hume checked his canvas bag under the bed. The money he had smuggled out of England was, unsurprisingly, still there. Taking such an amount out of the country was an offence under exchange controls legislation. Robert took Hume to three different banks where he changed his pound notes for dollars. No questions were asked of him. He only planned to spend a few days in Switzerland before travelling to Canada but what happened that night was to alter his schedule.[108]

That evening Robert told him, 'I will take you to a club where you can meet the most beautiful women in all Zurich.' Hume needed no second bidding, 'Okay, get cracking', he replied. The taxi took then to a brightly lit nightclub by Zurich's lake called Club Terass. Once they had passed the ingratiating manager, the interior was to Hume's delight; soft lights, a cha-cha band playing a 'sexy rhythm.' Red-coated waiters dashed from table to table. There was a floor show of chorus girls dancing the cancan. Hume recalled, 'Girls. Champagne. Music. I could buy anything in the joint.' After the austere prison regime of the past eight years, he was in his Seventh Heaven. He looked from woman to woman, but they all seemed accompanied. Then Robert pointed out a woman to him at the far side of the room.[109]

Over a year later, Hume recalled this moment, 'I couldn't take my eyes off the lovely girl who sat at the other end of the oval shaped bar.' She noticed him and smiled back. Robert told Hume, 'I think her name is Trudi . . . Trudi Sommer. She runs a hairdressing salon downtown. Nice kid. She's divorced.' Trudi was certainly attractive; born in 1931, she was shapely and slim with auburn hair. She had been divorced in July 1957 and when Hume met her she was feeling lonely. Another girl joined her; Marlis Hofner, her unmarried sister. Hume called across a waiter and bought two red roses from his tray. He had them sent over to the women and watched Trudi's reaction. She seemed pleased (later writing 'I was delighted but surprised') but shy and on catching Hume's face, smiled. Following up this favourable reception, he then sent over two glasses of cognac.[110]

Their response was disappointing, for an English-speaking barman came over to him and told him, 'The ladies say they must not speak to strangers. In any case, they are married [not strictly true; Marlis was engaged; Trudi was divorced from a travelling salesman], and there is no chance of a meeting.' Hume was not deterred, but sent a message back, apologising for his forwardness but explaining that he was enchanted by Trudi's loveliness. Robert, whom she knew vaguely, came over and reassured Trudi, who did not usually drink with strangers, 'Don't be afraid. This is a real gentleman from Canada. This is his first visit to Switzerland and he said he wanted to know someone from this lovely country.' She was impressed with Hume's appearance, 'He was wearing a light beige suit, looking very prosperous and attractive.' He grinned and waved. This broke her reserve and the two danced. Hume knew little German, but told her, 'You dance like an angel.' Hume, though did not, apologising for holding her too tightly and hurting her but despite this she later maintained that she felt a connection with him.[111]

She suggested that the four of them went elsewhere and they went to the hotel Hume was staying in. There he ordered champagne and oysters and turned on his charm. However, he had to talk through Robert as an interpreter. After the consumption of much champagne, Hume took the initiative and suggested, 'Let's have a party at your place', presumably meaning Trudi's, which was at Russenweg, just outside Zurich, near to both the police and the railway stations. She agreed, but rang for a friend, Irma, to come along and also Marlis' fiancé. Before arriving there, they bought a dozen bottles of champagne. Hume and Trudi spent most of the time there with one another and he managed to pile on the flattery by telling her, 'You are so beautiful. I have never seen so lovely a girl in Canada. It must be the air here.' He hugged her close and looked into her eyes. He told her that he was a Canadian test pilot, adding that he was in love with her and wanted to marry her. Despite having had at least one drink, Trudi was taken aback by Hume's declarations and told him, 'You hardly know me. You cannot marry as fast as you fly your planes.' He protested that if there had been a minister of religion who could marry them there and then he would desire that he did so. The party ended at 3 the next morning; Hume returning to his hotel.[112]

Hume was adamant that what he had told her was the truth and that for him it was a matter of love at first sight. Trudi was clearly not repelled by him for they saw much of each other in the next two days. Next morning he sent her red roses and invited her out to lunch, which she accepted. They also went for walks by the lake, to restaurants, dance halls and night clubs. He would usually call for her every lunch time and they would spend the afternoon together, before he returned her to her flat. Then he would call again later to pick her up for the evening. Hume laid on the flattery with a trowel, with comments like, 'Trudi, you are the most beautiful girl I have ever seen.' Another description of her was that she was 'thin, fair haired, small boned girl; with indefinite features, negative looking in repose, though quite pretty when she smiles.' She replied, 'Johnny, how much longer can we be together? Won't you have to go back to your work soon?' Hume told her he would have to leave for Canada tomorrow and that he would be away for many weeks. However, he promised that on his return they could get married. He did not think that she was yet in love with him but was sure enough of the situation that she would be in due course. Yet, she was smitten with this crazy, but fascinating man, 'We had a wonderful, wonderful time. I had never met anyone like him.'[113]

Next day they were in the airport lounge together. He ordered champagne and they kissed. He assured her of his return and of his devotion to her, 'Don't ever forget me. It isn't my fault that I have to go. I'll return and we'll get married.' Hume was upset about having to part from her but had to live up to his pretence of being a pilot in Canada. He also admitted, 'I didn't really like being in love' because he also desired to see himself as the 'tough-guy killer from Dartmoor' and 'This love stuff . . . was strictly for the women's magazines.' Once parted from her, he slipped into the airport lavatory and changed into his disguise as Johnny Bird before boarding the aeroplane to New York. No one asked any difficult questions.[114]

Hume was an avid writer of postcards to his new love. They show him as a very ordinary man but one who could not resist deception.

The very first postcard was sent by Hume to Trudi, apparently on 28 May, from Kloten airport, just before he left for Canada and the USA. It read 'Auf Wiedersehen! Johnny.'

He then sent her a number of postcards from Montreal, New York, Los Angeles and San Francisco. Oddly, most of the postcards depicted either cats or Indians with painted faces.

The first letters that he sent her were very brief. The first one was dated 21 June and sent from San Francisco:

> Dear Trudi!
> I have to go to Los Angeles, to clarify one or two things. But I think I most certainly will be back in Zürich on 28 June. I look forward to seeing you again.
> With love, Johnny

The next letter was dated 23 June and sent from Los Angeles:

> Dear Trudi!
> Sorry about the postponement, have important business in Los Angeles. But in one week's time I'll be back in Zürich.
> All my love, Johnny
> PS: Flying a new special aircraft. Have to rush, darling. Be a good girl. J.

Hume changed at Idlewild airport for a flight to Montreal. He spent a week there and every day he wrote to Trudi, telling her that he longed to be with her again. He then spent time in the USA, visiting places on the West Coast, such as Los Angeles and San Francisco. Trudi was still on his mind. But there was another topic that was not far away, and, in his opinion, wholly wrapped up with her: money. As he later wrote: 'How could I make enough dough to marry her and keep her? And how could I explain away lies about my dangerous job as a test pilot? I figured that with enough money I could get away with any pretence.'[115]

Hume's alleged plan was to rob a payroll wagon in Los Angeles. Whether Hume was ever serious about such a hare-brained scheme is difficult to know; but he desisted from the idea when he heard that a gang had already done so in recent times. Any repeat attempt would find a stronger guard there. So Hume spent money in the luxury spots of the West Coast. He dined at the Brown Derby restaurant – patronised by Hollywood stars. He swam in the moonlight off Santa Monica beach. He had someone photograph him standing in front of the Golden Gate bridge. He even took a trip to the now defunct fortress prison of Alcatraz.[116]

It was a rare old time. 'For days and nights I whooped it up', he later recalled. It was also expensive. 'It had been a crazy spending spree. The air fares, the presents, the hotel bills had made a big hole in the private bank I was carrying.' He could not, however, get Trudi out of his mind. He bought presents for her, scarves, shoes, dolls, dresses. Yet, the country was disappointing for him for it did not live up to the impression he had garnered of it from Hollywood films. He felt he was spending money in vain. It was time to return to Trudi and he claimed he felt great anticipation and excitement at the prospect.[117]

On 3 July he arrived at Zurich airport. After the disguise switch, he needed only an hour before he was standing outside his lover's salon, loaded down with presents and the inevitable red roses (all two-dozen of them). She was amazed to see him and left a client under the hair drier and almost pulled him upstairs to her flat. After intense kissing, he said, 'Trudi darling, I've come back to marry you.' When the last client had left the salon, the two were alone together at last. He later wrote:

> That evening in Trudi's flat I shall remember forever. We were in love and for the first time we were really alone. For the next few days and nights, it was one round of expensive pleasure for us. But, back to my hotel one night, I got a shock. I dug into my bag of cash and found less than £150 left. At the rate I was spending that meant two more weeks of life for Johnny Bird, ace test pilot.[118]

There seems little reason to doubt their love and it was confirmed independently. Hume showered her with gifts, a gold brooch, necklaces, earrings and bangles. He took her on car trips to Basle, Berne and Schaffhausen. Mrs Hast, a friend, recalled, 'Johnny and Trudi were terribly happy together and very much in love. He always seemed to have plenty of money.' Mrs Elizabeth Schmidhauser thought Hume was polite, generous and gentle. However, she knew that the wedding had been postponed once or twice.[119]

Hume had deceived Trudi in a number of ways. Not only did she not know where his income came from but he told her that he was supporting his elderly mother and that his father was a drunkard. He later admitted, 'Naturally I deceived Mrs Sommer. I didn't go around and tell the story of my life and give her the books about my life.'[120] Love was not enough for Hume. He needed a great deal of money without having to work legitimately for it. As before, crime beckoned.

Chapter 9

Bank Robberies and Murder, 1958–9

Hume decided that he would have to return to crime. But not the criminal enterprises he had been involved in during the 1940s. He needed to be his own man and he needed fast results. Nothing which required skill or accomplices for him. Banks seemed the obvious place to rob because they hold large sums of money and are relatively unguarded. All he needed was a gun, nerve and a lack of scruples. What follows is based on Hume's retrospective and self-justifying account and on contemporary newspapers. The relevant police file, held at The National Archives (MEPO2/2898), containing statements from 1958–83, is closed until 2035.

Hume left Zurich on 12 July, when he departed for Montreal (at least, that is what he told Trudi). She received, in fact, four postcards from him, all sent from London. They were dated 20 July (two on the same day), 23 July and 25 July. He told her that he was busy working (flying). The reality was far different.[1]

Hume spent a few days in London planning a raid and eventually, on the morning of Saturday, 2 August 1958, he went to the branch of the Midland Bank on Boston Manor Road, Brentford in west London, which was situated in a one-storey concrete prefab. He may have chosen Midland Bank because he had had an account with the Golders Green branch in the previous decade. Hume also thought that there should be a lot of money on the premises because he had learnt that the wages for several large factories in the locality had been delivered there recently and that he should be able to steal about £40,000, 'which isn't peanuts.' He entered the building and spoke to Frank Lewis, a 30-year-old cashier, and enquired about opening an account there. Lewis told him that he would need to speak to the deputy bank manager, Derek Higgins, but he was busy. The two men concluded that Hume would need to return later. Presumably the purpose of the visit was to familiarise himself with the interior of the building in preparation for his imminent raid, and to check that he would be let in just after the time it would later close. However, the risk in this was that the staff would have a better description of him than otherwise. 'Casing the joint' is a typical technique of bank robbers.[2]

Hume then went to the nearby Globe pub, 104 Whitestile Lane in Brentford. He had half a pint of beer there and took some pills to boost his forthcoming performance, for he was trembling. He had never robbed a bank before. It was 11.35 am and he knew that the bank would close at noon. There would be no other customers to complicate the robbery. As time went by he left the pub and sat on a roadside bench. He recalled, 'I felt more and more confident as I swiftly carried out last minute checks on the equipment I needed for the raid. At my side was the brown canvas travel bag which would hold most of the £40,000 in banknotes I planned to steal. In the pockets of my fawn raincoat were two paper carrier bags for the remainder of the loot.' He wore a white shirt and a blue gaberdine suit.[3]

It was now 10 minutes to zero hour. A little stray dog wandered over to Hume and he made friends with it. A good omen, he thought. He then took his automatic pistol from his pocket and shoved a live round into the breech. He looked at his watch. Still a few minutes to go. Just then a police constable walked by and halted by the bank for a few moments. He soon moved off. Hume stood up, braced himself and headed with confidence towards the building. He was positive that he could not fail and that success would be total.[4]

It was just after noon. The bank had closed its doors to its customers. Hume knocked on the door. Bank employee David Gutteridge opened it. Hume said, 'Sorry I am so late.' Doubtless remembering him, Hume was admitted and the door was closed behind him. It was locked. There were no customers there, just four members of staff. He then walked over to the counter, where Lewis stood. Hume recalled:

> So far, so good. My plan was working. Suddenly I blazed into action. I whipped out my automatic. I was a desperate man. It was now or never. On the other side of the bank counter, I knew from an informant, was the kind of lolly that was going to keep me in clover for a year or two. And no one was going to keep me from it.[5]

'This is a stick up', announced Hume to Lewis. The latter looked at Hume in disbelief. According to Hume he added, for good measure, 'and I'm not kidding.' He waved the gun at Lewis to show that he was deadly serious. Apparently Lewis swung around and called out something to a colleague. He then turned to face Hume and the latter thought that this sudden movement was an attempt to grab an inkstand and throw it in his face. Hume recalled, 'So I let him have it fast – in the stomach.' Lewis fell to the floor behind the counter with a bullet lodged just under his heart.[6]

Hume stood over the groaning man, holding a smoking gun. He then went to the side office of the bank where Gutteridge, Higgins and a 24-year-old cashier, Margaret Kirby, stood. Hume claimed they were terrified. He pointed his gun at Margaret and growled, 'All I want is money.' He said he would shoot her if the others did not obey him. They could see that he was in all earnest. They found a tin with £5 notes in and Hume's eyes goggled – he had not seen so much money since finding the cash on Setty's body – but this time none of it was discoloured by blood. One of the safes was opened and more money was given to Hume.[7]

Hume asked how much money he had got so far and was told that it was about £2,000. Hume thought that there would be far more. He claimed that he asked one of the men, probably Higgins as he was the senior employee there, 'What's in that big safe?', and he replied that there was no money, only books. Hume believed him, on the basis that he thought only criminals told lies.[8] He also ripped out both telephones from the offices. The staff were then herded into the manager's office.

Hume was nervous and this made the bank staff nervous. Margaret later recalled: 'Every now and then he threatened to shoot me. I had the impression he didn't like being laughed at. I thought we would have to be very careful not to jeer at him.'

There was concern for the injured Lewis. Margaret begged to be allowed to help him, but 'He wouldn't let me near Mr Lewis. He did not trust any of us. I begged him to hurry up with his robbing and let us get an ambulance. But he took his time, he kept pacing up and down the floor talking about Ireland.'[9]

They were occasionally threatened and Hume debated openly whether to shoot them or not. He pointed his gun at Higgins and pulled the trigger. There was a faint click and he said, 'Next time it's a bullet.'[10] The three were ordered to tie themselves up by the arms and the legs. 'If you're not tied up by the time I count to five, I'll shoot you all.' Margaret recalled, 'We believed he would shoot us all.' Adhesive tape was tossed over to them, whilst Gutteridge and Higgins were told to use their own ties.[11]

It seems that Hume believed Margaret was Irish, though she was actually from Blackpool. He said to her, 'You are Irish. I am a Roman Catholic. You know I will keep my word. I will phone for an ambulance in ten minutes.' He certainly seems to have been taken by her, noticing she was pretty and pulling down her skirt which had been raised above her 'shapely legs' when she had to tie herself up, 'A girl is entitled to her modesty even if she is tied up in a bank.' Finally, after nearly 50 minutes he told them that he had a friend in an automobile outside the front door who was armed with a Sten gun.[12]

Before he left, Hume opened the door of the bank just enough to check that the coast was clear. It was. He then returned inside and placed the spent cartridge in his pocket to dispose of later. As he slipped out, he took the keys and locked the door. He then broke into a trot along the Great West Road for he had almost a mile to cover before he reached his destination of Kew Bridge station. There were a few people about but none took any interest in him. He was out of breath when he reached his destination, but apparently used the telephone there to dial the operator and request that an ambulance be sent to the bank branch, or so he said.[13]

The train to Waterloo station arrived on time. The exhausted Hume flung himself into an empty carriage. Between stations he threw the bank keys out along the track (they were found three weeks later). He felt calm and content. Shooting a man had not troubled him, for as he rationalised, 'Nor did I have any qualms about what I had done. A man like me has no scruples about behaviour towards society.' Furthermore, he reasoned, 'It was because of lovely Trudi . . . that I robbed the bank. You see, I needed the money so we could get married.' He added, 'I risked my life and my liberty to carry out that raid. I did it for the love of Trudi. I wanted to be able to live in luxury with her.'[14]

The train journey did not take long, for Hume alighted at Putney station. At Putney he took a taxi to Cromwell Road air termini. Relaxing in the back seat, he puffed on a cigarette to calm his nerves after all that frenetic action.[15]

At Heathrow air terminus he locked himself into a lavatory and changed his clothes and appearance. Gone was the blue-suited Brown and now he was Stephen Bird, wearing a sports jacket and trousers, horn-rimmed spectacles, false moustache and with his hair plastered down. Apparently he was so confident in his disguise that he felt he could take part in the hunt for the perpetrator of that robbery he had committed. He did not do so, of course. Instead, he left the country and by the end of the day was back with Trudi. Or so he said. Trudi's recollection was that he came back by Swissair on 3 August.[16]

Hume arrived at Trudi's flat in Russenweg in 'a noisy, hectic, cheerful mood.' He gave her a doll he had bought in Paris. From his suitcase and his pockets he produced wads of banknotes (£1,300 in all, made up of 700 £1 notes, 200 10s. notes and 100 £5 notes); these he spread over her table, covering it. Trudi had no idea where these came from and he told her that it was his salary for flying on a special assignment. When Trudi asked why he had been paid in bundles of notes he merely shrugged. The money was hidden in the bedroom due to fear of burglars. Trudi was still confused but was unable to question him further because he changed the subject by insisting he wanted to visit her parents and so went out into the street and hired a car for the two of them.[17]

Back at the crime scene, 10 minutes after Hume had left the bank staff had managed to free themselves. Gutteridge climbed through a window and ran to a telephone kiosk to ring for the police and an ambulance. Lewis was rushed to hospital and the bullet was removed. He recovered. Eric Aires, the branch manager, arrived to see his staff, and when all those unwounded returned to work on the following Tuesday he declared he was very proud of them.[18]

Detective Superintendent Leonard Woolner of Ealing CID was in charge of enquiries. Road blocks were set up on routes from the bank after the robbery and three days later taxi drivers in west London were asked over their radio system if they had picked up a man with the following description; short and dark-haired and wearing a blue suit. On 7 August Midland Bank offered a reward of £1,000 for information leading to the gunman's arrest. A Belgian 0.22 revolver with six rounds of ammunition was found in Hounslow, 4 miles from the bank robbery and handed into the police but it was not thought to have been the weapon used. All the initial enquiries proved to be of no immediate avail. Hume had got clean away.[19]

Once back with Trudi, Hume was initially a happy man. He caressed her and talked of marriage. But his bliss was short-lived. He recalled:

> Next morning I bought a paper and settled down to read about my crime. I began to shake with rage. The paper said that I had missed a fantastic haul in the bank's big safe. I was livid. So that guy at the bank had lied to me by saying the safe contained no money. There were 40,000 smackers in it all the time. I tore the paper to shreds and stormed angrily round the room. Some day I would get even with that guy. Nobody lies to Hume and gets away with it . . . . That guy wants to remember for the rest of his life that if he had told me the truth a second bank man wouldn't have been shot later that year. Nor would a taxi-driver have been shot and killed in Zurich, and another man wounded earlier this year [i.e. 1959].

Hume had not been totally successful in this robbery. He had another cause for concern; the bank raid had only netted £1,300.[20]

Trudi tried to calm him down, and knowing nothing of the reason for Hume's rage, could not understand why her lover was so aggrieved. She wanted him to meet her parents, the Hoffners, to tell them about their impending marriage. The couple went to see them, in their house in Lotzwil, near Berne. Hume had met them previously and had gone for woodland walks with her father and also to the village hostelry to play skittles with him. He claimed to like them and on their third visit there the couple became engaged. Driving back to Zurich with Hume, Trudi admired her engagement ring. He kissed her goodnight as she was about to enter the flat. Then she said, 'Don't leave me alone – especially tonight. Don't waste money at that hotel. Why not come and live with me? We can save money and be married.'[21]

A few days later they went together to the city hall to ascertain what paperwork was needed for their marriage. That was an error, admitted Hume, for the official who looked from the photograph on Hume's passport (as the disguised Johnny Bird) to the real Hume was puzzled. He said, 'This photograph does not look much like you. I advise you to have it renewed.' He added that enquiries would have to be made about Hume in London. Hume claimed 'I was sweating and my hands were shaking.' Trudi asked to see his passport photograph and he admitted to her 'I suppose I have changed a bit.' To her the passport photograph was that of a complete stranger.[22]

Once they had returned to her flat they had a major argument. She kept asking him awkward questions which he was not able to answer properly. Hume knew that there was only one thing he could do to prevent this line of questioning. He later wrote, 'I forced her on to the divan and made passionate love to her.'[23]

That was, of course, only a temporary solution. Doubts and suspicions remained in Trudi's mind. She kept asking him about the evident discrepancies and why he should revert to such subterfuge. Hume could stand it no longer. He often flew into tempers and raved about her being a suspicious woman. She would try and calm him. Often these rows ended up with them making love. Hume and Trudi did make love on other occasions, too, once during an afternoon of hair appointments they had done so four times. However, 'As our love grew more passionate, Trudi became more and more demanding about the date of our wedding.' But Hume was reluctant to set a date until he had more money and that meant another bank robbery.[24]

For Hume, love was not enough. He lay alongside 'lovely' Trudi on the divan in her 'cosy flat' in Zurich, but his mind was not on love-making. He wanted more. He wrote, 'I was with a girl as gorgeous as technicolour, living the gay life that suited me – but my cash was running out.'[25]

Hume left Zurich on 11 August for Montreal via New York. His letters to Trudi give an insight into his activity there and the impression he wanted to create for her. He wrote to Trudi from New York on 13 August:

> My darling! Just a quick note to tell you how much I miss you and how much I love you and want to see you again. On my writing

desk in front of me is a photo of you, and when I look at it, I get sad because you're so far away.

We spent a total of 21 hours en route, the trip was obviously too long, especially since 5 hours had to be spent in Sabre (fighter) aircraft.

Be always a good girl, darling, and Johnny will soon be with you again. May God protect you, Trudi! With love, Johnny

Xxxxxxxx[26]

Two days later, on 15 August, he wrote from New York again:

Darling Trudi!

You can't imagine how much I miss you and how much I love you. I'm sad because I can't be with you again soon. They wanted to send me to South America, and then I wouldn't have seen you for three months. But I have averted this matter and reached a compromise, and I hope to be back on 6 September. Now that I'm not there, you can think about me, and if you want to have me forever, I would do anything to make you happy, and I must tell you that the happiest day of my life was the day we spent with your parents. Please tell them that. Give my regards to all. We shall both, when I'm back, go crab hunting again. I write this letter to you on Swiss-Air paper because I thought that a Swiss girl should have a letter written on Swiss paper. Your picture is in front of me, next to a glass with Kirsch, and I smoke a cigarette of the brand 'Hygis.' My thoughts are with you. Give my regards to everyone in the house, and to all at Burgwies, if they are there, and, Trudi, Johnny would be very happy if you could go to the photographers. Was it not a fearful disaster when the Dutch plane crashed and 99 people lost their lives? I hope that you think of me sometimes. I wish that everything you ever dreamed of will become true, Trudi, and when I fly at night I want to ascend and bring down the stars for you. I hope that Swiss-Air reached you and have told you that I landed safely in New York.

And now I say 'Auf Wiedersehen', my darling. Do not forget to think of me, as Johnny loves you so much. Auf Wiedersehen for today. All my love, Johnny.

Xxxxxxxx[27]

Trudi responded and Hume wrote to her from Montreal on 21 August:

Darling Trudi!

Many, many thanks for your postcards and letters. It was wonderful to read your handwriting. Tomorrow I will fly to Vancouver.

Since I, when I fly back to Zürich, most likely will pass by Japan, Singapore and India, it is better that you don't write to me in Montreal, or Vancouver, which is 2500 miles away from here. At the time when your letter arrives, I'll already be seeing you in Zürich. I'm certain that you can't imagine how much I miss you, my darling, and I think of you all the time. I love you very much, Trudi, and I hope that you're not anxious when we get married. I know that you don't want to make a mistake again with a marriage, but while I'm away you can take the time and think it through. Anyway I'm sure that I will always love you, and I know that I'll be a good husband to you. Forgive me if I'm a little jealous, but it is because I want you so terribly much.

I will try to fetch you soon and then I'll share all the joys and sorrows with you.

Many greetings for today!

All my love, Johnny

xxxxxxxxxxxx

Hume returned to Zurich on 27 August.[28] He had been in Canada, staying at the Realmount Lodge, Guy Street, Montreal where the proprietress, Mlle Yvette Berube, recalled that he was 'a very nice English gentleman, so quiet, so nice.' He stayed in room 24, paying $6 per night. Apparently he had a photograph of Trudi in his room. He told Trudi that he had a private aircraft and operated from Montreal, London, Yugoslavia and China. He was flying to Frankfurt on an almost daily basis in October. What he did on these trips is not known and Hume never divulged anything about them or even alluded to them. Whatever it was, it was probably not very lucrative. On his return to Zurich, Trudi told him that she was pregnant (the child may have been conceived on 3 July, a night that Hume said he'd never forget). The prospective father was surprised, but happy.[29]

Two months later the couple were devastated. They were in her flat when Trudi had a miscarriage. Hume rang for the family doctor and for an ambulance. Once in hospital, Trudi fell unconscious and Hume was excluded from the room whilst surgeons treated her. He was very anxious, waiting outside the operating theatre. When he could sit by her bedside he was in tears and he held her hand during the long night. Next day he bought her flowers, fruit, chocolates and a dress which fitted her. This was a side which many would have believed incompatible with Hume's criminal character, but that he was capable of being tender-hearted and loving is undeniable.[30]

Yet, the other side to his nature was never far away. Hume decided to try his hand at another bank robbery and resolved to steal from the same bank. He claimed that this was in revenge, 'that bank man was to blame. But I would go back to Brentford to get my revenge on him – and some more of that money he was so keen to protect.' This man had, he believed, cheated Hume not only of money but of the lifestyle he felt he was entitled to. He wrote, 'With that sort of money I should have been able to marry Trudi and live it up all over Europe.' Another reason for choosing the same bank is that security is often lax, even in the case of a bank that has already been robbed. Furthermore, Hume may have reasoned that if he could rob the bank once, then robbing the same one would be just as easy, if not more so, because he knew the surroundings and so felt secure there. The date for their marriage was set as 14 February 1959 to give him enough time to steal the money he thought they needed. On leaving the tearful Trudi he could hardly reveal the real reason for his departure, so he told her that far from being a test pilot he was actually a spy for the Western Powers and was about to set off on a dangerous mission in Eastern Europe. 'This is a big deal', he told her. 'Maybe I won't have to go away any more.' They made love that night with such passion, knowing they were soon to be apart. However, Trudi thought that he said he was going to London to obtain a copy of his birth certificate and other papers he needed in order to marry her.[31]

On 4 November, Hume visited a gun dealer in Berne, the only Swiss canton where the possession of a firearms licence was not required to purchase a gun. He bought a Belgian Walther 7.65mm pistol with a shoulder holster and twenty-five bullets. On either 9 or 11 November, he packed two guns (the other was a Browning. 22) and headed to London (telling Trudi he was flying to Montreal). As ever, he used his Johnny Bird passport and his disguise. He went through customs at Dover without any difficulties. In the lavatory he removed his disguise and became Donald Brown, before continuing the journey to London. Once there he stayed in a small hotel in Kensington. The next day he donned dark glasses and went to the scene of his first robbery, probably travelling on the District Line from South Kensington to Boston Manor station and walking down Boston Manor Road.[32]

When Hume arrived at the site of the bank he was in for a shock. The building was now derelict. However, there was a helpful notice stating that it had moved to a new location at Beecham House on the corner of Clayponds Road and the Great West Road, a quarter of a mile away, and so rather nearer Kew Bridge station. He cursed, knowing he would have to familiarise himself with a new building. Walking to it, he thought of the revenge he would have on the man he claimed cheated him out of tens of thousands of pounds, looking forward to that man's fear when he turned his gun on him. Wanting to savour these thoughts for a while, he returned to his hotel. At some stage he passed a police station and saw the reward poster for him and took it down, 'It made me feel good to know I was wanted. I tore the poster down and kept it as a souvenir.' To have successfully eluded the police was clearly an ego boost for Hume.[33]

Hume went back to the bank to consider how he should rob it. Seeing there was scaffolding outside the building, he managed to obtain a workman's overalls and cap and so climbed up the scaffolding. He was then able to look through the windows and get to know the inside layout. He decided to strike on Wednesday, 12 November. That day he went to a pub beforehand, as he had done prior to the earlier raid of three months ago. This time he chose the Pottery Arms on Clayponds Avenue. The licensee, Henry Mathieson, recalled talking to him for some minutes whilst Hume enjoyed a pint of beer: 'He was a short, stocky man, with black hair, and he was wearing a blue raincoat. He seemed quite casual, and was not a bit nervous. He kept talking about Lucozade, and when I asked him did he work there, he said, "Yes, I must get back".'[34]

As before, Hume took his two 'confidence pills' with his drink, then went to the toilet before loading his guns. It only took him a few minutes to get to the bank. He waited outside until the last customers had departed, as he had on his previous raid, and then entered at closing time. It was 3 pm. He later recalled, 'I rushed in, drawing one automatic from my shoulder holster, and the other from my trouser pocket. "This is a stick-up" I snarled.' Bank staff, however, recalled him announcing, 'I'm taking over.' Facing Hume was a man he had not seen on his last raid. This was John Bennett, a cashier. After a moment of temporary paralysis, he dived under the counter and pressed the alarm bell.[35]

Other bank staff, including Margaret Kirby and David Gutteridge, hid behind the counter out of sight and quickly made their way to safety behind locked doors. Hume would not be able to get at them or the money that was there. Alarm bells were ringing and his time at the bank was limited. Staff members were shouting for help from outside. Another was busy telephoning for assistance. Hume leaned over the counter and scooped up what little money he could and stuffed it into his blue holdall, placing one of his automatics on the counter. He then had another shock, as he recounted:

> Just as I jumped back over the counter with a fistful of 10s notes, a tallish man came from behind a pillar and rushed at me. For a few seconds we struggled with each other. Then, in a desperate effort, I flung him off and fired at the same time . . . He had a lot of courage.

Even with a bullet in his guts he tried to trip me up as I jumped past him.

The man was 52-year-old Eric Aires, the bank manager.[36]

When Stanley Wilkinson, the middle-aged security guard, arrived on the scene he described it thus:

The manager was lying on the public side of the counter. I knelt down and cradled his head on my knee, then he gasped, 'For God's sake get the ambulance.' There was a silence and then he spoke again, 'Will you please phone my wife. My stomach feels on fire. My God, my God, where is the ambulance?' I told him he would be alright and the ambulance was coming. I did not know what to do. I thought I had better leave him lying there and call an ambulance and so I ran back to my office and dialled 999.[37]

Dr Richard Moore of Brentford High Street arrived 15 minutes later and saw Aires being held by Wilkinson. Aires was taken to West Middlesex hospital for an emergency operation. Initially the surgeons were unable to remove the bullet and his situation was reported as being critical. However, he eventually recovered from the injury. CID officers from Brentford police station also arrived, and later fingerprint men from Scotland Yard. To no avail, roads were blocked off.[38]

Before all this happened, Hume was leaving the bank when a cashier threw a heavy glass stand at him, but it missed and hit a window instead. Hume was careful enough not to run out of the bank whilst the alarm was blaring out. He just walked outside quickly and on reaching the back streets ran as fast as he could. Once he was well away from the bank he broke into a run and arrived at Kew Bridge station. He bought a single ticket to Waterloo. As before, he went to the toilet to change his appearance. He became Johnny Bird again with glasses and moustache. He put the stolen money in a brown bag and ditched the blue holdall in the lavatory. He hoped he would not be recognised as the bank robber.[39]

Standing in the tiny waiting room, he had a new shock. There were two police officers walking along the platform. They took a good look at Hume. He gripped the gun in his pocket and wondered whether he would have to shoot them. If they suspected him he certainly would have and then contemplated shooting himself or committing suicide on the railway line (after the changes to the capital punishment system in 1958, it was still a hanging offence to murder a policeman). Yet, the policemen walked past and the danger was over. Little did Hume know it but the police were at each station on the line and checked both the train he was travelling on and the one thereafter at Waterloo, on the assumption that he might have boarded at Brentford Central as that was the nearest station to the bank.[40]

Hume then boarded the 3.23 train and found an empty compartment. He was then able to examine his takings. The notes were mainly 10s. notes and the total value was only about £350. The train stopped first at Chiswick and the next station was Barnes Bridge. Hume feared that the police might be at each station on the line, so as the train slowed down on its arrival into Barnes Bridge, he took the risk of breaking his legs and jumped off. Safe, he walked the few minutes to the main road and took a bus northwards to Hammersmith. There he took a taxi to London (Heathrow) airport.[41]

Having already purchased a ticket to fly to Zurich at 5.40 pm, he had just enough time to change his clothes, having previously dropped off a bag containing these at the left-luggage point. It was already past 5, but he quickly put on the grey sports jacket and trousers and caught the plane. He was in Zurich by the next evening and found Trudi in bed. He woke her up, and seemed very excited, as he had after his earlier bank raid, and wanted to take her to their favourite restaurant, the Burgwies. She dressed and saw him counting the money, spread out on the table, as before. He was angry and cursed, shaking his head at the amount there. When they arrived at the restaurant he drank a lot which was uncharacteristic of him. He recalled, 'That night I was dog tired – too tired to make love to the beautiful, slim auburn haired girl for whom I had risked my life and who now lay at my side.'[42]

Hume's raincoat and holdall were found by the police in the waiting room a few days later and were identified as being those belonging to the gunman, who they now realised must have taken the 3.23 train from Kew Bridge. Initially there were several suggestions as to the criminal's identity, and it was rightly assumed that he was the same man who had held up the bank in August, as confirmed by Margaret Kirby. However, some of the information forthcoming was misleading. A former convict from Pentonville prison thought that the man was a former inmate of two years ago who had talked about undertaking a similar crime. Detectives also enquired after a man who had disappeared from a hostel in Hammersmith after the raid. Boarding houses were searched for a man overheard talking about the robber in a pub. It was thought that the thief must be a local man because he knew about train times and the geography of the area. Two security guards claimed they saw a man casing the joint a day before the robbery. The bank offered a £5,000 reward to anyone providing information leading to the thief's arrest.[43]

Yet, though he had escaped, Hume had failed. Firstly, he had stolen very little money and, secondly, had not taken his revenge. But more importantly, less than two weeks after the robbery the police were sure of his identity. They did not know, however, where he was and asked Interpol to trace him in Paris. They stated they wanted Donald Brown alias John Lea Lee and this is what appeared in the *Police Gazette*. In public the name of Hume was not mentioned by the police but newspapers linked the cases together.[44]

But Hume was blissfully unaware of these developments. The day after he returned from London he awoke from a deep sleep to find Trudi at his bedside, with a newspaper under his nose. Expecting it to include a report about his bank robbery, he found it showed a notice of their impending wedding, just under three months away. It was in the *Zurich Gazette* and read, 'Bird, Stephen, Flugzeugingenieur, britischer, starutsangehbriger, in Montreal, Kanada. Sommer, Trudi, von Madiswil, BC [Berne Canton] Zurich.' Trudi was ecstatic. She said, 'I'm longing for the day to come, Johnny. Then we can have a home of our own and children.' Hume was despondent and thought, 'Even as she said it I wondered whether our marriage would ever take place. To get married I needed dough – lots of it. From both bank raids I made only about £1,700. You can get married on that sort of money but you can't stay married. And I wanted Trudi for keeps.'[45]

The weeks passed by quietly enough. Hume kept an eye on the newspapers to feed his ego and to check anything that might suggest his freedom was endangered. He was pleased that the papers described him in what he considered flattering terms and that he had escaped capture. He was also glad that about a month after the robbery Aires was let out of hospital and was on the road to recovery, though whether that was out of compassion or whether it meant that a murder charge was not hanging over him again is another question. Probably the latter was the case. He had been fortunate not to have killed another two men; as had they. He was pleased as his monetary worth soared when the Midland Bank raised the price on his head. 'I must be the only man in the annals of British crime who has had three prices on his head', though it was only two really– that for the Setty case was for the finding of Setty not for the discovery of his murderer.[46]

Hume seems to have made himself popular with others apart from Trudi. He often played skittles and drank beer and wine with the employees of the Zurich tram company. On one occasion he was at their bowling club and saw two tram drivers in uniform enter. Fearing that they were police officers coming to arrest him, he fled the building.[47]

Much of Hume's life with Trudi was ordinary enough. She recalled that his interest in aviation was still as strong as ever and he read many books on the topic, as well as detective fiction and about rocket science. He enjoyed evenings with her, at home or at skittle clubs, rather than at night clubs, and helped out around her flat, doing odd jobs for her, such as cooking and cleaning, as well as electrical jobs at the salon for her. He was kind and gentle towards her and only lost his temper with her twice. Once when they were play boxing and once when he picked a cherry from a tree and she said 'Look out for the police', Hume replying, 'You're always talking about the police.' With her parents he was equally helpful and also took their foster son, Ronald, aged 3, for walks, telling them he loved animals and children.[48]

All this was a far cry from the press image of him. Hume was often psychologically unstable, having said to Trudi, rather pathetically, 'Through you I have found a mother and father and sister for the first time.' On one occasion he talked of suicide, saying he would use poison if he didn't have a gun to do it and she dissuaded him from the act.[49]

However, after just three days in Zurich he left again: on 17 November he flew to Canada and stayed in the same guest house in Montreal as he had in August for four days, and did not return to Zurich until 12 December. He claimed he was working for an electronics firm there.[50]

Hume wrote a postcard to Trudi from Goose Airport, Labrador, on 21 November:

> Darling!
> It is terribly cold here. Lots of snow.
>
> >All my love, Johnny

On 22 November, he wrote to her from Montreal:

> Darling Trudi! I'm just back after having been to the other side of the country. I'm up to my ears, feeling tired and wishing I could be with you and that we could dine together. I think of you a lot and want to be back with you soon again.
>
> It's snowing a lot, and it's very cold; we have more than 2 meter snow, and the tarmac and everything else is frozen.
>
> I will fly from here next week, with a plane to Yugoslavia, and from there I'll try to fly via Belgrade back to you in Zürich.
>
> By now I think that you're finished knitting my pullover and that you're satisfied with your work.
>
> I hope you think of me, and don't look too much at other men.
> All my love, my darling
>
> >Yours Johnny
> >Xxxxxxxxxx[51]

Trudi had written him a letter on 20 November, and on 29 November Hume responded:

> My dear Trudi!
>
> Thanks for your dear letter. I'm pleased to hear that you've been to the doctor and that everything is in order. It has been snowing here continuously for three days, and it's white as in a church, but very cold. Don't worry darling, I don't drink too much Kirsch. Johnny is a good boy. I go swimming every day after work; it's good exercise.
>
> If it's as cold in Zürich as here, at least you have a warm, nice room in the evening. I have to work both Saturday and Sunday this weekend, but I shall think of Russenweg.
>
> When the winter shoes are in order I'm sure you'll wear them, and it must look pretty when you wear them in the shop.
>
> I have chains on my car tires that keep me from skidding, but it takes about one half hour until I get to the airport from here. I don't know when I can return, but as soon as I do I'll let you know. I think of you all the time and must tell you, that you're Johnny's favourite girl.
>
> Best regards, and I hope I'll see you soon.
>
> All my love, Johnny
Xxxxxxxxxx[52]
>
> PS: Lots of thanks for your kisses.

After the miscarriage, Trudi had worried about her chances of having children, and Hume had urged her to go and see a doctor to make sure everything was OK.

Two days later, on 1 December 1958, Hume wrote her this letter:

> Hello darling!
>
> Now I can tell you that I fly tomorrow to the northern, most Arctic region in Canada; it's very cold, -20 degrees in Montreal, and it has been snowing for two long weeks, in the street there is one and a half meter snow, and everything is as white as in a church. My God, I don't want to know how cold it is at the place I'm going to now, which is 1250 miles from here. I think you're my good girl who thinks a lot about Johnny. If that's the case it makes me very happy. Trudi, I must tell you that I haven't been sneezing once since I left you, and thus my cold must have been caused by the bedsprings or something else at Russenweg 3 (Hotel Sommer).

Yesterday they flew Canadian transport planes to Frankfurt and Berlin, and since I've been working hard for seven days I wish for nothing more than to fly together with them, and be with you quite soon.

I love you so much. A hundred greetings, Johnny xxxxxxxxx[53]

On 7 December, Hume wrote this final letter from Montreal:

Darling Trudi!

I hope you're alright, and that you wear warm clothes in this cold weather. I will be very happy when I'm back in Zürich, which will soon be the case. You can't imagine how much I miss you, and how much I try to get back to you soon. Don't forget to write and tell me how everything goes, and also what you wish for Christmas. I have bought you pretty nylons, and some nice toys for Ronald and Ernst, and I haven't forgotten to buy your father a handsome American pipe, which I know he has always wanted to have.

Don't worry about me, I'm fine, but it's very cold and it's the coldest month here for years. When I come back to Zürich it will be Christmas soon, and I'll have 10 to 14 days off work, and think that this is a good compensation for all your waiting. I have some good friends who want to come to our wedding, they will be at that time in Germany. I have bought you a hundred packages of cherries, and I'll bring you oranges from Florida too. Write to me soon.

Lots of greetings, All my love Johnny xxxxxxxx

In all these letters, never before published in English, Hume shows himself to be a very ordinary man in love, a far cry from the murderous image he presented to the world. With Trudi he could be relaxed and loving, as noted already. Yet, a male friend of Trudi's called Hans made fun of this and told Trudi that a man who is a test pilot would never write xxxx, only a stupid schoolboy would do such a thing. Hans also told Trudi that Hume's handwriting signalled something sinister, that he is a 'bad' guy. This troubled her.[54]

Christmas was spent with Trudi and her parents and was a happy time, partly because the hue and cry over him seemed to have evaporated (or rather was no longer reported in the press). However, on Christmas night he was drinking whisky and became angry and resentful. Trudi recalled him being silent, resentful and uninterested in the presents, but when she found him in tears he couldn't explain why. He was annoyed that Trudi's brother, Viktor, had not asked him to be his best man at his wedding, despite only having been acquainted with him for a few months. Ronald's arrival the next day cheered up Hume, who played with the little boy. Trudi remembered that when he had returned from his trips abroad he was like this; morose and bad tempered. Yet, his callous nature was never far from the surface. He and Trudi were driving back to Zurich one day and they passed a place where Trudi told him that a man had been killed by two others in what was in Switzerland a very notorious murder case (the killers were Ernst Deubelbeiss and Kurt Schurmann, whom Hume was later to meet in prison). Hume commented:

> 'Why is it important?' I asked her casually. 'What does it matter if there is one more, or one less person on this earth?' Trudi seemed shocked by my callousness. I noticed that she looked at me sharply. She must have seen something cruel in the lines of my face at that moment. She shivered. And the rest of the drive back to Zurich we hardly spoke a word to each other.[55]

Back at the flat, tempers flared and Hume said some very hurtful things about his fiancée. After that he became more nervous and restless as days went by. Presumably it was because he was unemployed and anxious about the imminent commitment of a wedding and so entrusting his future to a woman. He was also becoming paranoid; suspecting that each client who came to Trudi's hair dressing salon might be an undercover policewoman. He was beginning to have nightmares about people attacking him as he slept.[56]

Hume concluded that he would either have to call off the wedding or commit another bank robbery. Trudi was out of the flat shopping on 22 January 1959 when Hume went to his locked box and drew out an automatic from the holster which he strapped under his jacket. 'Already I was beginning to feel better', he recalled. He strutted around the room and made tough-guy faces at himself in the mirror. Then, without warning, Trudi returned and caught him by surprise (his gun was not on view). She kissed him and then looked down with a shock. She was standing on a bullet.[57]

She recoiled. Then she saw the bulge of the gun under his jacket. She then saw his travel bag and the reward poster which he had taken down before his last raid. She was shocked, 'Johnny, what are you hiding from me?' He looked ashamed, stood with his back to her in a corner, burst into tears and thumped the bed with his fist, saying, 'I can't marry you, Trudi. I am a bad, bad boy. I must go away and never come back to Zurich.' But he could not tell the truth. According to Trudi, he said, 'I spy for the Russians. I need a pistol because I am in fear of my life.' She said, 'Do you want to shoot me?' 'No, no, no', he replied. Trudi tried to take the gun from him, 'You must get rid of it' she urged and suggested he threw it into the lake. She took hold of the gun and stated, 'I will not give it back to you.' Yet, another version of events on this day was that he threatened to commit suicide by shooting himself with the gun, but Trudi persuaded him not to. If this was the case it shows that Hume's mind was in a very troubled place indeed, and his subsequent behaviour confirms that.[58]

Hume promised he would destroy the gun at a later date and then emptied the magazine and poured six bullets onto the table. The gun was put into a cupboard. Trudi asked what the matter was, 'Why do you call yourself a bad boy?', but he was unable to tell her, replying, 'Don't ask me why. Just believe me when I tell you who I am. Now I have told you I am a Soviet spy, you can fetch the police.' 'No, not the police. I want my Johnnie.' He told her that he had a secret and that she was too good for him. She put her arms around him and said, 'Johnny, no matter what you have done or what you are, I shall always love you. Forget what lies behind you. Let's start a new life together. Time heals all wounds and love makes them heal faster.' They made love that night. Yet Hume's mind was elsewhere, as usual. He was thinking about his gun in the cupboard.[59]

Trudi also told how one day she saw him in tears and asked what was upsetting him. He replied: 'It's nothing, just that I'm so happy I've met you and that you love me. I've been alone in the world and been afraid of women, of falling in love with women. The only one I ever loved was a dog.'[60]

Two days later, despite his promises to destroy the gun, it was still there, as Trudi discovered for herself. On 27 January, Hume told her that he had business in Zurich. On the following morning he rose early and told Trudi, 'I will telephone if I have to go away.' In the afternoon he rang her to tell her, 'I cannot go and will be home about 5 o'clock.' However, he returned that evening at 6.30 pm and rang Swissair to book a flight to London, via Paris, to travel on the following day.[61]

On the morning of Thursday, 29 January, he made coffee for Trudi, took it to her bed and kissed her over and over again. He held her tightly. He later alleged that he knew he would never see her again as a free man. Trudi recollected that he said, 'As I leave, look at me out of the window, out of the bedroom window and not from the drawing room window, so you can see better.' That day he left the flat forever, but took his two guns with him. He fed ducks on a lake and as night fell went to the English church in Zurich. He explained why, as a man without religion, he did so:

> It's very difficult to say what is going on inside one at such moments. Maybe it was the influence of Trudi Sommer. I was thinking about if there was really something about religion. I was thinking that you cannot enter paradise with a gun in your hand. I stayed all night in

the church, shaving in the padre's room, eating the Communion bread and drinking the wine. I took a cardboard box from the church in which I afterwards concealed the pistol in the bank robbery.[62]

It was to be another bank robbery and this time it was to be in Zurich. There is no evidence that Hume planned this raid at all and does not seem to have thought about his escape route. Yet, he destroyed his identity papers prior to the robbery and also secreted a razor blade and a vial of poison on his person. He later stated, 'I wanted to commit suicide. I was down to my last bean [allegedly it is claimed; he had £1,700 salted away]. Then I decided to try the hold-up first.' Either he was so self confident, having got away with two previous offences, and arrogant that he did not think he needed to take such precautions, or he had a fatalistic impulse that he somehow wanted to be caught. Hume wanted to stage a last show of bravado to demonstrate to the world that he remained a hard man. He certainly thought that robbing a Swiss bank would be easy because, 'The banks seemed a pushover. The staff are so kind, so gentle, so unsuspecting.' His mental state was probably not good (possibly he was suicidal) and his relationship with Trudi may have been troubling him. He later said, 'I knew already that it would fail but I did it anyway . . . I didn't want my conscience to brand me as a coward.'[63]

Three years later, Playfair and Sington theorised that the simplistic attempt to rob a bank might have been Hume's way of committing suicide. They suggested that he might not have known that there was no capital punishment in Switzerland and so he might be executed for his intended crime.[64]

It seems that at about 11.30 am on the morning of Friday, 30 January, Hume simply walked up to the Gewerbe Bank, Ramistrasse, a major thoroughfare in Zurich. He had a cardboard box and a 7.65mm Walther automatic pistol. Walter Schenkel, a 25-year-old bank clerk, came face to face with Hume. He recalled:

When Hume entered the bank he did not say anything and I did not see any pistol. There was an overcoat on the counter. I myself was directly behind the counter. The man then shot me [through the box from the church; Hume claimed he said '*Hande Hoch*' and then he 'shot without thinking']. I fell down but managed to set off the alarm system. Hume then fought with another clerk, Edwin Hug. He tried to open a drawer but appeared too nervous to do so. Then he pocketed some money, jumped over the counter and ran off.[65]

Hume's haul amounted to a mere 215 francs, or about £17 13s. in English money. It had been lying on a desk waiting to be put into a drawer. It was a miserable sum indeed, and, as we shall see, the true cost of the robbery was far higher.[66]

Schenkel managed to set off the bank alarm as he fell. Hug had been on the telephone to his wife when Hume had entered. He saw what was going on and kicked a wastepaper basket at Hume and then they fought, and he was slightly injured as Hume hit him with his gun and with his head. Another bank employee, the 16-year-old bank apprentice, Ulrich Fitze, who had just returned after running an errand to the post office, ran out of the bank after Hume.[67]

Fitze did so because the chief cashier ordered him to 'Follow that man.' Fitze had been told by his father to always obey the instructions of his superior without question and immediately. So he did so. He recalled, 'I knew I could follow him right across Zurich. I am fit and I knew he would be exhausted soon. After about a 100 metres I caught him up and tried to seize him. But he turned and pointed his pistol at me, and I let him go.' Then Hume began fiddling with his gun and dropping bullets. Fitze remained on his tail and, 'He turned again and threatened me with the pistol, which was hidden under his coat.'[68]

Hume ran down towards the river, first to Oberdorfstrasse, before turning left and then right. Here, standing by the taxi he drove for a living, was 50-year-old Arthur Maag, clean shaven, married to 47-year-old Elizabeth with whom he had two children, Yvonne and a son aged 12. Fitze saw him and shouted, 'Hold him, hold him!' Maag moved towards Hume and tried to stop him by stretching his hands out towards the running man. Hume recalled, 'I just saw him running at me . . . it was perhaps sixty feet. . . I fired, but I cannot say I fired to kill. It was one of those things.' Fitze witnessed the attack, too, and he later stated:

> He suddenly turned and shot the taxi driver from a distance of about 10–12 metres. I was 6–7 metres behind the taxi driver. There was not a word spoken. The taxi driver fell to the ground and the man continued to run away. I had a moment of hesitation when I passed the taxi driver, but I continued the chase.

Maag collapsed in the gutter, a bullet in his stomach.[69]

Hume had no personal animosity towards Maag. Tragically he had been in the wrong place at the wrong time. Hume merely saw him as an obstacle in his own escape attempt or perhaps as a route to his own death. And as Hume once wrote, 'If anything gets in your way or annoys you – get rid of it.' Another man was dead as a result of this bleak and egotistical creed. Or was this an act of self-destruction as Hume hoped to use the murder as a means of ending his own life?[70]

Afterwards Hume ran back to Obersdorfstrasse and encountered Gustav Angstmann. A 35-year-old pastry chef, Angstmann described what happened next:

> I was strolling quietly along the street on my way to work when I saw this mad looking chap running straight at me with a pistol in his hand. I went with a football tackle to try and stop him. The breath was nearly knocked out of my body. He raised his pistol and twisted round towards me. The other passersby came to the rescue. I'm fairly tough, but this is not my idea of something I want to do again. I guess I hadn't time to think.

Little did he know it, but Angstmann had been fortunate; Hume's gun was empty and later the discovery of four bullets along the route he had taken suggested that he had unsuccessfully tried to reload whilst on the run.[71]

Angstmann gave the gun to Fitze who held it and noted that the chamber was open and there were no bullets left in it. He returned it to the chef. He went back to see Maag who he found was dead. Then he returned to the bank with the loose bullets and gave them to the police.[72]

Another account suggests that Angstmann chased Hume into Scheitergasse, dodging into doorways when Hume turned around and pointed his gun at him, and then they had a tussle at Hecht Platze, near the River Limmat. When Hume was seized, women who had gathered nearby and knew what had happened to Maag, chanted, 'Lynch him! Lynch him!'[73]

Hume was not lynched but he was assaulted by members of the crowd. One man punched him. A woman beat him with an umbrella. Taxi drivers, angered at the death of one of their own, shouted, 'Give him to us – we will hang him.' Angstmann, who was holding onto Hume and, having run half a mile, 'was absolutely exhausted', later recalled, 'I told the people to wait until the police came, as it was no use beating him.' Hume concluded, 'I suppose a man in my position must expect that sort of thing . . . I was pretty glad when the police arrived.'[74]

Financial compensation was offered to all involved. The Swiss government later gave Maag's widow 50,000 francs. Angstmann was awarded 1,000 francs for his bravery in tackling Hume and said that he, deemed the hero of Zurich, was sure he deserved it all.[75]

Maag's place of death was marked by bunches of flowers. His funeral and cremation took place on the afternoon of 4 February. Thirty fellow taxi drivers formed a cortège and the firm Maag worked for took all their taxis off the streets for 4 hours. A police delegation and Councillor Albert Sieber were also in attendance.[76]

Schenkel was taken to hospital where he was operated on. Doctors were optimistic about his recovery on account of his youth and hardy constitution. Sure enough he was out of danger and soon on the road to recovery.[77]

The cause of all this misery was taken into police custody, into cell 13, and was photographed, 'His face had a hunted look. His eyes were shadowed. He looked cowed and hungry, almost animal like. He stared like a snared man.' Captain Hans Stoltz, Zurich's police commissioner and a qualified lawyer, aged 35, interviewed him. The interrogation started at 1.30 pm. With the captain were three police officers; one to write down the prisoner's words, one who was handcuffed to him and the last in case of emergencies. The man before them had just shot two men and so was deemed highly dangerous. Stoltz was not a happy man, as he said, 'But me, I'm really angry. I don't like shootings.' He added, 'A family here mourns for a brave dead man. Feeling is running high.'[78]

Hume did not say anything to the police at first. He merely smiled and presented his interrogators with blank stares. Stoltz tried him in Polish, English, Czech, French, German and Italian. Hume was weeping before long. It seemed that Hume tried to give the impression that he was insane. Stoltz later related, 'He stands in my office holding a finger to his head like this . . . and says "poof poof". Then he keeps on saying "Shoot me, kill me, give me to the electric chair". Then he weeps again. He's a good actor.' He also expressed regret at his actions but Stoltz was unimpressed by these mere words. Hume kept on repeating them.[79]

Hume's first account of himself and his actions was typically a tissue of lies. He claimed he was John Stanislaw, a Pole born in London, aged 35 and employed as a civilian on the American airbase at Wiesbaden in West Germany. He claimed he had arrived in Zurich on Tuesday, 27 January from Wiesbaden. He had slept rough on the outskirts of the Swiss city for three nights. A representative from the American airbase was contacted and said they had no knowledge of him.[80]

After 3 hours he admitted his name was Hume and this was confirmed after his fingerprints were taken and sent to the central identification bureau at Berne. It was then that he admitted the reason for robbery was that 'he had no money, no food for three days.' Later Hume showed the police where he had allegedly slept for three nights; alongside the reeds. Stoltz noted, 'We've had three very cold nights. Must have been chilly, but that's what he said.' They went down to the place. Hume told them he had ripped up his passport and put it there; it was looked for but never found. Trudi's flat was searched and the police removed Hume's clothing and found his passport in the name of Stephen Bird.[81]

Detective Sergeant Frey, a Swiss policeman involved in the interrogation of Hume, stated:

> He has been telling us a fairy tale about his being in the US Army in Germany. He said he was fed up with roaming around and decided to come to Switzerland because he had heard it was peaceful here. He said he arrived by airplane with only five dollars in his pocket

and slept in a lake shore park for three or four nights. When his money ran out he said he decided on the spur of the moment to rob the bank.

On 1 February, Hume was charged with murder, attempted murder and armed robbery. Dr Hugo Horvath, the public prosecutor, said he would probably stand trial in two or three month's time. He was certainly treated well and Frey recalled him wolfing down the contents of three or four bowls of soup 'like a hungry animal.'[82]

Hume's questioning had been intense. By 2 February four police typists had taken down a 40,000-word statement, consisting of Hume's life history, stating that he was an orphan. Presumably this was an attempt to gain sympathy. The habit of lying died hard. He was closely guarded 24 hours a day and night lest he try to commit suicide and two armed policemen watched him. For an initial period he was not allowed any exercise or any cigarettes (earlier when offered a cigarette, he had crammed it into his mouth and eaten it). He complained of his stuffy cell and refused to eat.[83]

There was great interest in Hume amongst the British press and over twenty newspapers sent journalists to Zurich to follow his story. This was not appreciated by the Swiss, who were annoyed at what they saw as the British conducting their own investigations (interviewing Trudi at length, for instance) and using, allegedly, ungentlemanlike methods.[84]

Dr Frey-Sulzer, a ballistics expert, examined the gun and remarked, 'The markings on the bullet we found in the body of Maag were identical with the marks used in the trial series with Hume's 7.65mm, pistol, as well as the markings on the shells. It is absolutely definite that all these bullets were fired from the same gun.' The gun and bullets were eventually sent to a Swiss crime museum. Dr Hans Soegrist had performed the autopsy of Maag and found that the main artery in the stomach had been severed by the fatal shot and that he had died almost at once.[85]

Until 7 February, Hume had been held at the police headquarters of Zurich whilst he was being questioned there, and so that he could be observed night and day in case he tried to commit suicide, for a razor and poison had been found on his person. Up to then, he still wore the blue jumper Trudi had knitted for him. He was eventually allowed cigarettes and was shaved every other day. Then he was transferred to the cells under the Zurich Court of Justice. He would remain there whilst Dr Horvath gathered the evidence needed for his trial.[86]

Hume was, of course, wanted by the police in London for questioning over the two bank robberies in Brentford. But there was no question of him being extradited. The more serious Swiss charge was to take precedence over the others. One suggestion, by a Dr Goodman on 6 February 1959, was that if Hume was tried in Switzerland and was given the minimum tariff of fifteen years, he could then be returned to Britain for trial over the bank robberies, but that he might then be acquitted. Yet, if Hume was not found guilty in Switzerland for murder, then he could immediately be extradited and tried for the robberies and if found guilty could be sent back to Switzerland and detained in prison there. This idea was not adopted.[87]

Hume was also suspected of a number of thefts that had occurred while he was staying at the St Gotthard Hotel, where he signed himself as 'John Bird, merchant.' Fritz Widmer, a hotel employee, commented, 'I thought he was an American.' The hotel porter was more suspicious and didn't think his American drawl was genuine. Although Hume was suspected of these crimes, his old suitcase only yielded poor quality clothing suggesting a commercial traveller.[88]

The Swiss and British authorities shared information about Hume. It was the end of a European search of several months for him. On 24 February 1959 the Swiss magistrates received information about Hume's history, about his conduct in prison between 1950 and 1958 and about the decision taken to release him in 1958. They wanted to know everything there was to know about the Setty case, Hume's divorce and why he was allowed to obtain a passport in another man's name. Not all the information was available, though, for there was no complete transcript of Hume's trial.[89]

The police were also concerned that he had at least ten aliases; John Stanislaw, Terry Hume, Brian Hume, Terrence Hume, John Lea Lee, Stefan John of Montreal, Stephen Bird, John Bird, J.S. Bird and McGregor. They were also looking into how he had left Britain in 1958. It was even suggested in one newspaper that Hume might have killed Stephen Bird for his passport, but there is no evidence of this.[90]

Trudi found out about Hume's crimes by reading about them in a newspaper. Apparently she had a nervous breakdown due to the shock and had to have a nurse from the hospital stay with her in her flat for a short time. However, by 4 February she felt well enough to give a lengthy interview to an English newspaper about her life with Hume. She ended it by telling how she had to pick him out of a police identity parade, and later stated, 'My heart went out to him. He was still the man I loved. And he was in handcuffs.'[91] Most women stand by their man even if the latter is accused of terrible crimes; Cynthia Hume had done so in 1949 and 1950; in 1949 Barbara Stephens refused to believe that her platonic lover of several years, John George Haigh, could have killed six people and then dissolved them in acid. Such is the power of love. It does not always last, however.

Hume had certainly been very dependent on Trudi for the past few months. Apparently 'his physical desires were insatiable and he craved her company.' But it was more than just physical; he always needed her when he was upset and often sought solace in her arms for hours, in tears, but was unable to tell her what was the matter. In fact, he 'often he told Trudi he hated everyone except her.' He needed a mother that he had never had as well as a lover, but he could not fully confide his criminal past or present to her, so she was unwittingly unable to fulfil all that he needed.[92] It seems he was incapable of intimacy, at least for any period of time, perhaps because he had a distrust of all women ever since his own mother had deceived him and denied parentage.

He wrote a letter to her:

> You will indeed hear a lot about the life I have led. I was pretty wild, much wilder than I think, but I have never done anything to hurt you or said an angry word to you. I sacrificed my freedom when you telephoned me that I should come back 10,000 kilometres from Canada to Switzerland with . . . all the police of Europe after me. There are not many men who would have done that for you, Trudi. I knew that if the English bank manager I shot at had died they would have hanged me. In coming back I've risked for you not only my freedom but my life.[93]

Hume protested in his written account of his life that he wept at the thought that he had ruined Trudi's life. He regretted that he had been the cause of some of her friends shunning her. She wrote to him whilst he was awaiting trial:

> Never in my life have I ever met a human being who trusted me so much. From the very first moment that you entered my life I knew that we belonged to each other. I have asked myself many times if I deserved such a good person. The answer I have satisfied myself with is that I could not believe there were such people in existence. Dear Johnny, even if we are now separated you can imagine that we are still together.'

She later added, 'There's no other like him. Everything in him comes from the heart . . . There's still almost day when I don't think of him.'[94] Possibly she was on the rebound after divorcing her first husband.

Hume wrote of the distress he must have caused her:

> I think right from the start Trudi guessed I was a bad lot, but she was too much in love to do anything about it. She liked me for the way I behaved and laughed and loved and not for what I gave her. It is a tragedy that such a wonderful and innocent girl should be linked

with my own notorious name. Perhaps, though, it is just as well our love affair ended when it did. Trudi always made me soft and sentimental. And I don't want to be soft.[95]

Despite his stated everlasting love for Trudi, according to a fellow convict the reality was far different. Apparently he was rather misogynistic, 'He seems to have loved Trudi, but now he does not want to hear anything about her. "Women bring me bad luck. Every woman talks. Every woman is a traitress."'[96] Hume spent the time before his trial in the 58-year-old Regensdorf prison, just to the north of Zurich, which was described as being:

A very severe prison indeed, inaccessibly situated on the top of a mountain and quite impossible to escape from. Most of the very few letters which Hume was allowed to write were addressed to the DPP [Director of Public Prosecutions] and other authorities, asking us if we would extradite him to stand trial for attempted murder on the Great West Road (the Midland Bank robbery). We were however, very reluctant to do so because our case against him was not a strong one, and in any event he was safely incarcerated elsewhere. The Swiss authorities also asked us to take him – because he was such a damned nuisance – but we refused: we were no keener to have him on our hands than they were. He was a very unpleasant man.[97]

Hume was certainly a difficult prisoner from the outset, but to a far greater extent than he had been when incarcerated in English prisons in 1949–58. He attacked a fellow prisoner and so was sent to solitary confinement. Because of this he was not allowed to walk in the exercise yard as other prisoners did and was constantly watched day and night. He was usually given a sleeping pill each evening and on the one evening a prison officer forgot to do so, Hume howled with rage, drumming against the cell door and threatening to kill the responsible officer. He constantly complained that he was 'treated like a dog.' As a fellow convict said, 'I am sure he is mad.'[98]

Hume was also seen as something of a fantasist, as he had always been. He pretended to like animals, 'They are better than any man', but hated bees. When he saw them he would dance around them, trying to kill them. He remained a fantasist, spinning tall tales about his own activities outside prison. He claimed to be the boss of an American gang, a Soviet spy and a Second World War hero. 'I think he believes in wonders', one convict claimed. The same man also believed, 'I think for the next 25 years he will hope to escape. He has already killed two men and he knows he has nothing to lose by any new crime.'[99]

He was interviewed by Dr Adolf Guggenbuhl-Craig, a 36-year-old Swiss psychiatrist, twenty times in order to assess his sanity and so determine whether he was fit to stand trial. He made a lengthy report and some of the highlights from it are as follows:

> It is not true to say that Donald Brown was not capable at the time of his act – through insanity, imbecility or severe mental disturbance – of recognising the wrong of his deed. He was not affected at the time in his mental health or in his consciousness, nor was he mentally retarded in such a way that his capability of recognising the wrong of his deed was impaired. I could find no damage of his mental functions. He showed above average intelligence, and his memory was good. He had no hallucinations or mad ideas. During the whole examination he only showed deeper emotion when he talked about these acts of violence. If he started to talk about these acts his face took on an expression that was so evil I often had shivers down my spine.
>
> Because he is so good at playing his various parts, he really knows the value of such qualities as friendship, love, honour, respect for other human beings, and respect of life and property. He is only really and truly himself in the part of a criminal.
>
> That this letter and the pose of the romantic outlaw is not genuine is shown in that he often quarrelled with Trudi Sommer; and he told me that he had really come back because of certain espionage opportunities. He did not want to play the part of Trudi Sommer's romantic lover, but that of a gentleman criminal and an international master spy. This explains the discrepancy in his statement.
>
> When I first saw him I was surprised. He did not in any way give the impression of being ruthless. Dressed with a casual elegance, he was very polite and respectful. Right at the start he told me that he was against psychiatric investigation, as he considered himself completely responsible for his actions, and wanted to be judged as such. When he first saw me he watched me very carefully and said he was completely harmless. He described his life as a chain of misfortunes, disappointments and bad luck, which had transformed him into an embittered man. However, his real character came out when he was transferred from a prison in Zurich to Regensdorf. He resisted this transfer with the most brutal force. When he got to Regensdorf he refused to see anyone.[100]

Dr Dieter von Rechenberg, his counsel, also interviewed him, but had a different interpretation of Hume's conduct, believing that he seemed to be acting a part before him and there is much to be said for this point of view. Hume's achievements in life had been minimal and he resented it so for his own sake and others he embroidered an invented and wonderful series of roles; that of war hero, master criminal and secret agent. There was a female interpreter. Hume displayed a romantic gesture with her and gave her a carnation. Dr von Rechenberg believed that Hume had a good side to his character and did love Trudi, yet even here he was probably playing a part.[101]

However, the psychiatrist was not wholly correct in his assessments. As has been noted, Hume did have feelings for Trudi. When she had suffered a miscarriage Hume visited her in hospital, sitting by her bedside overnight. He later visited her twice daily. When she was discharged he took good care of her.

Hume was also happy to see journalists, knowing they would print his utterances. One story was that he was involved in raiding army depots to sell guns to the IRA, a story which they later repudiated. He talked of his hatred for people and his love for animals, claiming he saved a cat from a rooftop when in the RAF and buried a dead rabbit in Hyde Park in 1958, perhaps because notable criminals often expressed similar sentiments.[102]

Hume used his time to write to Dr Leinhart, the public prosecutor. One of his letters, composed on 27 July, shows a subversive and aggressive spirit:

> Sir,
>
> As you without doubt know, I have spent the last 6 days (from Monday to Saturday) in the punishment cell. As far as I understand, I'm under your control and thus I must suppose that my punishment has been carried out by your orders. For your information: I can endure bread and water. Neither does it bother me sleeping on boards, having nothing to do, nothing to read, being without light and not allowed to smoke. The only truly irritating thing is that it's not allowed to wash oneself, to brush one's teeth, comb one's hair, or shave. Undoubtedly one can get used to this state, and I am sure you will agree with me that small boys would appreciate it.
>
> I've never heard in my entire life of such an unlikely thing as stopping prisoners from fighting each other! It would have been different if I had been fussing with a guard, but this was not the case here. God only knows what I would have received if I had given him a decent kick or even a proper whipping.
>
> I see now that you're trying to intimidate me. You would do me a favour, if you would stop writing to me regarding my case, or

provoke me about a problem that affects me. I only want to hear from you when the trial starts. And when we confront each other at court, we will undoubtedly be able to verbally express the mutual dislike that has accumulated.

Excuse me for being repetitious, but I've never heard such an incredible thing as stopping prisoners from fighting each other! At Dartmoor, there was a big note on the wall of the guards' room saying 'When prisoners are fighting each other, they do not fight with guards!' I find these words to be very true. It seems to me that the majority of prisoners here at Regensdorf just want to get a bunch of keys so they can become guards themselves. That's the only thing they want out of life. I don't know why the devil they didn't volunteer as prison guards, instead of becoming crooks!

Myself and 99% of the English prisoners believe in the words of the immortal George Bernard Shaw, who has said: 'The only one who is lower than a convict is his keeper!' I have no doubt that I will have enough influence over the years to come, to convert some of the prisoners here to my way of thinking.

You don't need to answer this letter. I have the impression that you're actually a harmless human being, but perhaps under the thumb of a more powerful one, who in reality is the one I can thank for all my inconveniences.

Donald Brown[103]

In another letter to Dr Leinhart, dated 16 May, Hume wrote:

I have nothing against you, because I have not yet seen you. I don't know how you look like, you can be a big guy or a small man. You can even have blood in your veins, instead of ink, like all other prosecutors. And you can even be a good person, especially when you allow me to buy a packet of cigarette papers. But it doesn't hurt me when you deprive me of it. Then I can even stop smoking . . .

Apparently, Leinhart didn't take offence at Hume's letters but seemed to be amused by them; perhaps he was used to such outpourings by defendants.[104]

Hume was deemed to be sane and so fit for trial for murder and other offences. The psychiatric report was not dissimilar in its conclusions to that of Dr Matheson a decade earlier; Hume was not mad but bad. Unlike the Setty case, the evidence against him in this instance was strong (he had been seen committing murder) and was not only circumstantial. However, unlike the case in 1950, Hume's life was not at risk as capital punishment had been abolished in Switzerland in 1942.

Chapter 10

The Swiss Trial, 1959

Hume had to wait nearly eight months before his trial in Switzerland; a rather longer time than that of 1949–50. Trudi visited him at least twice whilst he was in prison. He was initially reluctant to see her, for he accused her of betraying him to the police, another indication of his old paranoia. When she saw him in February she was able to calm him down and he told her, 'I would give a million if I could once again be with you.' He told her that when he had been in the chapel on the night before the bank robbery he had sat for a long time before the altar, considering his life and remembering that Trudi was Christian, though he wasn't, and whether he could be redeemed. Hume concluded, though, that it was too late for him. Trudi told him that the police suspected her of being guilty of receiving stolen goods but did not press charges due to lack of evidence.[1]

After having worked in a beauty salon in England, Trudi returned to Switzerland before the trial and saw Hume again. Once more, he was not initially disposed to seeing her, but relented and told her about a film, *Never Love a Stranger*, which he claimed reflected his life. He said that he did not want her to attend the trial because she might break down and cry, which would give the English journalists present good copy and that was something he wanted to avoid. He told her that his defence lawyer was 'an idiot' and that he could do a better job himself.[2]

The trial opened on Thursday, 24 September 1959, at Winterthur, Switzerland's sixth largest city, about 19 miles to the north-west of Zurich and where German is the chief language. The Court President, or judge, was Dr Hans Gut and there was a jury of twelve members, as in England. Dr Paul Leinhart was the prosecution attorney and Dr Dieter von Rechenberg the attorney for the defence.[3]

The difficulty is that, as with the 1950 trial, there is no available transcript of it. The *Celebrated British Trials* series only gives a very minimal version. Apart from this there are reports in the contemporary press. Rupert Furneaux's *Famous Criminal Trials*, 6, provides a lengthier account, as does a German journalist who later wrote a book about Hume, but none are complete. These sources have been used to provide the most complete version of the trial possible.

There were five counts in the indictment served on him. These were murder, attempted murder, armed robbery, threatening human life and breaking the immigration laws. Unlike his trial in 1950, there was no real doubt about him having committed any of these offences. He had not attempted to disguise himself for the bank robbery in Zurich and had been caught shortly after the attempted robbery and subsequent murder, running from the scene of the crime. The question was more about whether he was sane or not; did he need treatment in a medical institution or could he go to prison.

Hume arrived at the court house elegantly dressed in a sand-coloured suit, a white shirt, a silk tie with light streaks and wore expensive brown shoes. His face, hair and hands all looked well kept. Apparently, 'he looked like he was on his way to a summer party.' Although Hume would always claim he knew no German, this was untrue, and he was often able to prepare his answers before the interpreter had completed his sentences.[4]

Hume was viewed, not surprisingly, as being an extremely dangerous man. Thus he was brought to the court house in chains. Four Swiss policemen, all armed with guns, brought him in. He initially seemed agreeable, winking and grinning at the journalists present. Later that day he was less so, lunging at a photographer, and one of his guards had to jump between the two men.[5]

The proceedings began with an interrogation of Hume by the President. Dr Wach, the court interpreter, had to translate, for Hume's knowledge of German was limited. Right from the start, Hume decided to annoy those around him. When asked his name he shrugged and replied, 'Ask a silly question, Buster, and you get a silly answer.' When the question was repeated he said, 'If you don't know who I am by now, Buster, you want to get some thicker glasses.' He also objected to one of the jurors being there, 'I don't know his name but I recognize and I object to him.' The juror stated to Dr Gut he had never previously seen Hume.[6]

Unlike British trials, Hume was asked in detail about his antecedents and earlier crimes. He insisted that he had been born in Swanage in 1921, not 1919. When Dr Gut queried this, Hume told him, 'There was a lot of hokey-pokey with my papers.' His aggressive stance continued when he shouted, 'You can tell this guy here I am following his line of thought but it won't get him anywhere.' The President explained to him, 'We in Switzerland are always anxious to know exactly the personality of each defendant.'[7]

Hume's version of early life was then stated. He claimed, incorrectly, that his father had been an alcoholic who died when he was 3 months old by committing suicide. After talking about his formative years in an orphanage, he was asked to comment about his life there, and there was an exchange between Dr Gut and Hume, which provides an insight into his mind:

> 'I thought it was strictly uncomfortable, but then I might be prejudiced. It was typical of the conditions of the 1920s. Things were pretty bad.'

'Do you think that anything special occurred there which might have influenced you in later life?'

'I am not one to judge. Several things happened but I don't think they had any effect.'

'I really ask this question because in several publications it has been stated that events there influenced your early life.'

'Other people reached that consideration, I didn't. Children were very badly treated. I was hit on the head with a hammer or an axe but that has had no effect on my future life, or I don't think it has.'

'In several publications made after consultations with you it was stated that this bad treatment provoked a hatred in you against humanity in general?'

'It may have done. I said that treatment by my step-mother, or so-called mother, had a greater influence on anything I have done in my life. It was after I was eight years old, after the orphanage. I don't think that environment has anything to do with the creation in a man's mind that makes him turn to crime.

He added that his mother 'always treated me as a stranger. I always had to be out of the way; I wasn't part of the family and was always unwanted.'[8]

Hume was asked about John Williams's book about him and he replied, 'I have never heard of the fellow before and have never read the book.' He admitted he lied to Trudi Sommer and spoke about his school days, his early jobs and his brief wartime career. When reference was made to a Scotland Yard report on him, Hume interrupted:

'If this jury believes what is written by some son-of-a-bitch inspector, there's no sense in my telling you any differently. I read the report from Scotland Yard. If this guy is going to believe Scotland Yard then it's no good my telling him my story.'

'If it is wrong, say so.'

'You should have allowed me to get my discharge papers. Either you believe an inspector from Scotland Yard or the RAF discharge papers. You would not let me provide the discharge papers, so obviously you want to believe Scotland Yard.'

Hume talked about his RAF career and his life as a fraudster leading to his conviction. He complained: 'The Scotland Yard report contains only things against me. Why doesn't it contain things such as I once saved a child from a river, and another time I saved a cat from the roof because it was too dangerous for the police. The whole report is just to blacken me.'

Hume's war career as he had related it to Trudi was stated; allegedly one in which he had been a bomber pilot, had been shot down and captured as a POW. He had told how he had been beaten up by guards there. Why, asked Dr Gut, had he told these lies? 'Yes, I told her that. I had to tell her something. But it wasn't true.'

There was an exchange about Hume's subsequent black-market activities, and he admitted producing illegal whisky from distilled potatoes. He saw nothing wrong in this, of course, 'I don't believe that there was anyone at the time who did not have any activity on the black market.'

Not all there believed these stories; Norman Rae for one did not, believing it was all part of Hume's account of himself as a man who hated the world.[9]

Then he was asked whether he was married and did he have a child? The surprising answer was as follows:

> 'Yes, but it was not mine. The father was Stanley Setty.'
> 'Where is Stanley Setty?'
> 'He is not around any more.'

This caused laughter amongst the British journalists present, but Dr Gut asked:

> 'That is not enough. We have no English newspapers here.'
> 'He is dead.'
> 'How did he die?'
> 'Violence. Tell the President I am willing to give the facts of his death but am I to be tried for the Setty murder again?'
> 'You will not be tried for the murder of Setty but it is important to give the jury the picture, if you say that Setty was killed, because that could be done in many ways.'
> 'I fought this man with a knife. He had in fact a bigger chance to kill me than I had to kill him [as Setty also had a knife, or so he now claimed].'

He then explained that the fight was due to an argument over Setty's treatment of his dog and added:

> 'I had injuries on my hands and with all sincerity, it could have turned out either way.'

Dr Gut asked:

> 'Why did you kill Setty?'
> 'Because of jealousy.'

Hume was then asked why he had earlier claimed (in a newspaper article) that it had been because of Setty kicking his beloved dog and for refusing to leave the flat when asked. Hume explained that both had played a part but that jealousy was the paramount reason. He had fought Setty out of jealousy over his wife, remarking,

> 'I sort of had the strongest objections to her friendship with some-one else . . . a man called Setty. I found him in bed with my wife. Well, you know what they were doing.'

He claimed he stabbed him thirty-two times – a gross exaggeration but it was not picked up on in the court room. When asked what his marriage was like he replied,

> 'Rough.'

This is the fourth version of the murder that he is known to have supplied; and the first to mention that both men used knives in the fight. It contradicted previous statements and known reality; Setty was killed quickly and was wearing his suit with the money inside. Yet, no one questioned Hume's latest version of events.

Dr Gut continued with his examination into the Setty case:

> 'Is it true that after the death of Setty you stole things?'
> 'Yes. A lot of money. Ninety per cent of it was also smothered in blood as a result of the fight. There was a little money that was not smoth-ered in blood. That I used. It is a fact that Scotland Yard only found two or three of the two hundred £5 notes in Setty's pocket. Only two of them could be used. The others were partly smothered in blood and damaged by a knife and could not be used. The fight took place all over the room, and in several rooms there was blood everywhere – on the furniture and on the floor. I sent one carpet to be dyed, but the police found bloodstains on the floor and carpets. I sawed off Setty's head and legs, and the parcels were thrown from an aircraft.'

Hume showed his aggressive side, never far from the surface, in the court, and he said to the interpreter, 'You tell him [Dr Gut] that if it comes to a slanging match, I will rip him to bits physically.' The interpreter did not see fit to translate this remark. The President told the court that Hume served eight years in prison for the crime and Hume added, sarcastically, 'Thanks very much for that, anyway.'[10]

The President then turned to a later stage of Hume's criminal career. He asked if Hume was a Fascist and he replied that was the worst thing anyone could say to him and was an attempt to blacken him.

> 'When you was released from Dartmoor, what were your plans for the future?'

'I had no plans. One can't look into the future.'
'You obtained a second passport under the name of Stephen Bird?'

Hume was less aggressive in his reply, but took a tone calculated to annoy:

'If you think so, it will be so.'

The President was in no mood to accept such comments without making a reprimand:

'You only make yourself ridiculous by such answers.'

He questioned Hume further on the matter of his passports, but was treated to dumb insolence and did not receive a reply. Dr Gut reiterated what he had already said:

'As long as I have been in this criminal court, you are the first person to refuse answers. It will not work in your favour.'

As ever, Hume revealed his violent side, though spoke in a barely audible voice:

'Tell him to get lost.'

This puzzled the interpreter and Hume repeated what he had just said, softly but clearly.[11]

There were other instances of Hume's acerbic manner. He referred to the judge as 'this guy, the old fellow, this bum.' Yet, he did apologise to Dr Gut and this was accepted.[12]

Hume also behaved in other unconventional ways. When listening to Dr Wach, he picked his teeth and cleaned his hand nails with toothpicks. He would then throw these at the jury. He walked about the court and even sat on the jury bench at one stage. He helped the judge hold up large photographs of the bank interior for the jury's benefit. At one point he smirked at a young girl who later remarked, 'I cannot bear him to look at me.' Little did he know it but this was Yvonne Maag, his victim's daughter, who shrank from him and hid from his view.[13]

Further questioning failed to elicit any responses for some minutes. Then the President asked:

'Why did you need the pistol?'
'I felt lonely.'

This reply is typical of inadequate and insecure people who feel that they need the reassurance and power provided by a gun over the law-abiding majority who do not need the psychological crutch provided by a firearm.

Hume was then questioned about the Brentford bank robbery of August 1958. He initially refused to answer, 'sat with one leg crossed over the other, his arms crossed, staring out of the window in total silence', and kept this up for 11 or 12 minutes. However, after consultation with his lawyer, he stated that he had taken part in the robbery and that it was a result of two to three weeks' planning in London. The President pressed him for details:

'Did you plan the bank robbery like a military operation?'
'Yes.'
'How did you carry out this robbery?'
'I went through the door and held up the cashier with the pistol. I had been reconnoitring, and returned just before closing time. I went in and held up the clerk.'
'How did he react?'
'He didn't react quickly.'
'What did you do then?'
'The clerk thought it was a joke. I showed him I wasn't kidding. I shot.'
'Did he fall down?'
'Yes.'
'What happened then?'
'I went through and held up the three other clerks.'
'What did they do?'
'I robbed the Midland Bank. I got about £1,500 sterling. I plead guilty. Is this sufficient for the jury?'[14]

Hume also showed his contempt for the British police. He boasted that he had hoodwinked the officers over his descriptions of the three men he had invented as having given him Setty's corpse to dispose of. On the topic of the Brentford raids, after the evidence from Scotland Yard had been read to the jury and his opinion was asked, he replied, 'If the jury believes some inspector at Scotland Yard, what's the sense in my answering questions?' And as to the fate of those he had shot in Brentford, he replied, 'I don't give a damn.'[15]

The President then abandoned questioning him about the bank raids and asked about Trudi's knowledge of the provenance of Hume's income. He acquitted her of any awareness of the robbery; that had been his secret and his alone. He confirmed that he had arrived in Zurich on 3 August and had remained there for a short time. He was asked if he had made any trips with her and said that he might have done. Then Hume became angry again and shouted, 'I know you are trying to crucify me. I have admitted doing the raid.

The President knows that I have insulted a friend of his, Dr Horvath. He is trying to crucify me under the old pals act.'[16] The interpreter denied that this was so and the President continued his questioning.

The second bank robbery was then the subject of questioning. Dr Gut asked:

> 'When you went back to London to do the second bank raid were you not afraid that you would get caught? You must have been aware that the police were on your track.'
>
> 'I have weak nerves. That's why I often do uncontrollable things.'

How was all the money he stole accounted for, to which Hume merely shrugged his shoulders. He was also asked about Trudi:

> 'Is it true you told Trudi Sommers that you did not want to marry her?'
>
> 'Yes, I didn't want her to fall into the abyss.'[17]
>
> 'What was the reason for your trips to East Germany?'
>
> 'I was in prison with Dr Klaus Fuchs, and he gave me a message to take to his father in Eastern Germany [Fuchs denied this], but the principal reason for my trips to the East was to compare Communist countries to the West.'
>
> 'Did you also work as a spy?'
>
> 'I took some photographs of the United States military airport in Maine, United States, and took them to Eastern Germany and delivered them to the East German Government.'[18]

Hume then admitted to owning three automatic pistols; one of which was still hidden; at the Stadthof Hotel in Zurich, along with a passport under the name of Brown. He told the court he returned to London to rob another bank as revenge and there he shot the manager who had leapt at him:

> 'We fought for a while, and then I fired. I did not know how badly he was hurt, but when I went to Canada I found out from the newspapers that he was in a serious condition.'

Hume then told of his trip to Canada, where he claimed he worked for an electronics company and came back to Switzerland with £1,700 and stayed with Trudi. Then he said he wanted to rob a bank in Zurich:

> 'I must be honest and say that I have no regrets over what happened in England; I didn't give a damn about what happened over there. I did have a conscience, as the judge is undoubtedly aware, over the Swiss raid. I couldn't reconcile myself to doing it. I was going to do it several times but it fell through.'[19]

At some stage on the first day of the trial, he added for good measure that he stole machine guns from a British arsenal 'for Ireland', but there is no corroborating evidence that he had done so as his visits to England in 1958 were of limited duration and chiefly concerned with his two bank robberies in Brentford. Presumably this was a product of his imagination in order to depict himself as a major criminal.[20]

Hume had certainly been verbally and occasionally physically aggressive during the first day of the trial. He was, of course, a violent man by nature and so perhaps this is not surprising. Yet, he may also have been acting in such a way so as to appear to be insane or at least suggest this in the minds of some of the jurors in order to secure a more lenient sentence. Norman Rae made the following observation:

> Every day since . . . Hume, knowing this was to be his swan-song, has baited, bullied, boasted and blustered his way through the most fantastic performance of his life. He has wise cracked his way through hours of questioning; he has spat insult after insult at the patient, long suffering court officials and then turned to wink and grin at me. He has nothing to lose by his arrogance and he knows it.[21]

The President made a plea for more decorum: 'I think Hume has enough to face without making the court unnecessarily hostile to him. Here in Switzerland we have a tradition of courtesy to the prisoner in the dock and we would like it to continue.'[22]

As the trial was reported in the British press, Hume's statement about the parentage of Alison Hume, never hitherto made public, did not pass by unremarked (Cynthia, as far as we know, had no knowledge of the statement in 1950 which alleged this). David Jacobs of M.A. Jacobs & Sons, solicitors of London, issued a statement that night:

> I have been asked by Mrs Cynthia Webb, formerly the wife of Mr Brian Donald Hume, who is at present on trial for murder in Switzerland, to say that the statement alleged to have been made by Hume during the course of the trial to the effect that Setty is the father of his child is completely untrue, and that Mrs Hume, as she then was, gave evidence at the Central Criminal Court, when in 1950 Hume was on trial for the murder of Stanley Setty, that she had never met Setty in her life. In 1951 Mrs Webb's marriage with Hume was dissolved on the grounds of her husband's cruelty, and he is the father of her child.[23]

Hume probably uttered these comments because, as in 1950 when he spoke to the police in Wormwood Scrubs, he held his wife in contempt and perhaps this was a way of attempting to make her life as unpleasant as he could through wounding and untrue comments.

On the second day of the trial, 25 September, Hume was serious and subdued after his boisterous conduct on the opening day. He even showed some remorse; offering to pay compensation out of his 20,000 francs in banks abroad to the people who had suffered as the result of his actions. Yet, there is no evidence that he had such cash, so this may well have been an empty gesture. Hume was again in the witness box. He was questioned about his actions and motivations during the period prior to the bank robbery in Zurich, most of which have already been recounted in the previous chapter. He claimed he had only returned, at great personal risk (a reward having been placed on him), because of Trudi. He thanked the President for not calling her as a witness at the trial.[24]

The questioning then turned to the robbery in Zurich itself and Dr Gut asked:

> 'Is it right that you put the cardboard box on the counter and shot through it?'
> 'Yes. Afterwards, it's easy to realise that the man could have been killed, but at the moment I just shot without thinking.'
> 'You have already told us that the manager of the Brentford branch of the Midland Bank was badly injured. So you had to take into account the possibility of killing?'
> 'Yes, but regarding the English bank manager, I must say that he jumped on me and threw me to the floor. He was the one who attacked me. I think he got what he was out for. I didn't have the pistol just for shooting around, but for necessity.'

He then went through the actual robbery and was asked:

> 'Why did you do it anyway?'
> 'It's difficult to say. I didn't want my conscience to brand me as a coward.'
> 'Did your conscience not remind you that persons might be killed or wounded by shooting, even though you did not believe yourself in your success?'
> 'I didn't think it would be absolutely necessary to shoot anyone.'[25]

There was some discussion about whether Hume had taken any precautions for after the raid when he entered the bank, and what he said. Hume then made another interruption, again to boost his own ego:

'Will you tell the President that if I went there to start blasting and shooting . . . They know that I am a very good shot with a pistol and shot apples in two at twenty-five yards, and if I had wanted to shoot those two I could quite easily have shot the pair of them. At such close range I could not have missed.'

There then followed an exchange between Hume and the President in which there was disagreement as to whether there was any dialogue between Hume and Schenkel when the former arrived at the bank. Hume claimed Schenkel did not speak with him.[26]

The two debated Hume's intentions, with Hume stating:

'If I was going to liquidate them I would have blasted straight at his head.'
'Is it right that you put the cardboard box on the counter and shot through it?'
'Yes.'
'Did you aim your pistol?'
'No, it was just a snap shot as Schenkel moved.'
'Do you realise in what direction you aimed the pistol?'
'Just at the body.'
'What do you have to say about the shot at the clerk? You said you did not want to kill. You shot him just to get him out of the way. Did you take into account that you could have killed him?'
'Afterwards. It's easy to realize that the man could have been killed but at that moment I just shot without thinking.'
'You went there with the intention to shoot in the same way as the raids on the Midland Bank at Brentford. You should have known that you could kill a man.'
'I didn't think about the consequences.'
'But, generally speaking, shooting without aiming could kill a man.'
'Yes, that's clear.'[27]

The shooting of Maag was then discussed, as was the crowd mobbing him. Hume expressed his respect for Fitze:

'This young fellow Ulrich Fitze the bank apprentice deserves any reward from the Midland Bank if they want to give it. This young guy followed me all the way. The others only joined in afterwards.'[28]

It was now time for the first witness for the prosecution to be called and Dr Leinhart took over the role previously adopted by the President. His first witness was Schenkel. He contradicted Hume's statement that he spoke during the initial stage of the robbery. He gave his version of events, that he was shot by Hume, but managed to sound the bank's alarm system. Leinhart asked the lad:

'Are you claiming any damages?'
'Well, the bank paid me and I suffered no financial loss. There is no compensation for pain.'
'I have a nice surprise for you. Hume is going to give you £200.'

This was from the fees that would otherwise come to Hume for the story he was to contribute to a newspaper.[29]

Edwin Hug was the next witness and gave his evidence about Hume's activities at the bank that day. Mrs Hug told the court that she had waited 10 minutes to ring her husband back and Hume laughed and caustically remarked, 'Does she love her husband? Why didn't she call back for ten minutes if she was so upset?' She gave him a fierce glance.[30]

The trial was halted over the weekend and resumed on Monday, 28 September. Further witnesses were called by the prosecution, describing the bank raid and its aftermath. These included Schenkel, Hug, Angstmann, Fitze and Emil Abderholden, the bank manager there. A Zurich ballistics expert, Dr Frey-Sulzer, was summoned to tell how the bullets from a pistol Hume was alleged to have used to shoot Maag had been sent to Scotland Yard for comparison with those bullets used in the Brentford bank robberies. Dr Leinhart asked Frey-Sulzer if Maag could have been saved if a doctor had been on the spot and he was told that there was no chance. During the questioning of witnesses, Hume was allowed to confirm or deny their evidence. Whilst not denying the shooting, it was important that the court established who had done most to arrest him in order to award them the appropriate amount of reward money.[31]

Hume could not resist taunting one of the witnesses called, one Jakob Schlatter, who had helped pursue him after the bank robbery in Zurich. He said of him, 'He is a paper hero. He ran up and pulled my hair – I think he went to a girls' school.' All that Schlatter knew about the business could have been written on a postage stamp, Hume claimed. However, he was complimentary towards Fitze, 'He is a good boy. He is the only guy who chased me all the way. He should get the reward.'[32]

On the fourth day of the trial, Tuesday, 29 September, the defence produced their psychiatric expert, Dr Guggenbuhl-Craig, their only witness save Hume. He had already examined Hume in prison as well as reading extensively on the case. We have already seen that the doctor's report stated that Hume was sane and full of hate, and he read out his report in court.[33]

Hume was then invited by the President to comment on the statements just made. Principally, did Hume believe he was of diminished responsibility? He said, 'I accept that but I want to talk to him for about an hour if possible, if he can spare the time', and the President granted him that wish. Firstly, the doctor was asked which leading psychiatrist (Hume named several) did he follow and was told that it was Carl Jung. He challenged the doctor's findings by accusing him of merely forming his opinions about him based on the newspaper accounts of his bank robberies and of his behaviour in prison. Dr Guggenbuhl-Craig said that he had formed an opinion on Hume prior to having met him, 'But I was agreeably surprised when I met you for the first time. I would not have thought you were a murderer.'[34]

Hume's reply gives an insight into his character:

> I want to empathise this, and I am very likely upsetting my lawyer, that there is nothing that has happened to me physically that had had any effect on me. I want to empathise this and I want the jury to know this, that when I have performed in England any form of violence, that I have done it with determination. But this business in Switzerland was completely against my nature. I could have shot a number of other people and there was no determination or organised plan behind it. It was just something as crazy as going back to England. In England nobody could have stopped me.

The psychiatrist denied having a hostile attitude, as Hume alleged he had, on the basis that he thought Hume had Communist sympathies or tendencies. The psychiatrist stated, 'It is not my job to accuse you of anything. It is only my job to understand you. I did say it would be quite wrong to believe that simply because you were a Communist you were an abnormal character.' When pressed by Hume as to how his report had been formulated, he stressed that his evaluation of Hume was in part due to what he had read about him and what he had learnt in conversation with him.[35]

Dr von Rechenberg told the court, 'Most often accused people seek refuge in psychiatry. I once said I would like just once to defend a man who does not do this but who stands by the deed that he has done. And that is what has happened here.'

It was now time for the final speeches for the prosecution and defence. Dr Leinhart called for a conviction on all five counts of which Hume was accused. He then listed six 'moments of destiny' in Hume's life and made some criticisms of the British judicial system, too. The first moment was when Hume was released from Dartmoor prison on 1 February 1958:

> 'It was a mistake that no probationary period, no control, no super-vision was ordered. It was a mistake that he was able to change his name without any precautionary steps being taken. If Brown (Hume) had been determined to lead a new life, then a new passport would have been perfectly in order. But he did not improve himself. Thus he was let loose on humanity.'

The next key moment was when Hume received £2,000 from the *Sunday Pictorial* for his story. 'That money was given to him to dispose of as he wished', and he used it to travel and not work. Another key moment was:

> 'I should like to name a failing in the law of England – that it is not possible for an appeal [by the Crown] if it is subsequently discov-ered that a person has been incorrectly or insufficiently sentenced. Brown was able to announce to the whole world that he was the murderer of Setty. He was not brought before a court and punished, because he had been acquitted by that court. This would have been grounds for an appeal under Swiss justice.'[36]

Dr Leinhart then added that great injustice had been done to Mrs Som-mer as she had been taken into custody on suspicion of concealing evidence against Hume. This charge had been dropped. Although she was offered com-pensation, she declined as she preferred to take money from newspapers for her story rather than from the Treasury.[37]

Dr Dieter von Rechenberg then spoke. He agreed with all the points made in the indictment, 'Hume has admitted he is guilty and that he is fully respon-sible for his acts', but whilst he was 'not the defender of the British Crown', wanted to stress that there were parts of Switzerland where the legal system was similar to that of Britain. He was concerned, though, that there was noth-ing known of Hume's formative years and declared, 'If indeed the anomalies of Hume's character have their origins in meningitis, then the case of Hume has a tragic quality. Then it is possible to have pity for the accused.'[38]

The trial concluded on Wednesday, 30 September. Hume had pleaded guilty. He smiled at those assembled and said, 'This is the end.' The jury left the court room to consider their verdict.

Victor Sims was, naturally, covering the trial for the *Sunday Pictorial*. He observed:

> The sensational trial, at which the cocky killer snarled, sneered and hurled abuse at the judge, was almost over. Handcuffed and chained, Hume was hustled from the court by armed police guards to await the jury's return. Cameramen's flash bulbs popped as Hume jerked the guards to a halt, 'I must speak to Herr Sims' he called out. The guards dragged him away. He was taken along a corridor to a sealed off room at the end of the court building. But one guard turned back and beckoned me to follow him. Then came an amazing interview. Bolts were drawn. A door burst open. Hume was sitting at a table that was bare except for a half-eaten slab of chocolate. Two guards were unlocking the chains that bound his wrists to his ankles. Around the room, backs to the wall, stood five police in steel blue uniforms. Three had pistols in shiny black leather holsters. Two more stood at each side of a large window, tommy guns cocked to stop any attempt at escape.[39]

Hume greeted Sims like an old friend, he shook hands and told him that the police officers had really been very good to him. Sims sat down opposite Hume, who seemed calm and unperturbed about the jury's deliberations. He was still concerned about his public image. 'I hope you will tell everyone that I am taking it like a man.' Hume looked up at the clock and then leaned towards Sims, 'Let's talk . . . fast', he urged, being, of course, unsure how long the jury would take to reach a verdict.

Sims noted:

> His wild dark eyes burned into me as he said, 'I didn't do this murder. It was the other Donald Hume. You see, there are two Humes. One wants to be normal. The other doesn't want to be a coward. It was the second Hume who pulled the trigger. I will possibly have to serve a life sentence because of him.'

As with most criminals, he was trying to distance himself from all responsibility for his actions, but it also suggests that he was not the monster as depicted by the press.[40]

A slip of paper fell to the floor. It was a note to Hume from the Director of Regensdorf prison, advising him of a small fine for damage to his cell during a fight with guards there. Hume then displayed the angry side of his character, which was never far from the surface. He justified his violence, 'Well, they wouldn't tell me why they were shifting me. And I get mad at people who try to boss me about.' He then talked excitedly about two books he had written whilst in prison. One was titled 'Scream Loud and Die.' He wrote another about a police officer who shot a man's dog and was murdered for it (shades of his 1958 version of the murder of Setty here). After some laughter and chatter about his Brentford bank robberies, 'his face twisted in rage and he raved at the findings of the psychiatrist who examined him in jail who said he was over-sexed and incapable of loving anyone.'[41]

Hume vehemently denied that the psychiatrist could be correct. He told Sims, 'I may be more over-sexed than some of the Swiss. But I treated Trudi better than any of them. I'll always love Trudi. I'm crazy about her', he stormed. He then asked a guard to show Sims his possessions. The cardboard box contained all Hume's worldly possessions, 'a pathetic collection', thought Sims. These were a little toy mechanical Mickey Mouse which Trudi had won at a fair and he said he would keep it. There was a crushed red rose she had sent him in prison. There was a love letter she had sent him and a blue pullover she had knitted for him. Then there was his will, with Trudi as the sole beneficiary, though given that he had no monetary possessions, this was very much a token gesture and echoed the one made by the equally penniless John George Haigh when facing the gallows ten years previously.[42]

Hume was at pains to stress the genuine nature of their love, he wanted to be seen, of course, in a positive light:

> 'Trudi and I have made a secret love pact. She has promised me that she will never marry anyone else. No matter how long they manage to keep me in jail – and I am warning everyone that there is still a lot of the old Donald Hume in me – I know that Trudi will always keep in touch with me.'

Sims asked if Hume had any regrets about killing Maag or injuring Lewis and Aires in Brentford. His response was swift: 'The only thing I am sorry about is all the trouble I have caused Trudi.' This indifference to the sufferings of others is typical psychopathic behaviour. It is worth noting that the abortive bank robbery and shooting of Maag took up a mere two sentences in his 1959 press confession compared with pages about the Brentford robberies; clearly not an episode on which he wished to dwell, unlike his earlier 'triumphs.'[43]

Hume smoked casually and mused on his fate:

> 'You know, it would be better for me if they were out there deciding whether I should be sentenced to death. The easiest thing in the world is to die. The hardest thing for someone like me is to live.'

Footsteps could be heard outside. The jury had clearly finished their deliberations – they had taken almost 3 hours – and Hume was about to be brought back to the court room to hear his sentence. He was chewing chocolate, cracking jokes. Hume stood up as the guards put his chains back on him. As they did so, he thrust a large sheet of papers into Sims' hands and said, 'I shall probably be an old man by the time I get out of here. This is the true story of a criminal that everyone ought to read.' Sims later admitted to having nightmares about that interview, dreaming that Hume and he switched places and that he was trying to convince the guards to release him, which they refused to do.[44]

Once everyone was back in court, the jury gave the verdict of guilty on all counts and so Dr Gut made the following statement:

> 'The Court, on the verdict of the jury, finds the accused guilty first of murder, secondly of attempted murder, thirdly of robbery, fourthly of repeatedly threatening and fifthly of offences against the Swiss federal laws concerning sojourn and residence.'

He addressed Hume and added:

> 'Persons sentenced bear their imprisonment better if they take it with a certain amount of goodwill and cheerfulness, and the burden is less heavy to bear if one feels that the punishment is just. You will find the punishment harder to bear if you oppose it inside yourself.'

The plea of the defence that Hume was medically unfit and should be placed in a care facility was rejected. He was deemed not to be mad but merely bad.[45]

Hume then received the court's sentence. It was life imprisonment with hard labour. Should he be released for good behaviour, he would then be barred from Swiss soil for fifteen years. He also had to pay 1,750 francs towards court costs. As with most of those sentenced, he had nothing to say on his own behalf at this point. As Sims wrote, 'He knew it was bound to happen. I knew it was bound to happen too.' Before he was led away, he said, 'I am satisfied with the way the trial went. I knew it was bound to end this way. I got what was coming.' However, his anger flared up within him once again, for when he was being taken away, he suddenly ran down the stairs of the court house, dragging the guards to whom he was handcuffed, with him. Outside he kicked out at a photographer and had to be thrown into the awaiting van to take him to Regensdorf prison. This was the country's prison reserved for the most dangerous of criminals; not only murderers, but in the 1960s terrorists, too. Oddly enough he asked for a trumpet so he could play in the prison band. The President added, later, 'Life imprisonment for this kind of man means for life. He will never be let out of gaol not this one.'[46]

Hume spoke to a journalist after sentencing, 'I have led a bad life, but I take my punishment like a man. I want the English people to know I took my punishment courageously. If I smile it will be said I have no character. If I do not smile people will think I do like Swiss justice.'[47]

Hume learnt that the first three months there would be very severe. He was not allowed to talk to anyone, except when the prison officers spoke to him. He would be awoken at 5 am each day. He was only allowed to write one letter per month. His only visitor would be the prison chaplain. He could work in his cell but not with metal. He was to be allowed reading materials. Other privileges would accrue thereafter if he was well behaved.[48]

Norman Rae later talked to the judge and the latter told him, 'The sentence was life imprisonment. And that means life. Hume will never be set free and the prison authorities will take good care he does not escape.' Rae referred to Hume as 'the man the world may never see again.'[49]

Hume was now described thus:

> Plumpish, ruddy, full-lipped and crowned with thick dark hair, it can register a pleasant smile. But the heavy eyebrows that tend to meet over the well-marked nose suggest a violent temper. There is, too, a sour downward twist to the mouth, and the hard jaw line shows ruthlessness. But the really frightening thing about the face of Donald Hume is the eyes. The eyes are round, grey and penetrating. In moments of rage they stare out with a frozen unblinking malevolence.[50]

Chapter 11

Later Years, 1959–98

The later years of Hume's life are less well documented, but are not unknown. Even so, the available evidence is far more scanty, partly because some of it (chiefly medical records) is withheld from researchers for decades to come and partly because for most of the period he was in secure custody and so his scope for action was very limited.

Sims took Hume's papers back to England and as he had done in the previous year, showed them to officials at Scotland Yard. They were then published, with photographs, over four issues of the *Sunday Pictorial* in October and November 1959. Apparently this was in the public interest, 'Because of the lessons that can be learnt from the confession of a double killer' and 'Because it provides a terrible warning to anyone who might be tempted to follow the same vicious path.' Once again, Hume was in the limelight at home. He ended his articles with this, 'And believe me, there's still a lot of the old Donald Hume left – even if he is serving life imprisonment in a lousy Swiss jail.' Apparently Trudi persuaded him to write these and that the fee, £1,200, be paid to his victims; the Maags receiving £1,000.[1]

Hume used the articles, as he had done in 1958, to justify his actions. He did not deny that he had robbed two banks in Brentford and shot bank staff there. He did so, he said, because of his love for Trudi and the need to have money for their life together. His second robbery was justified in his eyes because one of the cashiers had lied to him and so this man was to blame for the subsequent crimes committed by Hume. These crimes were painted as being successful as Hume initially eluded the law. He said very little about the robbery in Zurich which had ended in failure and dealt with the killing of Maag with extreme brevity. There was a great deal about his love for Trudi. He was the romantic hero, a criminal, but one that was dashing and motivated by the highest of ideals. The lot of his victims was downplayed or dismissed. As with all criminal autobiographies, it attempts to portray the subject in the best possible light, though it is possible that Hume believed his own propaganda.

Journalists had made Hume well known as a monster. But after his incarceration at Regensdorf they began to lose interest; he was now old news. Hume was disappointed, for he always asked visitors if there was anything about him in the press and became depressed by the negative answer. According to Playfair and Sington, the press 'helped to make him, take the view that he's now an old story, a dead story, a story very much told.' Only if he escaped would he be news and apparently criminologists agreed.[2]

Midland Bank paid out the £6,000 reward money it had offered in 1958 for anyone helping to apprehend the robber of their Brentford branch. The money went to the public prosecutor of the canton of Zurich and they distributed it thus. Fitze was given the most; 14,000 francs, then the Maag family, 12,000 francs. Angstmann, Schenkel and Hug each received 10,000 francs. Five others received between 1,000 and 7,000 francs. Meanwhile, Trudi signed a contract for £400 for her to appear in a film about her life with Hume (it does not seem to have ever been made). Yet, another newspaper stated that she was eager to make money out of Hume but quickly disappeared from the limelight. Another account states that she was an advisor only and that although Hume initially agreed, he became suspicious of her involvement in it and love turned to hate.[3]

Mrs Webb's ordeal was not over. On the first day of Hume's second trial, when asked if he had been married with a child in 1949, he said, 'Yes, but it was not mine. The father was Stanley Setty.' This was reported in *The Times* newspaper and Cynthia was even more upset than she had been in 1958 when the *Sunday Pictorial* reported Hume's words about her, which implied her immorality and secret meetings with Setty. On 27 May 1960, at the Queen's Bench Court, barristers argued her case against those for *The Times*, before Mr Justice Pearson (Sir Colin Hargreaves Pearson, 1899–1980). Cynthia's barrister argued that these words were defamatory and libellous with the 'plain suggestions of illegitimacy and bastardy.' Those acting for for *The Times* claimed that 'it was part of a fair and accurate report of judicial proceedings publicly heard before a criminal court of competent jurisdiction.'[4]

The case was heard over three days. There was much discussion over whether the said phrase was crucial for an understanding of the trial or was merely salacious. The defendants could not plead unintentional defamation because it was clear that these words were derogatory. Nor had the newspaper made an apology to the plaintiff. There could be no blanket ruling as to whether a newspaper was privileged to report remarks made in court; each case had to be heard on its own merits.[5]

On the last day of the hearing, 2 June, the judge stated that the defence could show that Hume was a British subject, had been tried in an English court in 1950, had been sentenced, had subsequently been wanted for robberies in England and then was put on trial for murder in Switzerland. The words objected to were part of an accurate report of the trial. Was there a qualified privilege for reporting a foreign court? It was concluded that because the Swiss trial examined Hume's previous crimes, the comments he made about his wife were germane because, according to Hume, her alleged activities resulted in Hume's jealousy and so provided a motive for his killing Setty. This is was what Hume then said. It was not fact that was being reported. Thus the judge gave judgement for the defendants.[6]

The first book to be solely concerned with the Hume case was written by John Williams, who worked on the *Sunday Pictorial*. It was first published in 1958 and was reissued with amendments and additions in the following years. The introduction was written by Sims, who had obtained the confession from Hume in May 1958. It was reviewed in one newspaper, who stated it was 'full of interesting material and makes, despite rather excessive popularisation, a lively and instructive read.' The reviewer thought that the section on Hume's immediate post-war business interests was its best part but that it 'rather skimps his trial in Switzerland', which is covered in a page compared with the earlier trial which is detailed in three chapters. Overall, though, the verdict was favourable for presenting 'a fairly well rounded picture of him.'[7] It was reprinted the following year with a few supplementary comments about his life in gaol. It does not consider the whereabouts of Mrs Hume on the day of Setty's murder and it accepts as true Hume's statement in 1958 as to the murder of Setty, as well as some of Hume's statements on the day afterwards without mentioning the contrary ones by Mrs Stride. Needless to say, the author was unaware of the statement made by Hume in Wormwood Scrubs in 1950.

Williams provides much information about Hume's initial spell of incarceration in Regensdorf prison, as prisoner number 22. He was obliged to wear a brown prison uniform with a red number tag. His head was shaved. By Christmas, though, after three months in solitary confinement, he was allowed to receive parcels from the outside world. The faithful Trudi sent some and then she visited him on New Year's Day 1960, bringing red roses for him. Yet, his behaviour deteriorated as 1960 progressed. He told another correspondent that he was planning to break out soon. He also became unruly, throwing stones at the chaplain during Sunday services and breaking the windows of the prison bakehouse.[8]

The Governor, Emil Meyer, tried to treat Hume as a reasonable human being, but without success. New prisoners were usually designated as Class One and placed in solitary confinement, but most progressed to Class Two within six months and were permitted to mix with their fellow prisoners. Notes sent to Hume to reprove him for his conduct were failures. He had to be assigned three prison officers when in the exercise yard. Occasional visitors, such as British journalists, reported him to be irrepressible and cocky. He told them he would soon be out of prison. Yet, the regime was not severe. He was allowed a typewriter to write stories and a small library of books.[9]

In August 1960, following rumours that he was plotting to escape (Hume alleged, 'I've been given a large map to stick on my cell wall. I'm marking places I'm going to – and don't kid yourself it won't come along soon'), prison officers searched his cell and found nothing suspicious. But he resisted them and was given ten days' solitary confinement with a strict diet of bread, water and soup. This only made him more aggressive, shouting at the staff, hurling things around his cell and throwing stones whilst in the exercise yard. He was named 'The Monster of Regensdorf.' This title probably appealed to his vanity as a 'tough guy.'[10]

The failed prison break-out had, apparently, been made with one Ernst Deubelbeiss. This man, along with Kurt Schurmann, had kidnapped and murdered a banker in 1951 for political reasons. Apparently, Hume and Deubelbeiss competed to be the toughest prisoner in Regensdorf. The episode showed that Hume, contrary to later protestations, may have had some knowledge of German, unless his fellow inmates knew some English.[11]

The following year saw an even more extreme outbreak of violence. Hume had been frustrated in not being allowed his favourite brand of cigarettes. So he broke up his bed in the cell and made the pieces of iron into lethal weapons. He threatened to kill the first man who entered his cell. Eventually tear gas grenades had to be thrown into the cell before the prison officers rushed in and overpowered him. This led him being incarcerated into a specially built double-doored solitary cell and Meyer called a press conference to explain why he had to take such drastic steps, 'Where I need one warder for the average prisoner, I need three for Hume.'[12]

Yet, on the other hand, Hume tried to portray himself as an essentially gentle man. He was known by the prison officers as the 'Crazy Birdman' because he fed his bread ration to the birds. Hume claimed, 'I have on the whole a great deal more sympathy for wildlife than human life. I would not harm a fly.' This is similar to Haigh's statement in the press in 1949 that he would prefer to kill a human than a dog.[13]

The question of Hume's extradition was raised on 17 October 1960 by Dr von Rechenberg, but was turned down. A year later, Hume requested an extradition, possibly because of the special conditions under which he was now housed. The Swiss Embassy in London was involved in the matter in April 1962. Yet, they were told, 'Mr Barry advised them that there would be no purpose in extraditing Hume, as this could not be done in respect of a crime committed in another country and secondly there was not now sufficient evidence to extradite him.'[14]

Hume wanted to be extradited in order to serve his sentence in a British prison. The Foreign Office and the public prosecutor were unsure whether this would be legal. The former believed that Hume's solicitors might be able to release him under habeas corpus and the public prosecutor stated, 'This is a risk the department of the public prosecutor has no wish to take in view of Hume's past history.' In 1962 the police thought there was still a good chance of convicting him over the bank robberies. The Foreign Office's view was, however, 'the British authorities do not wish to have Hume back at any price.'[15]

In 1965 Hume wrote to Sir Frank Soskice (1902–79), Home Secretary. He still wanted to return to England, the country he'd been so happy to leave in 1958, but now he claimed to be insane. He cited the example of another British bank robber called Brian Cowell who had shot a policeman dead during a bank robbery in Mannheim, West Germany, in 1957. Cowell, in early January 1965, had been found to have been suffering from schizophrenia and so was deported to Britain and sent to Broadmoor. Again, his pleas were no more successful than before.[16] It seems probable that Hume was far from insane at this point, but wanted to be returned to England, and having read about Cowell in the press, tried to convince Soskice that he was of a similar mental condition.

The Swiss authorities turned down Hume's pleas for deportation on the basis that there were insufficient grounds to do so and because British officialdom had not made that request. Hume became angry about the latter and blasted what he saw as the hypocrisy of liberal pressure groups. He wrote, 'These organisations in England show no interest yet they go into apoplectic fits if a coloured guy gets three months solitary in South Africa. There are some real great guys in the Labour Party . . . but there are others who will not help unless you are in a South African nick or in Alabama.'[17] Clearly, Hume could not differentiate between his own violent crime and those who protested against racial injustice.

Hume was now convict 133 in cell 36. It was only 8 by 10ft. Papers were strewn about the place. Hume collected news cuttings about his exploits and trial, and these were plastered all over the walls. He spent time writing to politicians in Britain. The chaplain thought the room was 'always utterly untidy, a mess' and that Hume was a 'most pitiable sight.' On one occasion a British diplomatic visitor was harangued by Hume as being an imposter.[18]

Prison inmates have a great deal of spare time. One of Hume's recreations was painting. This was only possible because a Quaker organisation had given him painting materials. One painting was a *Present for a friend of a friend* and it showed a gleaming bullet amongst flowers and represented the revenge of a man on a woman who had jilted him. He also painted the Virgin Mary and much more. He held an art exhibition in his cell, which a journalist referred to as 'a psychiatric firework display . . . The colours startle. Geometric patterns explode through still life. Animals are portrayed in loneliness and sympathy.' Hume wanted to offer the animal pictures to the World Wildlife Fund for sale, the Christian picture to the English church at Zurich (he was also an apparent convert to Catholicism) and another painting was for his mother, whom he alleged he was still in touch with up to 1949, not until the 1930s as he had told Sims.[19]

There was a hiatus in his painting because he had learnt that his application for repatriation had been turned down. This led to him attacking prison officers with broken glass. He then lost his privileges and was placed in an underground cell in the darkness, labelled as prisoner 22.[20]

Hume painted at least three pictures in 1964. One was *The Unhappy Clown*, an oil painting measuring 50 by 33.5cm. It shows a wolf's head in a cap, with the following message, 'Don't ban the bomb (a reference to the Campaign for Nuclear Disarmament in Britain). Remember 1066 and Bill the Conqueror.' The other was also an oil, and a little larger, 59.6 by 44.3cm, titled *The End of the Mermaid*. It shows a woman's head with a 1960s hairstyle, a mermaid's tail and ten penguins swimming around her. Possibly the female figure represented Trudi. Another picture is a still life mounted, oil on board, 60.5 by 45cm showing a green bowl and oranges, together with a blue decapitated head, which presumably is a reference to the fate of Setty. These were transferred to the Guttmann Memorial Trust in 1968 and then to the Institute of Psychiatry, Bethlem Royal Hospital, in 1984 and are now in the Bethlem Museum of the Mind. Hume exhibited his works whilst at Regensdorf.[21]

Hume also painted two more pictures which can be viewed as being semi-autobiographical, relating to his own experiences. One was *Dartmoor Prison Quarry* showing a convict working with a pickaxe, which is presumably meant to be himself. The other is *The Lynched Thief's only Mourner* and shows the lower legs and feet of a hanged man with a backcloth of Alpine scenery and a dog at the man's feet. The man is clearly Hume, as he might have been had the crowd in Zurich had their wish following the murder of Maag, and the dog is meant to represent Tony; his only friend (Trudi had clearly been forgotten by this time). Both show a degree of self pity on the part of the artist.[22]

Hume played a minor part in the 1965–6 re-investigation into whether there had been a miscarriage of justice in the trial and execution of Timothy Evans, a man he had met in Brixton prison in 1949. Judge Daniel Brabin led the investigation and submissions from all interested parties were welcomed. As Hume had met Evans, he wrote to the inquiry to give a different version of events than that offered in 1958. This time he alleged that Evans had indeed confessed to him to murdering his daughter. He also penned a few acerbic words about Ludovic Kennedy (1919–2008), a journalist whose book *Ten Rillington Place* (1961) made the case for Evans' complete innocence. According to Hume, 'I know him from experience to be a phoney who has used the Evans case for nothing else than to further his literary ambitious and make money out of it.'[23]

In 1962 he had been reading, in *The Sunday Times*, extracts from Hugh Thomas' book on the Spanish Civil War. This led him to asking for a copy of the book, because he insisted that he had fought in that war on the Republican side in his young Communist days and he wanted to correct the author on his facts, which allegedly ran contrary to his experiences. This was another instance of his fantasy of having taken a heroic part in events which he had not.[24]

Hume was interested, eventually, in reading English newspapers brought in by the British Consul, after first tending to tear them up. He also spent time writing letters to British politicians who he thought could assist his cause. These included George Brown (1914–85), Foreign Secretary from 1966–8, and backbench Labour MP Michael Foot (1913–2010).[25]

In 1970 a former inmate of the gaol gave a statement about Hume's condition in the prison:

> His window is heavily screened and God alone can imagine what the air in the chamber (thirteen feet by six feet six inches) must be like.
>
> He has no bed, merely a mattress on the floor, and his food is passed to him through a hatch in a steel grille and which is faced with steel plate. Outside this is the normal cell door of heavy wood, steel lined.
>
> This is where he lives and is treated like an animal from prehistoric times.
>
> His sole excursions are twice daily trips to empty his chamber pot into a sink 20 yards from his cell, and daily half hour sessions pacing to and fro under the gaze of a few guards.
>
> He sees and speaks to scarcely anyone, but his shouts and cries can be heard by the inmates on all sides of him.
>
> Understandably, in England, he would have been certified insane long ago.
>
> His cries remain unanswered. More strongly caged than any zoo animal, he remains behind his steel plated bars and fed food that

would cause riots in any English jail, and raise the eye brows of the average pig.

Hume has always been a violent man. When the door to his cell is opened for any reason, there are always three guards because they know that if he had a small chance he would attack anyone.

I can honestly say that I think what keeps him alive is the hate he feels for everybody.

Hume no longer resembled the smart chap he had once appeared. He resembled a scarecrow, having grown his hair long and was bearded. Then he had it all shaved off and looked like a skinhead. He refused to wash or bathe and when he was forced to change clothes once a week his old clothes were burnt.[26]

Hume's appalling state was caused by his own behaviour. He slept on a mattress because he had broken his bed and the prison authorities were not going to give him that opportunity again. Privileges had been withdrawn because he had abused them. For instance, in early 1970 he had begun to use his oil paints to daub paint over his body, his clothing and his room and had done so repeatedly and so there was no more painting for Hume. His aggressive behaviour led to his visitors, other than legal advisers from Zurich, stopping coming. He alleged that he could not mix with other prisoners because he claimed that he had not troubled to learn German (though as noted this is almost certainly incorrect), and in any case as the British Consul, Hugh Gilmartin, noted, 'He makes such a racket at night, shouting and bellowing that his fellow prisoners frequently complain.' Had he not been in solitary confinement he would undoubtedly have faced a beating.[27]

Prison conditions in Regensdorf were poor. Swiss prison reformers argued in the 1960s that the cells were narrow and gloomy. Hygiene was poor. There was little in the way of therapy or rehabilitation. Meyer imposed strict punishments on any inmate who broke the rules.[28]

Apparently Hume was deemed Switzerland's worst prisoner ever for he continued his vicious and aggressive ways. Three guards were always needed to attend to him whether at feeding times or when he was in the exercise yard. Dr Arthur Bachmann and Emil Meyer considered him to be the greatest problem facing the Zurich judiciary and the latter claimed Hume gave him sleepless nights. They deemed Hume was evil and lacked any human emotions. The question they pondered in 1970 was whether Hume was also mentally ill. Switzerland lacked any hospitals or prisons for people deemed 'homicidal lunatics' and though Britain was not enthusiastic about extraditing him, considered that Britain would have a moral duty to house him if he could be certified as insane.[29]

One inmate told how Hume was planning to batter his way out of prison by using a sawn-off leg of an iron bedstead. His moods varied from being affable to being savage. He had bursts of uncontrollable violence, smashing his cell and trying to attack both prison officers and even the governor.[30]

The Revd Thomas Quinn, chaplain to the British community in Zurich, had seen Hume in the summer, but did not despair, 'It is difficult to communicate with him. I hope to see him again soon and to establish some sort of relationship eventually.'[31]

It was difficult to know what should be done with him. Mr Werner Schlegel, Secretary of the Zurich Justice Department, was unable to have Hume removed to a psychiatric clinic in Switzerland because Hume needed a permanent guard of three men and he could not be easily isolated from other patients. The British Home Office refused to take him, 'I regret to inform you that the difficulties which would be raised by such a transfer would be insurmountable.' This was because the crime for which Hume was held in Switzerland was a crime he had committed in that country. There was no provision for him being detained in England on a charge made by a foreign court if he was brought over. This upset Schlegel as the case came up for review in 1974, and when it did, the outcome was that Hume would have to remain in Regensdorf.[32]

A psychiatrist stated that Hume was no longer sane as he had been in 1959, claiming he was suffering from 'incarceration psychosis.' This meant that he was no longer always in touch with reality and this could lead him to indulge in bizarre behaviour, which fits the symptoms known and stated above. This form of mental illness was not uncommon amongst long-term prisoners, but in Hume's case it was even more pronounced because he only spoke broken German and so could not fully communicate with his fellow prisoners. Hans Joerg Braunschweig, a Swiss official, said that Hume's deteriorating mental state meant that he needed to be in an English gaol or clinic where the surroundings and fellows would be more familiar and so would stand a chance of retaining his former health. Schlegel agreed, 'We feel this is a desperate and tragic case. A lot of people seem to have lost interest in Hume.' The British newspaper which published this lengthy article concluded that the Home Office had left Hume to die in a smelly foreign cell, 'Evil as he was, in the name of humanity, should we allow this to happen?'[33]

Hume was not without visitors. Ann Riley, aged 23 and a trapeze artiste from Eastleigh, Hampshire, met him having been part of an act that had performed for the prisoners. He was pleasant and quietly spoken but egotistical, telling her, 'Good afternoon, madam. You have heard of me I am sure. I am Donald Hume.' He showed her his paintings and talked of his love for animals. He boasted he had the record for being in solitary confinement the longest – 107 days – and told her that he blamed his mother's early treatment of him for making him at war with society. Ann also stated:

> He counts the life of an animal higher than the life of a human. What upset him when he was arrested was that they did away with his dog because they could find no one to look after it. I think he is crazy but he fascinates me. I feel no empathy for what he has done but he is paying for what he has done and if it is possible to help him a little there is no harm in it.

Ann visited him several times and helped supply him with artistic materials.[34]

Father Marcos Periera saw him regularly from 1968–74. However, his visit in December 1974 may well have been his last for he reported:

> I took some fruit, cheese and biscuits, things I know he likes. In the past he welcomed me and chatted freely. But this time he shouted that he did not want to see anyone. He switched off the light and took a menacing step towards me, screaming loudly. I hurriedly left and a guard slammed the doors shut. It was a most unnerving experience. Physically he is a mass of muscles. As strong as an ox. He does exercise daily – there is little else for him to do. But I am worried about his mental condition.[35]

Hume's lawyer found him to be a difficult case, too. Braunschweig reported, 'When I last went to see Hume he behaved most strangely. I was smoking a pipe. As soon as he saw it, he put his nose in the air, turned his back and declined to see me.'[36]

Some time later, Monique Fischer, a prison social worker, expressed similar concerns:

> He is a very difficult man. Very violent, still. I can talk to him only through bars because it would be too dangerous otherwise. He is under constant observation by at least three guards. He spends nearly all his time in his cell sitting and listening to the radio, although once or twice he has tried to paint. When he's out on exercise he marches about like a soldier, moving briskly and swinging his arms. He is in good health physically, but he is living in another world. It is impossible for anyone to visit him alone. This has been

expressly forbidden by the Justice Department after trouble a few years ago when he became very violent.[37]

Hume was deemed 'highly dangerous.' Therefore, he was sent for psychiatric examination and it was eventually decided that he should be released as an undesirable alien and discussions be entered into with the British authorities for his despatch there. The Swiss concluded that Hume was insane in April 1976.[38]

It is possible that Hume was suffering from paranoia. All his life he had claimed that he had been persecuted. Prison psychosis was another assessment. Hume had not made friends in prison, possibly due to a limited knowledge of German. Dr Walter Riebi, a Swiss psychiatrist of the Justice Department, seemed to confirm that, writing, 'His state of mind is that of being permanently persecuted. He has had times when he delivers wild speeches in English to an imaginary crowd. When on daily exercise in Regensdorf prison yard he has had to be accompanied by several warders as he may at any time act with extreme violence.'[39]

Since at least 1971 the Swiss authorities began to press to deport Hume. The Foreign Office insisted that he stayed where he was. There was another request in 1974. In August 1975 the Swiss had Dr Lieselotte Meier study Hume and compile a report. It recommended that Hume be repatriated. Herr Weilenmann of the Zurich Department of Justice informed the British Consul General there, Mr P.D. Stobart, of this on 18 August, promising to include a translation of the report made by Dr Meier and arguing that Hume be sent to a secure institution in Britain. British officials were sent a copy. Part of the report read as follows:

> As he would be just as lonely and shut off in the local psychiatric institutions, as in Regensdorf, because of language difficulties it is essential that he be transferred to a mental home in more familiar surroundings, ie the serving of his sentence here must be interrupted, but only on condition that he is placed in a British mental home. In any case his condition here is untenable for himself for psychiatric and human considerations.
>
> The state of his illness does not appear to be reversible at present. Whether it can be cured in his own country can be neither confirmed nor denied with certainty . . . he has no perception of his disturbed behaviour . . . [we must] not allow him to be regarded as fit for further confinement here in Regensdorf.[40]

One British official wrote, 'It would seem difficult, in this situation, to avoid at least considering the transfer of Brown [Hume].' A letter put the situation thus, 'We have to steer a rather delicate course here. While we would clearly prefer not to have him back, it is not easy after all these years to be totally negative of a proposal for the return of a British subject to the country.' There was the fear that the Swiss might, 'in exasperation simply deport Hume here and leave it to us.' In that case it might be difficult to detain him, so collaboration with the Swiss was necessary.[41]

Although the principle that Hume should be returned had been conceded, grudgingly, a second opinion was wanted. The Home Office was involved by December 1975, Roy Jenkins (1920–2003), Home Secretary from 1974–6, noting on 21 December, 'We must be careful as we possibly can that nothing goes wrong. Release or escape or any slip up would rightly cause great public concern.' It was decided that Dr Patrick Gerard McGrath (1916–94), Superintendent of Broadmoor from 1959–81, be sent to Switzerland to evaluate Hume for himself. On 3 March 1976, ministers agreed that Dr McGrath would go to the prison and so provide them with a full psychiatric assessment of Hume. They wanted him to be able to decide whether he could be compulsorily detained in Broadmoor. After having studied previous reports, Hume was examined by the doctor on 5 May for 2 hours and for a further 90 minutes the following day. The Foreign Office did not want to appear to the Swiss to be over eager to accept him but on 6 July decided to indicate their 'reluctant acceptance of a marginal responsibility.'[42]

The Foreign Office told Emerson on 12 August that it was planned for Hume to return in eight days' time and this was confirmed on the 16th. In the company of two Swiss police officers ('Those two with me are fine fellows, but it wasn't good in jail', said Hume), he arrived at Heathrow airport on Friday, 20 August 1976, on Swiss Air Flight 804, having travelled on an emergency passport under the name of Henry Simpson. He was handcuffed and manacled, his left arm chained to his right leg. He told a detective there, 'Look what they've done to me. And they even made me shave my hair. But I have taught them a lot over there – nearly all I know.' Despite the chains, he performed a little jig for the assembled reporters. They were met by Dr McGrath and other officials, including Dr Peter Scott (1914–77), a psychiatrist used to dealing with those involved in crime, and the airport's own medical inspector, a Dr Cooper.[43]

He arrived at the Broadmoor Institution, Crowthorne, Berkshire, 90 minutes later. Broadmoor was Britain's first purpose-built establishment for the criminally insane, founded in 1863. Under section 26 of the Mental Health

Act of 1959 two doctors examined him and decided he was suitable for incarceration there because of his mental health. He was initially due to be detained there for one year, but this could be extended dependent on subsequent medical re-examinations. Mr C. Emerson wrote in 1976, 'A Tribunal discharge of such a notorious character as Hume is rather unlikely in the foreseeable future.' Dr McGrath put it more strongly, writing in 1979, that there was 'an extremely remote prospect his patient will ever be released.' This was because he knew Hume had no next of kin whom he was in contact with and that he wanted that protection from the press that only Broadmoor could provide (the press would need the superintendent's permission to contact him and that would not be granted).[44]

Whilst we have no account of Hume's arrival at the hospital, fellow patient Ronald Kray, who was admitted three years later, did write about what happened to him and it is probable that Hume's experience was similar. The van taking him left the main road and turned into what appeared to be a large park, and through a tiny window in the van he saw a sign on a white board, 'Broadmoor Special Hospital. Private Property.' They drove up a hill, which became steeper, passing pine trees which seemed to make the day darker. Then the hospital came into full view. 'It was big. Big and silent. Depressing really. All dark red bricks and high walls.'[45]

They drove through two large wooden doors, then through padlocked gates into the main courtyard. It was quiet and deserted. The various accommodation blocks were situated around the courtyard. The patient was taken to the admission ward and met by male nurses and a social worker. His height and weight were measured. He was given a bath, watched by the nurses. A cup of tea was provided and he was then locked up in a bare room, 9 by 6ft, containing only a mattress and without any natural light. That evening he was allowed a cigarette, was told what would be in store for him in the next few weeks and that the first few days and weeks would be the most difficult.[46]

All patients entered the hospital through the admission ward, which was on the bottom floor of Somerset House, one of the accommodation wards. The daily routine began at 7 am when patients' rooms were unlocked. They then emptied out their chamber pots, washed and shaved and lined up as the razors were counted lest anyone used them for violent purposes. The new arrivals then went into the day room, where they sat down until 9 am, when they returned to their rooms. The day room had five rows of chairs and a television at the far end. There was also a small table and chair, where men could write letters, and also a snooker table. Staff looked on, to report any conversations, but most men said little or nothing. This was what happened for the first few months.[47]

Near the day room was the dining room. The food served was plain and simple but apparently not too bad, certainly by prison standards. There were china cups and proper knives and forks, again unlike prison where they were plastic. All knives and forks were counted at the end of each meal. Breakfast was at 8 am, lunch at noon and tea at 5 pm.[48]

Apart from all this, doctors, psychiatrists, education officers and social workers saw the patients. They explained the simple rules to the men and stated that if the inmate behaved himself, he would get privileges, a better room, choice of where to work, use of a radio and so on. Failure to adhere to these meant a hard life; solitary confinement in Norfolk House, known as the punishment block and somewhere no one wanted to spend time.[49]

It should be noted that the Broadmoor Institution, as it has been known since 1948, and which is run by the Department of Health, with its headquarters at Alexander Fleming House in south London, not the Home Office as previously had been the case (the latter runs the prison service), is not a prison, despite its forbidding appearance of high brick walls and barred windows. Furthermore, the blue/grey uniformed staff there, though nurses, are members of the Prison Officers' Association. Convicted criminals with mental health problems are sent there. They make up about two-thirds of its population, but other inmates are people who have not been tried but are deemed to have psychiatric issues. Along with Rampton and Moss Side in Britain, it is designated as a special hospital. Its inmates are not prisoners but patients. In the 1970s it was overcrowded; with accommodation for 450 people it housed 750 and included women as well as men (segregated, of course). This situation had been recognised in the previous decade but little had been done about it. It was more of a place for detention than treatment given that there was only 1 psychiatrist per 100 patients. Rehabilitation was seen as being for psychiatric hospitals, not for Broadmoor.[50]

However, in theory, the aim was 'to treat patients in safety and to return them safely to society.' A consultant psychiatrist was responsible for each patient, to supervise them, to advise on their possible transfer and discharge. The patients were accommodated in a number of houses, all named after English counties, with Monmouth House offering maximum observation to Essex House where less supervision was deemed necessary. Each house had a departmental nurse, and each was divided into wards, all with a charge nurse.[51]

Life was very much a routine. A typical patient's day was as follows, as explained by fellow patient Ronald Kray (1933–95), a former gangster, who was a patient here until his death. The staff unlocked the patients' rooms at 6.55 am. The patients had 25 minutes to wash, shave, dress and make their beds. From 7.20 to 8 am they went to the day room and had a cup of tea. Break-fast followed at 8 am in the dining room. Half an hour later they returned to the day room and received any necessary medication. From 9 until 11.45 am the inmates went to the occupation areas, escorted by staff. The occupation officers instructed them. The school, dentist, optician, group therapy and shop could be visited at this time, too.[52]

At noon the patients went to the dining room for lunch. Half an hour later, they trooped out under escort to the ward, where they again received any nec-essary medication. The next hour was spent in the day room or rest rooms with various recreational activities open to them. They could have a cup of tea, chat to friends, watch television, read library books or write letters, whichever they chose. The next 2 hours were spent at the occupational activities followed in the morning. At 4 pm they had tea and there was a patient count. Half an hour later there was more free time; they could bathe, wash their clothes or use the recreation or rest rooms. At 6.30 pm there was time spent in the open air, either gardening, playing football, tennis or badminton, walking with friends or just relaxing. At 7.20 pm they returned to the ward and answered the roll call. Supper was at half-past, followed by any recreational activities they wanted to pursue, or in tending to domestic chores. Some played cards, snooker and table tennis. Others listened to the radio or to records or cassettes. At all times the patients were observed by staff. At 8.30 pm they changed into bed clothes and reported to the night room to receive any medication. At 9 pm they were locked into their rooms.[53]

Patients were encouraged to undertake occupational therapy and this com-prised a number of different activities; arts and crafts, carpentry, painting, toy and model making, printing, bookbinding, making radios and televisions, all with a qualified instructor. There were also numerous sporting and other activities; football, cricket, bowls, tennis, gardening, table tennis, whist drives, billiards, chess and bingo. Social events, such as dances and discos, were held regularly. There was also a patients' library and regular film evenings – in 1980 films shown included *Escape from Alcatraz*, *Dracula*, *The Amytville Horror*, *The Godfather II* and the pornographic film *The Bitch*. It is unknown if Hume availed himself of any of these. Possibly his age debarred him from the sport-ing events, for he was almost 60 on arrival at Broadmoor.[54]

Broadmoor could also be a very dangerous and unpleasant place. One patient, Michael Martin, was restrained by the staff and died shortly afterwards in 1984. David Francis was killed by two fellow patients in 1977. Charles Bron-son wrote that many of the staff were bullies and some of the doctors were hostile, too. Drugs could be used on patients.[55]

Those who were there at the same time as Hume included fellow murderers such as the aforementioned Kray and Peter Sutcliffe (1946–), the Yorkshire Ripper. He probably also knew an occasional famous visitor introduced to Broadmoor by Dr McGrath, television personality and disc jockey Jimmy Saville, OBE, who occasionally 'kindly presented' awards at competitions. He was deemed 'a remarkable man' by Kray and was 'well thought of by the patients.'[56]

In his autobiography Kray wrote the following in his list of 'Broadmoor Legends', described as 'special people, fellers who stand out from the crowd':

> H-for Hume, Donald. Like others here, Donald was found guilty of murder. He got a lot of publicity in the fifties after he murdered a man in Germany. He was sent to prison there and he had a tough time. After many appeals, the Germans finally agreed to him being sent to Broadmoor. I remember him saying to me once, 'Compared to prison in Germany, this place is like Buckingham Palace.'[57]

Charles Bronson also expressed considerable respect for Hume. He later wrote, 'Don was knocking on a bit but when I met him, his hair was grey and he'd slowed down and accepted his fate.' Bronson considered Hume to be 'a legend' and 'one of the best' and told other patients that he was something special. Bronson was amazed that no one had ever made a film about him. Bronson clearly admired him, 'Get on this. Hume also killed a guy and slung him out of a four seater plane over the Channel. Real James Bond stuff.'[58]

In a letter to the author, Bronson made some additional comments about Hume. Hume lived in Cornwall House at Broadmoor. According to his fellow patient:

> Down the field he was always polite, respectful and a humble man. His eyes shone. He still had the fire going in him. He was too strong willed to allow the asylum to crush him. On one of our on site roof protests, he shouted up to me 'Sling some slates off for me.' He had a great sense of humour. Yes, a good sort of chap with old school morals . . . very difficult to maintain your sanity in such a place (he did). So has my respect (Always).

Hume also said to Bronson, 'Let 'em think your mad, but never let 'em think your silly.'[59] Bronson added that Hume 'had decades of madness sucking away at him' and 'not too many in prison or asylum can fly a plane . . . and never forget the years he spent in the Europe prison system. He drove them f——s mad. They couldn't control him. They flew him back in chains.'[60]

There was some concern about Hume being in Broadmoor. Peter Thompson, a former inmate, thought that his being there would tarnish the name of the place and set its image back fifteen years, as some of the patients there were not criminals. There were 850 patients and 400 staff and resources were stretched. As a killer, Hume would need special supervision by officers to stop him escaping or harming others. The tabloid press was also allegedly unhappy at his presence, with one stating, 'Hume is a mad dog, a pitiless killer who for the sake of every man, woman and child should be locked away for the rest of his life. But will it happen?' They thought his cause would be supported by a 'tightly knit band of progressive propagandists [who] will move into action. Arrogant people who imagine Providence has given them a monopoly on mercy.'[61]

As with all new patients, Hume was initially isolated from the others in order that psychiatrists could assess his mental state. To do this they studied the reports from Regensdorf prison and also interviewed him.[62] Yet, by March 1977 he was still lodged in the same place, Norfolk House, where new arrivals usually only stayed for three or four months. Psychiatrists were uncertain whether he had really changed or was merely putting on an act. If he turned violent then he would be placed in Monmouth House, where security was highest.[63]

In early 1977 Hume was employed in the kitchens. A report stated, 'The chubby faced man with cropped grey hair standing at a sink, washing dirty pots and pans, has a friendly word for anybody who wants to talk to him. He smiles at people passing by and is pleased if they respond.' He appeared a changed man, 'docile and friendly', compared with his time at Regensdorf when he was often anything but. Yet, the staff kept him away from any form of food preparation, especially that involving knives and choppers. Hume seemed to appreciate being in Broadmoor, 'He is like a friendly uncle . . . and he is glad to be back in Britain. In Switzerland his cell was tiny and he felt like a caged animal. Now he has a lot more room to move about. He is causing no trouble at all.'[64]

Hume never wrote about his experiences in Broadmoor and as his medical notes are unavailable until 2099, they will remain unknown for many decades. For some of the tabloid newspapers he, as ever, provided good copy. In 1982 it was alleged that his prize possession was a portable tape recorder which he carried everywhere in order to listen to his favourite music – Nazi marching songs and gunfighter ballads. Hume was still attracted to violence and wanted to imagine himself as the man of action even though that was no longer the case. It was also reported that he had his own room and even a colour television.[65] Most of the patients led very routine existences within the walls of Broadmoor and so presumably Hume was no exception. He probably spent time being employed in the workshops, perhaps working on electronic and electrical projects as he had in Dartmoor prison. Patients received a small wage for these tasks; between £3.50 and £5 per week.[66]

Yet, in 1978, when there was a visit by several members of the European Commission of Human Rights, Hume was eager to talk to them about the conditions he was living in. He told them that they should investigate Regensdorf prison instead. He was positive about Broadmoor, telling them, 'I am enjoying life in Broadmoor. The people know what they are doing. It is a very well run place.' However, he also looked forward to being released, and soon enough.[67]

However, Ronald Kray noted that 'The place itself is bloody grim' and could do with a lick of paint. There was the loss of liberty, not much to do and a regimented lifestyle with lights out at 9 pm. Yet, on the whole, 'Life here is much better than in prison, you get a lot more privileges.' He recalled, 'We were treated more like hospital patients than criminals . . . the people who work here are kind and that's the main thing.' Patients could buy cigarettes but not alcohol. Bedrooms were similar to those in prison, but had a colour television, a cassette player and a radio. Books were available. Kray read and wrote a lot. He had plenty of correspondents and visitors. It is unlikely that many people wrote to Hume or visited him apart from lawyers and doctors.[68]

Patients could receive money for undertaking various chores and could obtain pocket money, all of which could be spent in the hospital shop. There were also concerts and plays, sometimes staged by the patients' theatre group, The Broadhumourists, and sometimes by outside groups. Some patients wrote poems and short stories in the *Chronicle*, the inhouse magazine written by patients; one-such poet being Ronald Kray. Hume's only known contribution to the magazine was a letter, at least it is presumably by him, judging by the initials, which read as follows:

> Dear Editor,
>
> I'd like to put on record a note of congratulations to Bob W. [patients are always referred to by Christian name and initial of surname only], the Sports secretary, for the improvement in the records he plays at socials. The records are more up to date, and the order in which Bob plays them is perfect for dancing. Keep it up Bob! I used to be among the worst moaners when the records left me disgruntled, so you really do deserve credit for such good work now.
>
> D.B.H.[69]

One wonders which music Hume liked; perhaps that of Abba, Blondie, Elton John or Rod Stewart, rather than the hits he would have known in the 1940s and 1950s.

One of the major questions that arose when Hume was in Broadmoor was whether he could ever be tried for the bank robberies in Brentford. As the police noted a month after his arrival there, 'Hume is in Broadmoor and I assume, likely to remain there. What action, if any, do you want taken with regard to the Brentford robberies?' Certainly in 1976 both the police and prosecution service wished to try him. However, the main issue was Hume's mental condition; whether he would ever be sane enough to plead. In 1976 he was in need of 'fairly prolonged observation and treatment.' He would not be discharged and thus liable for a trial unless his mental state improved. The time lag was another factor to be considered, as noted in 1983, 'Even if the witnesses are available I do not see how we can possibly prosecute for the bank robberies, serious as they apparently were – some 25 years after the events.'[70]

The principal problem with the time lag was that the police officers who had worked on the robberies were now all retired. However, it was felt that most of the witnesses could be tracked down. Yet, some believed that the identification of Hume by witnesses might be questionable. His features had changed considerably over the decades. In 1983, Derek Higgins, once the deputy bank manager whom he had threatened in print, had correctly identified him but when he had been asked to do that previously he had not been able to do so. Furthermore, the forensic evidence which had been collected at the time, such as fingerprints, had long been disposed of.[71]

Dr McGrath wrote that it was an 'extremely remote prospect his patient would ever be released.'[72] Hume went before the Mental Health Tribunal on several occasions, once in 1979 and the next in May 1983. He corresponded with Benedict Birnberg, a London solicitor, about the second of these. He was certainly aware of the risk of him having to stand trial for the Brentford robberies and asked his solicitors in 1979 if there was any realistic chance of this happening on his release. He was advised that he would be liable to be arrested and charged if he was released. Apparently, 'There is ample evidence to convict Hume with both offences', but this was far from clear in reality.[73] In 1983 the DPP stated it would now be 'inappropriate to institute any criminal proceedings against Hume in respect of the offences committed in 1958.' Two years later the police came to the same conclusion.[74]

According to the legislation, Hume could only be released if ordered to be so by a near relative, the Mental Health Tribunal or the managers of a mental health hospital. Initially, 'it is not at present the inclination . . . to direct an early release.' The police and the public prosecutor both wanted to be told if this was a possibility. Yet, the Tribunal was an independent body and could tell a patient he could leave with a seven day notice and they alleged, 'We would not be in a position to give any prior notice to you.'[75] By March 1985 it was considered that Hume was no longer a restricted patient and that rehabilitation was deemed possible.[76]

Most patients in Broadmoor remain there on average for about five years. Yet, Hume was there for a dozen years. This was probably partly because of his reluctance to leave and so face a possible charge on account of the Brentford robberies. Secondly, he had committed two murders and so was viewed as being potentially dangerous to the public. Dr McGrath and his successor from 1981–3, Dr Edgar Udwin (described by Bronson as being 'Some evil swine of a doctor'), who had been the psychiatrist who had authorised the release of the poisoner Graham Young in 1971 who had gone onto kill again, probably did not want to run that risk of Hume reoffending. Finally, Hume had no family or friends whose care he could be released into and mental hospitals elsewhere were often reluctant to accept potentially dangerous people and so used delaying tactics at least.

Gordon Rowe, who ran a private home for the 'mentally handicapped' in Stoke Poges, Buckinghamshire, in the 1980s, got to know Hume at Broadmoor. Apparently, Rowe believed that Hume had hidden proceeds from a bank robbery in Switzerland, though there is no evidence that he did and it seems inherently unlikely. Rowe lobbied the superintendent to allow Hume to be released into his care and also discussed this with Hume. Hume decided not to accept the offer, which was probably just as well for him, given Rowe's crimes.[77]

Yet, Hume was not to stay there indefinitely. Numbers at Broadmoor were being reduced from 750 in the 1970s to about 500 in 1985. Hume was released from Broadmoor on 19 April 1988. He had been a parole patient for the previous four years, being allowed out for shopping trips and other excursions, always accompanied. His mental health was clearly seen as having improved to the extent that he was no longer a danger to the public and that he might eventually be discharged into the community. Hume was described as being 'plump, with close cropped, almost white hair.' He was transferred to St Bernard's Hospital in Southall, west London, for a trial period. This was a hospital for low-risk mental patients, though there was a secure unit there, opened in 1986. Dr Ian Tresseadon (1958–) was assigned to him. He declared, 'He is on leave with us from Broadmoor and it is intended he may go on to somewhere outside of the region depending on how well he gets on here.'[78]

St Bernard's Hospital is a large psychiatric hospital established in 1831, and expanded significantly in the decades following its opening. Patients there could be voluntary or referred by their GPs. Numbers were falling in the 1980s and 1990s from 1,100 in 1985 to 390 in 1992 as patients were prepared for life in the outside world rather than being permanently institutionalised. At this hospital, patients were encouraged to take part in organised recreation and other activities. They were allowed to wear their own clothes. Facilities in the hospital included a library, hairdressing salon, hospital shop and sports ground. Patients would receive a small allowance of pocket money.[79]

On arrival a patient undergoes a full physical examination. Their mental state is studied and assessed in order to ascertain the most appropriate treatment. This may take several days. Each patient is then allocated a consultant who is assisted by junior doctors. As treatment progresses, the doctor will discuss with each patient when he is ready to leave and make arrangements for discharge. Many will need to continue with treatment as an outpatient or with their new GP.[80]

Paul Howard Lang was hospital librarian there from 1982–2014 and recalled meeting Hume. He stated that Hume had a great interest and knowledge in aircraft. He was also very physically active, could scale walls and enjoyed gardening. On one occasion he was topping and tailing a root vegetable with the machete knife he was given, attacking the plant with great gusto. He was a very polite man, Lang remembered, always calling him 'Sir' (staff at Broadmoor had insisted on this and so Hume retained the habit he had learnt) and asking other members of staff if he could buy them anything. It was only later that someone pointed out to the librarian what crimes Hume had committed. After that he treated him with a degree of caution. Towards the end of his time at St Bernard's, Hume was allowed off the premises to nearby Hanwell and West Ealing, accompanied by a member of staff, to acclimatise him to the outside world.[81]

It is not known when Hume was discharged from St Bernard's as a cured man; Lang thinks he was only there for about a year, so it would have been towards the end of 1989; as with Broadmoor, patient records are closed for a century after the patient's demise. By 1993 Hume was living at 2 Thompson House, 200 Wornington Road in north Kensington. This was a basement flat with two bedrooms and a bathroom; probably social housing. The other resident was Mrs Ada Elizabeth Sullivan (1911–93), an elderly widow. After her death Hume lived there alone, as Donald Brown, for the remainder of his life.[82]

Hume's later years and demise are scantily documented. Apparently, 'he had been a wide traveller since his release', though one wonders how he had the income to indulge in much travel, for presumably he would have been dependent on state benefits; his age, too, may have inhibited such activities. All we can state for certain is his demise and that is also shrouded in mystery. At 7 am on Thursday, 9 July 1998, the corpse of an elderly man was found on the grassy area behind the Copper Beeches Hotel (named after the Hampshire-based Sherlock Holmes story of the same name, perhaps?) on 107 Cliddesden Road in Basingstoke, by an unnamed guest. The police were called, but they could find no means of initially identifying him.[83]

The police believed that it was not a case of foul play and the body remained in the mortuary for a week. Eventually, dental records were checked against former patients of Broadmoor. They matched those of Hume. Why Hume was in Basingstoke can only be conjectured. Possibly he was visiting the vicinity of his former grammar school (which had by then been closed down), though it is unknown whether the brief time he had spent there was the source of fond memories now that he was almost an octogenarian. Brian Ferkin, the coroner's officer, stated, 'We just do not know why he was in Basingstoke, but I remember hearing about his crimes at the time.' The hotel made no comment.[84]

The hotel is about a mile from the centre of town. Its grounds are just behind the hotel and can only be accessed by walking through an archway by the hotel. Presumably Hume was not a guest there, or there would have been a record of his being there. He may have been visiting someone there or he may have been there by chance and decided to have a look inside. It is an unanswerable question. A newspaper stated that he 'was a few miles from his home' and if this is true, then it does at least suggest that.

Hume's death certificate stated, however, that he died of heart disease on 9 July 1998 at North Hampshire Hospital, Basingstoke, where the post-mortem was carried out the following day. There was no inquest and the death certificate was signed by Andrew Bradhey, Coroner for North East Hampshire. He was subsequently buried on 30 July in an unmarked grave (plot F720) in Basingstoke Cemetery on Worting Road, not far from his old grammar school. No money was available for his burial and presumably there were no mourners present.[85] In the following month his daughter was married; whether this was a coincidence or whether she did not wish to marry in her father's lifetime is another question.

The death was reported in some, though not all, newspapers, and often where it was, it was but a brief paragraph. From being a nationally notorious figure in 1949–50 and in 1958–9, he was now almost forgotten; unlike fellow Broadmoor inmate Ronald Kray who died in 1995 and whose funeral was given a great deal of media coverage. A local newspaper, however, did give him a full front-page headline, with pictures, titled 'Mystery of the Beast.' As well as giving a brief description of his criminal career and his death, it referred to him as being 'evil', 'one of Britain's most notorious post war killers' and 'one of the world's most deranged murderers'; epithets which Hume may well have not been wholly dissatisfied with.[86]

Hume had not made a will, probably because he had very few possessions of any material worth. Yet, the probate court at Winchester decided that what he had should go to Betty Fitzgerald Blaikie (his sister, who was a few years younger than him), of 8 Kilbride Avenue, Dunoon, Argyll, in the Highlands of Scotland. Hume's half-sister Margaret had pre-deceased him and so, as he was presumably estranged from his daughter, Alison, Betty was deemed his next of kin. The grant does not state the value of Hume's estate, though it is safe to surmise it was very little as his grave was unmarked.[87]

Comments about Hume have been variable. Rebecca West, in 1976, noted: 'My impression was that though Hume was a horror – an infantile, grouchy, complaining, envying horror – he had not got to the point of murder, then, though he was to come to it. I think he was inspired by the trial and imprisonment.'[88]

Retired Superintendent MacDougall had no doubts about Hume's guilt and denied the existence of any 'secret' evidence as West implied and gave the following personal view: 'I should say he was at times unbalanced, but sane in the legal sense. He had a violent temper, though he was not abusive to the police. Incidentally, he had no idea at all of aeroplane navigation.'[89]

Williams, in his study of Hume, acknowledged that Hume had a very hard childhood at the orphanage and was unacknowledged by his mother who went on to treat him unfairly. Yet, he goes on to state that Hume had had chances in life to escape from the effects of his horrendous upbringing. He had had kindness shown to him in London in the 1930s by Mr Fox and Mrs Clare, but he had treated them with disdain. Hume had had little opportunity to shine in wartime, but made a success of his business. Yet, that had collapsed. Williams concluded that Hume could not forget the chip on his shoulder and the grudge he felt against society and so continued to make life miserable for himself and others.

Rupert Furneaux deemed Hume one of that rare class of murderers who kill repeatedly and compared him to George Joseph Smith, Peter Manuel, John Haigh and John Christie, though these four would now be deemed serial killers, unlike Hume. He considered Hume enjoyed killing and was a methodical killer, unlike the majority who slay for emotional reasons.[90]

Playfair and Sington, unlike every other writer on Hume, tried a more sociological approach to Hume, refusing to see him as a monster, but as a symptom of a wider social malaise. He was abnormal but not insane. They suggested that he and his crimes were the consequences of society considering psychopaths to be offenders who needed to be dealt with punitively, not people to be cured. Hume had the potential to lead a peaceful and useful life and would have benfitted from time in a mental hospital, where he could have been studied in order to ensure that society could be protected from similar individuals who might repeat their crimes. Knowledge was needed and this could only be gained by a study of the man himself in order to ensure that a cure for him could be found and in order to solve the social problem that he embodied. They deemed that Hume was mentally imbalanced but not legally insane and as a liar and a fantasist he had been pursuing a reckless and hopeless quest for self recognition in a hostile world.[91] Andrew Garve, in a lengthy account in a volume dealing with five criminal cases, wrote:

> He was, first and foremost, a show-off. He was a crude, brash, superficially attractive man of no moral or intellectual substance, but with great drive and enormous ego. He was a little man who wanted to be big. He longed to stand out, to be noticed, to shine and impress. Conceit was his downfall . . . He consistently over rated his own ability and cleverness.[92]

There have been three books written about Hume. Since Williams' book published in 1958, an account in German, Curt Cäsar Winter's *Der Teufel kam nach Zürich*, which is novelisation based on reality about Hume's life and crimes, appeared in 1961. This is all but unknown to British crime historians, but contains much useful information about his life with Trudi and his trial in 1959. Since then there have been chapters about Hume in murder anthologies, articles in three crime magazines in the 1990s and a volume of the *Celebrated British Trials* series edited by Ivan Butler (1976). The latter book is more sceptical than Williams had been and nowhere definitively states what happened in Hume's flat on 4 October 1949, though it does not explicitly question Hume's confession of 1958, either. The case often features in true-crime compilations, but in limited detail. These works have tended to be synopses of Williams with minor updates but little fresh information or analysis. Hume's confession to the *Sunday Pictorial* has largely gone unchallenged.

In contrast to dramas featuring the other prominent post-war killers, Chesney, Christie, Haigh and Heath, there has been little in the way of television and dramatic interest in Hume, despite the hopes of Bronson, as previously noted. Dr Camps featured in a 50-minute television programme about the case as part of the series *Accessory after the Fact*, broadcast on BBC2 on 13 April 1972 and repeated the following year. This included interviews with Tiffin, who spoke about thinking that the floating bundle might have been a burial at sea and how he was tempted to let it drift away. Fryer spoke, too, and was very respectful about the memory of his late employer, Setty. In May 2001 there was a 30-minute documentary about Hume's crimes shown on television in a series titled *Crimes and Trials* and in 2002 the History Channel featured the case in an episode of *Ultimate Crimes: A Question of Doubt*, which also dealt with other criminals. However, in 2011 Sir Timothy Ackroyd and Beryl Bainbridge wrote a play about Hume, titled *The Fuse*. This was performed at the National Liberal Club on three occasions in March 2015. A short film directed by Edward Andrews was also produced to promote the play. This was 7 minutes long and shot as a 1940s' film noir short, in black and white, with atmospheric music but no dialogue. It shows Setty kicking Hume's dog and later the two men in a pub. Hume puts a pill in Setty's beer, presumably rendering him unconscious. He is then seen on his way to his trial at the Old Bailey. It can be viewed on http://vimeo.com/128270184.

Last Words

The big question about Hume's criminal career concerns Stanley Setty. Only two or perhaps three people ever knew the answer – Setty, Hume and possibly Mrs Hume – and the first two, at least, are dead. Only one spoke about what happened (Setty being dead could not do so and Mrs Hume flatly denied any knowledge of any criminal act carried out in her home). Hume gave four versions. In the first, made in 1949 in order to save his life from a death sentence for murder, he admitted disposing of the corpse (never denied) but not of the killing or dismemberment (allegedly committed by three men). The second was made in 1950, possibly to get his now-estranged wife into trouble and blame her for the murder, of which he was not guilty. The third, made in 1958 when he was safe from a retrial but needed money and wanted to show himself as a tough guy, had him stab Setty to death after a fierce fight because of his hatred of Setty based on the latter's behaviour towards his dog and his wife. Finally, in court the following year he claimed that his wife was having an affair with Setty and after he caught them together the two men then fought with knives and the wounded Hume was victorious, stabbing Setty over thirty times.

Clearly at best, only one of these can be wholly correct. Or perhaps none are. We need to assess the evidence, chiefly that gathered by Dr Camps. Setty must have arrived at the flat on the evening of 4 October at some point after 6 pm. It is unknown if Hume was there at that time (he said not) or whether he arrived some time later as he claimed (Mrs Hume was certainly there, as she said). Setty had had at least one or two drinks that evening. He was killed in the front room of Hume's flat; being stabbed five times in the chest in a matter of seconds, with blood flowing freely. No one outside the flat, even those below, heard anything of this quick and quiet murder. This would have required some strength and speed and so Hume is indicated as the killer. The body was then dissected for disposal by Hume that evening and probably bundled up on the following afternoon and thrown out of the aeroplane on that day and the next.

The murderer had Setty's flat searched three days after the killing, and had a female accomplice to arrange it so that Setty's brother-in-law, Ouri, was absent. The killer went there to check whether there were any incriminating documents, and the accomplice must have been someone he trusted.

These facts call into question all of Hume's accounts. The first was an invention to save his neck from hanging; the second was nonsense, and was meant to embarrass his now-estranged wife. The third was to make him money by providing an entertaining tale and stoking his ego by presenting himself as a hard man, fighting and killing a much bulkier man. The fourth was similar to the third, with a terrific fight taking place, though one in which both men had knives. The number of wounds on the real corpse gave the lie to the last story. The idea that a woman who has just given birth and lost another baby was in a physical or mental condition to have an affair and to commit murder is the stuff of fantasy of a particularly nauseating kind, but which gives an insight into Hume's capacity for hatred and delusion.

Why Setty was killed is another mystery. If it was money – and given the Humes' poverty this seems not impossible – then it was a botched job as the stabbings ruined most of Setty's wad of £5 notes. The cash found on him came in useful for the Humes, but it was probably an incidental benefit.

Or, perhaps more likely, Hume and Setty were discussing business over a drink or two and Hume saw red over Setty's behaviour or words. Setty had certainly been drinking (though not to excess) and might have acted in a manner that was offensive. Setty was almost certainly taken by surprise and after a drink or two was, perhaps, unable to react instantaneously.

Hume had not meant to be a killer. There is little or no evidence that he was a violent man up to that time. His action was unpremeditated and caused by defensive instincts, but was deadly for all that. Having war souvenirs to hand allowed him to act quickly and without thought. A premeditated killing would also be unlikely to take place in the killer's home where the evidence of the deed would be likely damning for the killer.

It is clear that Hume felt a great deal of anger towards Setty; writing that at the time of the murder 'I was in a rage' and that hitherto there were 'the weeks my anger had smouldered against this man' and afterwards 'he deserved it.'[1] This was probably caused by a number of different factors; paranoid fears that Setty was seeing his wife behind his back, anger at Setty's mistreatment of Tony and envy at Setty's wealth and status. All his life he had felt anger and hostility towards society and Setty epitomised all he feared and hated. A few additional careless words from Setty lit the fuse to the dynamite that lay within Hume. That both men had imbibed alcohol recently released all sense of restraint.

The actual stabbing would seem to have been unpremeditated. As Camps suggested, it could have been carried out quickly and quietly. Stabbing, or any murder of another adult, is usually the work of a man. Presumably Hume then dismembered the corpse on the evening of the stabbing, as Camps suggested.

We can be certain that Hume took the parcels from the flat and disposed of the corpse roughly as he said he did as this is backed up by witnesses. The question thus has to be why he did so. If, as seems certain, he was the murderer, the reason is obvious enough. The other question is who arranged to have Setty's flat searched as it would appear that this was a two-person job – Hume and possibly Mrs Hume? She may well have been acting under duress or prompted to save a beloved husband and father to her daughter by making the telephone call to Ouri. Both are understandable motives. The final conclusion can only be that Setty was murdered on the evening of 4 October at 620b Finchley Road and then dismembered before Hume disposed of the remains.

Cynthia's involvement was, at most, passive, but it is possible that she knew what happened; in the small flat it would have been unlikely for her to be unaware of the arrival, quarrel, killing and dismemberment of Setty. She was in a difficult position; though as far as is known and as is evidenced by a newspaper interview in January 1950, she was standing by her man and the father of her daughter. This may have meant committing perjury, but if the alternative was having her husband hanged, it was the lesser of two poor alternatives. It is also likely that she contacted Ouri on her husband's behalf two days after the murder, in order to decoy him away from the flat. However, it is also possible, that, caring for Alison upstairs and listening to a radio play, she did not know what happened below; the schoolmaster in the flat below heard nothing. Also, the tiredness due to sleep deprivation as a result of having a newborn to look after would have made her less aware of anything else.

It could have been the 'perfect' crime from the point of view of Hume (not so for the victim, of course). Setty contributed unwittingly to his own demise by not telling anyone where he was going. Therefore, had the (partial) corpse not washed up on the Dengie Marshes and been brought in by Tiffin, it is unlikely that Hume would ever have been apprehended. None of those questioned by the police in the days after Setty was reported missing made any reference to Hume. It was only when the partial corpse was found that he came to the attention of the police. The fatal flaw in murder and disposal (so common in crime fiction) was that the weight came loose from the wrapping that the corpse was inside. Were it not for this then it could, as did the rest of the body, have fallen to the bottom of the sea and the Setty case remained an unexplained disappearance.

However, another point worth pondering is that Hume was not by nature a violent man. His previous conviction was for fraud and few fraudsters graduate to commit murder (John George Haigh being an exception). Yet, his wife claimed he had attacked her, but this is impossible to verify (there is no evidence he was ever violent towards Trudi). Secondly, in his confession to the newspaper he was telling them what they wanted to hear. We know he had an inventive imagination – remember his statement to the police in 1949 and his RAF fantasies. And the motive for this story was monetary – a commodity he stood in desperate need of. He knew that he could not be tried for murder again so he was free to make up whatever story he chose, true or not, and to confess to murder could not harm him now. Nothing in his story about the murder can be confirmed by witnesses or by evidence and if he did not commit the murder it was unlikely that the real killer would step forward and risk their neck in confessing.

All through his life Hume had sought both wealth and the adulation of others. He was not very successful on either count; certainly not in the long term. He had brief success in the mid-1940s as a legitimate businessman. He had limited fame as a criminal in 1949–50 and 1958–9, and enjoyed a brief spell of good living in the few months he was in Switzerland in 1958–9. However, for eight years of his life he was resident in the austere surroundings of British prisons; from 1959–76 in the grim atmosphere of Regensdorf prison; from 1976–88 in the relatively less austere (but still regimented and restrictive) Broadmoor and finally a year or two at St Bernard's. A total of nearly four decades, or half his life (and a rather larger proportion of his adult life), during which he lacked both freedom and wealth. Save for very brief periods of success, Hume's life had been a miserable failure. He seemed to be an attractive personality and secured the love of both Cynthia and Trudi (in both cases briefly), and was affectionate towards both, but never seemed to show any regard for his daughter whom he apparently disowned. He never made any lasting friends and probably led a lonely life in old age. In order to compensate for his disappointments he created a rich fantasy life for himself as a heroic war pilot, an aviator, a spy and a great criminal. In his murders and bank robberies Hume acted not only violently but impulsively, and with no thought for his long-term future or his victims. He killed two men and shot another three. The emotional harm he caused to the women in his life should also be remembered. It is to be hoped that all those he damaged were eventually able to recover.

Notes

Chapter 1

1. Census returns, 1891 and 1901, indexes to BMD.
2. Mervyn Miller, *English Garden Cities: An Introduction* (2010), pp. 23–30.
3. 1911 census.
4. Barnet Local Studies Centre, Hendon Education Committee Minute Book, 1911–1913.
5. *Hampstead and Highgate Express*, 27 July 1912, India Office List, 1918, p. 565; *The Times*, 20 July 1912, wills.
6. Birth certificate; *Kelly's Directory for Dorset*, 1921.
7. *Sunday Pictorial*, 1 June 1958.
8. Census returns, 1901, 1911, parish registers.
9. Ibid.
10. TNA, CRIM1/2033.
11. J. Williams, *Hume: Portrait of a Double Murderer* (1960), pp. 18–19.
12. *Sunday Pictorial*, 1 June 1958, street directories; Williams, *Hume*, pp. 19–20.
13. A. Pitcher, *Mapledurwell, Up Nately and Andwell* (n.d.), pp. 51–2, 61.
14. Hampshire Record Office, 86M82/PJ1.
15. Ibid.; *Sunday Pictorial*, 1 June 1958; 1939 registers.
16. A. Pitcher, *Herriard and Lasham* (n.d.), pp. 45–8.
17. TNA, CRIM1/2033.
18. Ibid.
19. J. Arlott, *Basingstoke Boy: The Autobiography* (1990), pp. 35–6, 45.
20. Ibid., pp. 37–8.
21. TNA, MEPO3/3144; Hampshire Archives, Grammar School Pupil Roll.
22. *Sunday Pictorial*, 1 June 1958.
23. D. Webb, *Crime is My Business* (1953), p. 16.
24. *Sunday Pictorial*, 1 June 1958; Williams, *Hume*, pp. 25–7, 29; TNA, KV2/2902; MEPO3/3144.
25. Williams, *Hume*, pp. 26–9.
26. Ibid., pp. 28–9.

Chapter 2

1. Williams, *Hume*, p. 30.
2. *Oxford Dictionary of National Biography* (ODNB), 58, pp. 476–7.
3. TNA, MEPO3/3144.
4. Ibid.
5. TNA, CRIM1/2033.
6. TNA, MEPO3/3144.
7. Ibid.
8. Ibid.
9. *Sunday Pictorial*, 1 June 1958; TNA, CRIM1/2033; MEPO3/3144; Williams, *Hume*, pp. 34–5.
10. TNA, MEPO3/3144.

11. Ibid.; R. Dahl, *Going Solo* (1986), pp. 207, 209.
12. Metropolitan Police, CRO File: Hume.
13. Ibid.
14. TNA, MEPO3/3144; CRIM4/1687.
15. TNA, MEPO3/3144; *London Gazette*, 21 November 1947 and 11 July 1950; *Sunday Pictorial*, February 1950.
16. Williams, *Hume*; Sunday Pictorial, 1 June 1958; Webb, *Crime is My Business*, p. 17.
17. Webb, *Crime is My Business*, pp. 15–17, 21; *News of the World*, 29 January 1950.
18. Metropolitan Police, CRO File: Hume.
19. *Sunday Pictorial*, 1 June 1958; Webb, *Crime is My Business*, p. 16.
20. *Sunday Pictorial*, 1 June 1958; R. West, *Train of Powder* (1954), p. 206; *News of the World*, 29 January 1950; *Gloucester Citizen*, 21 January 1950.
21. *Sunday Pictorial*, 1 June 1958; *People*, 29 January 1950; TNA, MEPO3/3144.
22. *People*, 29 January 1950.
23. *Portsmouth Evening News*, 18 June 1951; *Yorkshire Evening Post*, 18 June 1951; *People*, 29 January 1950.
24. West, *Train of Powder*, pp. 204–5.
25. TNA, MEPO3/3144.
26. Ancestry certificates; TNA, CRIM1/2033.
27. TNA, MEPO3/3144.
28. *Sunday Pictorial*, 15 and 22 June 1958.
29. *Sunday Pictorial*, 6 February 1950.
30. Ibid.
31. TNA, CRIM1/2033.
32. *Sunday Pictorial*, 5 February 1950.
33. TNA, KV2/2903.
34. *Daily Telegraph*, 27 January 1950.
35. *Sunday Pictorial*, 1 June 1958; *Hereford Times*, 2 November 1949; *Gloucester Citizen*, 21 January 1950.
36. Metropolitan Police, CRO File: Hume.
37. TNA, MEPO3/3144, *London Gazette*, 21 November 1947.
38. Metropolitan Police, CRO File: Hume.
39. Ibid.
40. TNA, CRIM1/2033.
41. TNA, MEPO3/3144; *Hereford Times*, 2 November 1949.
42. TNA, MEPO3/3144; CRIM1/2033.
43. Ibid.

Chapter 3

1. TNA, HO334/1102/79338; census returns, birth and death certificates, TNA, HO405/48518.
2. Manchester directories, Ancestry.co.uk; *Manchester Guardian*, 2 August 1928 and 15 October 1959; *News of the World*, 23 October 1949; TNA, HO405/48518.
3. *Manchester Guardian*, 28 April 1928, 4 October 1938.
4. Manchester directories, Ancestry.co.uk; *Manchester Guardian*, 2 August 1928.
5. *Manchester Guardian*, 22 June 1928.
6. Ibid., 28 April 1928.
7. Ibid., 2 August 1928.
8. Ibid., 28 April 1928.
9. Ibid.
10. Ibid., 10 May.

11. Ibid., 14, 22 June.
12. Ibid., 2 August 1928.
13. Ibid.
14. Ibid. and *Cheltenham Chronicle*, 4 August 1928; *Yorkshire Post*, 2 August 1928; TNA, MEPO3/3144.
15. Metropolitan Police, CRO Files: Setty; TNA, MEPO3/3144 and BT226/5547; *Daily Express*, 24 October 1949; TNA, HP405/48518.
16. *Manchester Guardian*, 4 October 1938 and 15 October 1959.
17. TNA, H0405/48518.
18. Ibid.
19. TNA, MEPO3/3144 and BT226/5547; *Daily Express*, 24 October 1949; www.niceklinthema-chine.com/2013/04/warrenstreet-at-the-time-of-the-murder-of-stan-the-spiv-setty-by-Brian-Donald-Hume-in-1949/.
20. Ibid.
21. Ibid.
22. Ibid.
23. Ibid.; *Daily Express*, 8 October 1949.
24. Ibid.; *Daily Express*, 7, 8 and 24 October 1949.
25. *Daily Express*, 24 October 1949; *Daily Mail*, 25 October 1949.
26. D. Webb, *Deadline for Crime* (1955), pp. 8–10.
27. *Daily Mail*, 25 October 1949.
28. TNA, MEPO3/3144; Sunday Pictorial, 1 June 1958.
29. Webb, *Crime is My Business*, p. 6; *Kelly's Directory* for London, 1950.
30. *Picture Post*, 19 November 1949, pp. 25–7.
31. *Sunday Pictorial*, 1 June 1958.
32. Ibid.
33. Ibid
34. TNA, MEPO3/3144.
35. Ibid.; *Daily Express*, 7 October 1949.

Chapter 4

1. TNA, MEPO3/3144.
2. Ibid.
3. Ibid.; *Daily Express*, 7 October 1949.
4. Ibid.
5. Ibid.
6. Ibid.; *Daily Express*, 24 October 1949.
7. Ibid.
8. TNA, MEPO3/3144.
9. Ibid.
10. *Daily Express*, 7 and 24 October 1949; *Daily Mail*, 25 October 1949.
11. *Sydney Morning Herald*, 15 September 1957.
12. *Dundee Courier*, 19 October 1949; *Western Morning News*, 11 October 1949; TNA, MEPO3/3144.
13. *The Times*, 26 October 1949; *Evening Standard*, 6, 8 and 15 October 1949; Islington Library, Diary of Gladys Langford, 1949–50.
14. TNA, MEPO3/3144.
15. Webb, *Crime is My Business*, p. 20; I. Butler, *Celebrated British Trials* series, (1976), Vol. 5, p. 72.
16. TNA, MEPO3/3144.
17. Ibid.
18. Ibid.

19. Ibid.
20. Ibid.
21. Ibid.
22. Ibid.
23. Butler, *Trials*, Vol. 5, pp. 72–3, 77–8.
24. Ibid., pp. 40–1.
25. TNA, MEPO3/3144.
26. Ibid.
27. Ibid.
28. Ibid.
29. Ibid.; *Sunday Pictorial*, 8 June 1958.
30. Ibid.
31. Ibid.
32. Ibid.
33. Ibid.
34. Ibid.; *Sunday Pictorial*, 22 June 1958.
35. TNA, MEPO3/3144.
36. Ibid.
37. Ibid.
38. Ibid.
39. Ibid.
40. West, *Train of Powder*, p. 197.
41. Ibid., p.193.
42. G.H. Totterdell, *Country Copper* (1956), p. 8.
43. TNA, MEPO3/3144.
44. *ODNB*, 9, pp. 582–3.
45. Butler, *Trials*, Vol. 5, pp. 46–7; TNA, MEPO3/3144; Totterdell, *Country Copper*, p. 238; F.E. Camps and H. Holden, 'The Case of Stanley Setty', *Medico-Legal Journal*, Vol. 19/1 (1951), pp. 3–4.
46. TNA, MEPO3/3144; Totterdell, *Country Copper*, p. 238; G.K. Murphy, 'The Case of Stanley Setty', *The American Journal of Forensic Medicine and Pathology*, 1/3 (1980), p. 245.
47. Camps and Holden, 'The Case of Stanley Setty', p. 4; P. White (ed.), *Crime Scene to Court: The Essentials of Forensic Science* (1998), pp. 267, 270.
48. R. Mayes, 'Alcohol discovered in the urine after death; Ante-mortem ingestion or post-mortem artefact', *Medical Science Law*, 45/3 (2005), pp. 196–200.
49. *Daily Telegraph*, 25 October 1949.
50. *Evening News*, 25 October 1949.
51. TNA, MEPO3/3144; J. Thorowald, *Dead Men Tell Tales* (1966), p. 177; P. Hoskins, *The Sound of Murder* (1973), p. 33.

Chapter 5

1. TNA, MEPO3/3144.
2. Ibid.
3. Scotland Yard, CRO Files: Hume.
4. TNA, MEPO3/3144.
5. TNA, MEPO3/3144; *The Times*, 16 November 1949.
6. TNA, MEPO3/3144.
7. *Sydney Morning Herald*, 15 September 1957.
8. TNA, CRIM1/2033.
9. Scotland Yard, CRO Files: Hume.

10. *Sunday Pictorial*, 12 February 1950.
11. TNA, MEPO3/3144.
12. *The Times*, 16 November 1949.
13. TNA, MEPO3/3144; *Evening Standard*, 26 October 1949.
14. *Evening Standard*, 26 October 1949; Camps and Holden, 'The Case of Stanley Setty', pp. 8–10.
15. *The Times*, 26 October and 2 November 1949.
16. TNA, MEPO3/3144.
17. *The Times*, 31 October 1949.
18. *Sunday Pictorial*, 12 February 1950; *The Times*, 29 October 1949; *Empire News*, 30 October 1949; *News of the World*, 30 October 1949.
19. Webb, *Crime is My Business*, pp. 21–2.
20. *Empire News*, 30 October 1949.
21. TNA, MEPO3/3144.
22. *Sunday Pictorial*, 12 February 1950.
23. *The Times*, 17 September 1976; Webb, *Crime is My Business*, pp. 22–3.
24. Camps and Holden, 'The Case of Stanley Setty', p. 14.
25. *Sunday Pictorial*, 6 November 1949.
26. *The Times*, 16 November 1949; *Manchester Guardian*, 16 November 1949.
27. *Evening Standard*, 25 November 1949.
28. *Yorkshire Evening Post*, 6 December 1949.
29. *The Times*, 8 November 1949.
30. *Sunday Pictorial*, 12 February 1950.
31. Ibid., January 1950.
32. TNA, CRIM1/2033.
33. Ibid.
34. Ibid.
35. Ibid.
36. *Sunday Pictorial*, February 1950; TNA, CRIM1/2033.
37. *Sunday Pictorial*, 26 January 1950.
38. Ibid.
39. D. Brabin, *Rillington Place* (1966), p. 178.
40. *People*, 29 January 1950; *Sunday Pictorial*, 6 November 1949; 12 February 1950.
41. *People*, 4 November 1949.
42. F. Tennyson-Jesse, *Trials of Evans and Christie* (1957), p. xx.
43. Brabin, *Rillington Place*, p. 178.
44. *Daily Express*, 7 February 1958.
45. *Manchester Guardian*, 8 December 1965.
46. John Eddowes, *The Two Killers of Rillington Place* (1994), pp. 70–3.

Chapter 6

1. *Evening Standard*, 18 January 1950; *Sunday Graphic*, 29 January 1950; Islington Library, Diary of Gladys Langford; Webb, *Crime is My Business*, pp. 6, 28.
2. W. Bixley, *The Innocent and the Guilty* (1957), pp. 19–23.
3. *ODNB*, 33, pp. 661–2.
4. *Who's Who, 1950*, p. 853; *ODNB*, 28, p. 802.
5. C. Humphreys, *Both Sides of the Circle* (1978), p. 173.
6. Butler, *Trials*, Vol. 5, p. 29.
7. *Who Was Who, 1961–1970*, p. 671.
8. Butler, *Trials*, Vol. 5, p. 30.
9. West, *Train of Powder*, p. 199; *News Chronicle*, 19 January 1950.

10. TNA, CRIM1/2033.
11. Ibid.
12. Ibid.
13. Ibid.
14. Ibid.; *Daily Telegraph*, 19 January 1950.
15. Butler, *Trials*, Vol. 5, pp. 38–9.
16. Ibid., p. 39.
17. Ibid., pp. 39–40.
18. Ibid., pp. 40–1; TNA, CRIM1/2033.
19. Butler, *Trials*, Vol. 5, p. 41; *Daily Telegraph*, 19 January 1950.
20. West, *Train of Powder*, pp. 211–12.
21. Butler, *Trials*, Vol. 5, pp. 18–19, 41–2; West, *Train of Powder*, p. 205.
22. *Who Was Who, 1971–1980*, p. 2314; Butler, *Trials*, Vol. 5, p. 42.
23. Butler, *Trials*, Vol. 5, pp. 42–3.
24. Ibid., p. 43.
25. Ibid., pp. 43–4.
26. Ibid., pp. 44–5.
27. TNA, CRIM1/2033.
28. Ibid.
29. Ibid.
30. Ibid.
31. Ibid.
32. Ibid.
33. Ibid.
34. Ibid.
35. Ibid.
36. Butler, *Trials*, Vol. 5, p. 48; *News of the World*, 22 January 1950.
37. Butler, *Trials*, Vol. 5, pp. 48–53.
38. Totterdell, *Country Copper*, p. 245.
39. Humphreys, *Both Sides*, p. 173.
40. Bixley, *Innocent and Guilty*, p. 168.

Chapter 7

1. Butler, *Trials*, Vol. 5, p. 53.
2. Ibid., pp. 53–4.
3. R. Howe, *The Pursuit of Crime* (1961), p. 95.
4. Butler, *Trials*, Vol. 5, p. 54.
5. Ibid., pp. 54–5.
6. Ibid., p. 56.
7. Ibid., pp. 56–7.
8. Ibid., pp. 57–8.
9. *Manchester Guardian*, 24 January 1950; *News Chronicle*, 27 January 1950.
10. Butler, *Trials*, Vol. 5, p. 58; *News Chronicle*, 24 January 1950.
11. Butler, *Trials*, Vol. 5, pp. 59–60.
12. Ibid., pp. 61–3.
13. Ibid., pp. 63–4; *Daily Telegraph*, 25 January 1950.
14. Butler, *Trials*, Vol. 5, p. 64.
15. Ibid., pp. 64–5.
16. Ibid., pp. 65–6.
17. Ibid., pp. 66–7.

18. Ibid., pp. 67–8; Islington Library, Diary of Gladys Langford.
19. Butler, *Trials*, Vol. 5, p. 69.
20. Ibid., pp. 69–70.
21. Ibid., p. 70.
22. Ibid., p. 71.
23. Humphreys, *Both Sides*, p. 173; Webb, *Deadline*, p. 28.
24. West, *Train of Powder*, pp. 225–6.
25. Butler, *Trials*, Vol. 5, p. 72.
26. Bixley, *Innocent and Guilty*, p. 168; Hoskins, *Sound of Murder*, p. 39.
27. Butler, *Trials*, Vol. 5, pp. 72–3; *News Chronicle*, 25 January 1950.
28. Butler, *Trials*, Vol. 5, pp. 73–4.
29. Ibid., pp. 74–5.
30. West, *Train of Powder*, pp. 237–9.
31. Butler, *Trials*, Vol. 5, pp. 75–6.
32. Ibid., p. 76.
33. Ibid., pp. 76–7.
34. Ibid., pp. 77–8; Camps and Holden, 'The Case of Stanley Setty', p. 14.
35. K. Simpson, *Forty Years of Murder* (1978), p. 191.
36. Butler, *Trials*, Vol. 5, pp. 78–80; TNA, MEPO3/3026.
37. Butler, *Trials*, Vol. 5, p. 80.
38. Ibid., p. 80.
39. Ibid., p. 81.
40. Ibid., p. 80.
41. Ibid., p. 82.
42. Ibid., pp. 82–3.
43. Ibid., pp. 83–4.
44. Ibid., p. 84.
45. West, *Train of Powder*, p. 240.
46. Butler, *Trials*, Vol. 5, p. 84.
47. Ibid., pp. 85–6.
48. Ibid., p. 87.
49. West, *Train of Powder*, pp. 240–1.
50. Butler, *Trials*, Vol. 5, p. 87.
51. Ibid., pp. 89–90.
52. Ibid., p. 90.
53. Ibid., p. 124n.
54. Humphreys, *Both Sides*, p. 173.
55. Butler, *Trials*, Vol. 5, pp. 92–3.
56. Ibid., pp. 93–4.
57. Ibid., pp. 94–5.
58. Bixley, *Innocent and Guilty*, pp. 169, 175.
59. Butler, *Trials*, Vol. 5, p. 95; *News Chronicle*, 27 January 1950.
60. Ibid., p. 96; *News Chronicle*, 27 January 1950; *Daily Express*, 27 January 1950.
61. Ibid., p. 96.
62. *Sunday Graphic*, 29 January 1950.
63. *News Chronicle*, 27 January 1950.
64. TNA, MEPO3/3144.
65. Murphy, 'The Case', p. 245.
66. West, *Train of Powder*, pp. 222–4, 246.
67. Hoskins, *Sound of Murder*, pp. 39–40.

Chapter 8

1. *Sunday Pictorial*, 30 January, 6 and 13 February 1950.
2. P. Wildeblood, *Against the Law* (1955), p. 114.
3. Ibid.; TNA, DPP2/2906; *Sunday Pictorial*, 12 February 1950; MP: CRO Files: Hume.
4. Wildeblood, *Against the Law*, pp. 114–15, 121, 142, 158.
5. *Yorkshire Evening Post*, 18 June 1951; *Liverpool Echo*, 18 June 1951.
6. G. Playfair and J. Sington, 'International Psychopath: the Case of Donald Hume', *Encounter*, 104, May 1962, p. 11.
7. TNA, MEPO3/3144.
8. Ibid.
9. Ibid.
10. Ibid.
11. Butler, *Trials*, Vol. 5, p. 72.
12. Ibid.; Webb, *Crime is My Business*, pp. 31–4; *Birmingham Daily Gazette*, 19 June 1951.
13. TNA, MEPO3/3144.
14. *Sunday Pictorial*, 12 February 1950.
15. Ibid.
16. Butler, *Trials*, Vol. 5, p. 124; Sir H. Scott, *Scotland Yard* (1954), p. 176; West, *Train of Powder*, pp. 243, 246; *Evening Standard*, 27 January 1950.
17. Webb, *Crime is My Business*, pp. 6, 31, 35.
18. Camps and Holden, 'The Case of Stanley Setty', pp. 2, 13.
19. Bixley, *Innocent and Guilty*, pp. 165, 169, 175.
20. TNA, MEPO3/3144.
21. TNA, MEPO3/3144; Scott, *Scotland Yard*, p. 217.
22. *Yorkshire Post and Leeds Intelligencer*, 20 October 1951.
23. TNA, MEPO3/3144; *Western Morning News*, 18 April 1950.
24. TNA, KV2/2903; Wakefield Archives, C118/226, C188/224/A/2; *Daily Herald*, 13 October 1950.
25. TNA, DPP2/2906.
26. Letters, *Encounter*, July 1962, p. 93.
27. TNA, DPP2/2906; Wakefield Archives, C118/224/A/2.
28. Ibid.
29. TNA, MEPO3/3144.
30. *Sunday Pictorial*, 20 June 1958.
31. Playfair and Sington, 'International Psychopath', pp. 8–9; Howe, *Pursuit of Crime*, p. 96.
32. Metropolitan Police, CRO Files: Hume.
33. TNA, DPP2/2906, HO343/117.
34. *Sunday Pictorial*, 6 July 1959.
35. *Spectator*, 24 May 1962.
36. Ibid.
37. Ibid.
38. *People*, 5 February 1959.
39. *News of the World*, 27 September and 4 October 1959.
40. Williams, *Hume*, p. 9.
41. Ibid., p. 10.
42. Ibid.
43. *Empire News*, 8 February 1959.
44. Ibid.
45. *Sunday Pictorial*, 20 June 1958.
46. Playfair and Sington, 'International Psychopath', pp. 14, 16.
47. Ibid., p. 14.
48. Hoskins, *Sound of Murder*, pp. 41–2.

49. *Sunday Express*, 7 February 1958.
50. Letters, *Encounter*, July 1962, pp. 93–4.
51. *Sunday Pictorial*, 25 October 1959.
52. Ibid.
53. Metropolitan Police, CRO Files: Hume.
54. Williams, *Hume*, pp. 10–11.
55. Ibid., p. 11.
56. Ibid., p. 12.
57. Ibid., pp. 12–13.
58. Ibid., pp. 13–14; *Southend Standard*, 1 and 8 May 1958.
59. Ibid., pp. 14–15; M. Molloy, *The Happy Hack: A Memoir of Fleet Street in its Heyday* (2016), p. 22.
60. Williams, *Hume*, p. 15.
61. *Sunday Pictorial*, 1 June 1958.
62. Ibid., 20 June 1958.
63. Ibid., 1–28 June 1958.
64. Ibid., 1 June 1958.
65. Ibid., 8 June 1958.
66. Ibid., 1 June 1958.
67. Ibid., 8 June 1958.
68. D. Kynaston, *Austerity Britain, 1945–1951* (2006), p. 270.
69. *Sunday Pictorial*, 8 June 1958.
70. Ibid.
71. Ibid.
72. Ibid.
73. Ibid.; *Daily Express*, 7 October 1949.
74. *Sunday Pictorial*, 8 June 1958.
75. Ibid.
76. *Sunday Pictorial*, 15 June 1958.
77. Ibid.
78. Ibid., 8 June 1958.
79. Ibid., 15 June 1958.
80. Ibid.
81. Ibid.
82. Ibid.
83. Ibid.
84. Ibid.
85. Ibid.
86. Ibid.
87. Ibid.
88. Ibid.
89. Ibid., 22 June 1958.
90. Ibid.
91. Ibid., 22 and 29 June 1958.
92. Ibid., 12 February 1950.
93. Ibid., 29 June 1959.
94. Ibid.
95. *Sunday Pictorial*, 29 June 1958.
96. Ibid.
97. Howe, *Pursuit of Crime*, pp. 96–7.
98. TNA, MEPO3/3144.
99. Playfair and Sington, 'International Psychopath', pp. 10–11.

100. *Neue Zurcher Zeitung*, 2 February 1959.
101. *Manchester Guardian*, 9 June 1958.
102. *The Times*, 17 July 1958.
103. Humphreys, *Both Sides*, p. 173.
104. *Time Magazine*, 16 February 1959.
105. *Sunday Pictorial*, 1 November 1959.
106. Ibid.
107. Ibid.
108. Ibid.
109. Ibid.
110. Ibid., 1 November 1959; *Daily Express*, 5 February 1959.
111. Ibid.
112. Playfair and Sington, 'International Psychopath', p. 14; *Daily Express*, 5 February 1959.
113. Playfair and Sington, 'International Psychopath', p. 14; *Sunday Pictorial*, 1 November 1959.
114. *Sunday Pictorial*, 1 November 1959.
115. Ibid.
116. Ibid.
117. Ibid.
118. *Daily Express*, 5 February 1959; *Sunday Pictorial*, 1 November 1959.
119. *Daily Express*, 4 February 1959; *Daily Mail*, 4 February 1959; *Daily Telegraph*, 5 February 1959.
120. R. Furneaux, *Famous Criminal Cases, VI* (1961), p. 72.

Chapter 9

1. Curt CäsarWinter, *Der Teufel kam nach Zürich* (1961), p. 57.
2. *Brentford and Chiswick Times*, 8 August 1958; *Sunday Pictorial*, 26 October 1959; *News of the World*, 3 August 1958.
3. *Sunday Pictorial*, 25 October 1959.
4. Ibid.
5. Ibid.; *Brentford and Chiswick Times*, 8 August 1958.
6. *Sunday Pictorial*, 25 October 1959.
7. Ibid.
8. Ibid.
9. *Brentford and Chiswick Times*, 8 August 1958.
10. Ibid.
11. Ibid.
12. *Middlesex County Times*, 8 August 1958; *Sunday Pictorial*, 26 October 1959.
13. *Sunday Pictorial*, 26 October 1958.
14. Ibid., 1 November 1958.
15. Ibid.
16. Ibid.; *Daily Express*, 6 February 1959.
17. Winter, *Der Teufel*, pp. 63–4.
18. *Brentford and Chiswick Times*, 8 August 1958.
19. *Middlesex County Times*, 8 August 1958; *The Times*, 4 August 1958; *Brentford and Chiswick Times*, 8 August 1958.
20. *Sunday Pictorial*, 1 November 1959; *The Times*, 4 August 1958.
21. *Sunday Pictorial*, 1 November 1959; *Daily Express*, 6 February 1959.
22. *Sunday Pictorial*, 1 November 1959.
23. Ibid.
24. Ibid.
25. Ibid., 8 November 1959.

26. Winter, *Der Teufel*, p. 65.
27. Ibid., pp. 65–6.
28. Ibid., pp. 66–7.
29. *Daily Express*, 6 February 1959; *News of the World*, 15 February 1959.
30. Winter, *Der Teufel*, pp. 74–5.
31. *Sunday Pictorial*, 8 November 1959; *Daily Express*, 6 February 1959.
32. *Sunday Pictorial*, 8 November 1959; *Daily Telegraph*, 5 February 1959.
33. *Sunday Pictorial*, 8 November 1959.
34. Ibid.; *Brentford and Chiswick Times*, 14 November 1958.
35. *Sunday Pictorial*, 8 November 1959.
36. Ibid.
37. *Brentford and Chiswick Times*, 14 November 1958.
38. Ibid.
39. *Sunday Pictorial*, 8 November 1959; *Brentford and Chiswick Times*, 14 November 1958.
40. *Sunday Pictorial*, 8 November 1959.
41. Ibid.
42. Ibid. and *Daily Express*, 6 February 1959; *News of the World*, 15 February 1959; Winter, *Der Teufel*, pp. 102–4.
43. *The Times*, 13 and 15 November 1958; *Manchester Guardian*, 15 November 1958.
44. *The Times*, 24 November 1958; MP, CRO Files: Hume.
45. *Sunday Pictorial*, 15 November 1959; *Daily Express*, 4 February 1959.
46. *Daily Telegraph*, 5 February 1959.
47. Ibid.; *Daily Express*, 6 February 1959.
48. Playfair and Sington, 'International Psychopath', pp. 8, 15.
49. Ibid., p. 15.
50. *Daily Express*, 6 February 1959.
51. Winter, *Der Teufel*, pp. 106–7.
52. Ibid., pp. 112–13.
53. Ibid., pp. 113–14.
54. Ibid., p. 118.
55. *Daily Express*, 6 February 1959.
56. Ibid.
57. Ibid.; *Daily Express*, 7 February 1959.
58. *Daily Express*, 7 February 1959; Playfair and Sington, 'International Psychopath, p. 12.
59. *Daily Express*, 7 February 1959.
60. Winter, *Der Teufel*, p. 36.
61. *Daily Express*, 7 February 1959.
62. Ibid.; Butler, *Trials*, Vol. 5, pp. 116–17.
63. *Empire News*, 1 February 1959; *The Times*, 26 September 1959; Williams, *Hume*, p. 184.
64. Playfair and Sington, 'International Psychopath', p. 12.
65. Butler, *Trials*, Vol. 5, pp. 117–18.
66. *Manchester Guardian*, 29 September 1959.
67. Butler, *Trials*, Vol. 5, p. 118.
68. *News Chronicle*, 29 September 1959; *Manchester Guardian*, 29 September 1959.
69. *News of the World*, 27 September 1959; *Daily Mail*, 29 September 1959.
70. Williams, *Hume*, p. 165.
71. *Sunday Graphic*, 1 February 1959; *News of the World*, 1 February 1959; *Daily Telegraph*, 2 February 1959.
72. Furneaux, *Famous Criminal Cases, VI*, p. 85.
73. *Daily Express*, 2 February 1959; *News of the World*, 1 February 1959.
74. *Manchester Guardian*, 26 and 29 September 1959.

75. *Sunday Graphic*, 1 February 1959.
76. *Daily Telegraph*, 4 February 1959; *Neue Zurcher Zeitung*, 4 February 1959.
77. *Neue Zurcher Zeitung*, 1 and 3 February 1959.
78. *News of the World*, 1 February 1959; *Sunday Pictorial*, 1 February 1959; *Daily Express*, 2 February 1959.
79. *Daily Express*, 2 February 1959; *Daily Telegraph*, 2 February 1959.
80. *Daily Express*, 2 February 1959; *Neue Zurcher Zeitung*, 1 February 1959.
81. *Daily Express*, 2 February 1959; *News Chronicle*, 4 February 1959.
82. *Empire News*, 1 February 1959; *The Times*, 2 February 1959.
83. *Daily Telegraph*, 2–3 February 1949; *Daily Mail*, 5 February 1959.
84. *Neue Zurcher Zeitung*, 3 and 4 February 1959.
85. Furneaux, *Famous Criminal Cases*, VI, pp. 85–6.
86. *Empire News*, 1 and 8 February 1959.
87. Ibid.; TNA, DPP2/2906.
88. *Daily Telegraph*, 4 February 1959.
89. TNA, MEPO26/234.
90. *Evening Standard*, 1 February 1959; *Daily Telegraph*, 5 February 1959; *Daily Herald*, 6 February 1959.
91. *Daily Express*, 4 and 7 February 1959.
92. *News of the World*, 4 October 1959.
93. Butler, *Trials*, Vol. 5, pp. 119–20.
94. *Sunday Pictorial*, 15 November 1959; Playfair and Sington, 'International Psychopath', p. 15.
95. *Sunday Pictorial*, 27 September 1959.
96. Ibid.
97. Butler, *Trials*, Vol. 5, p. 126.
98. *Sunday Pictorial*, 27 September 1959.
99. Ibid.
100. Butler, *Trials*, Vol. 5, p. 119.
101. Playfair and Sington, 'International Psychopath', p. 15.
102. Ibid., pp. 13, 15–16.
103. Winter, *Der Teufel*, p. 247.
104. Ibid.

Chapter 10

1. Winter, *Der Teufel*, pp. 231, 234.
2. Ibid., pp. 250, 254.
3. *News of the World*, 4 October 1959.
4. Winter, *Der Teufel*, pp. 260, 290.
5. *The Times*, 25 September 1959; *News of the World*, 27 September 1959.
6. Furneaux, *Famous Criminal Cases, VI*, p. 70.
7. Ibid., pp. 70–1.
8. Ibid.; Winter, *Der Teufel*, p. 262.
9. Furneaux, *Famous Criminal Cases, VI*, pp. 72–3; *News of the World*, 4 October 1959.
10. Butler, *Trials*, Vol. 5, p. 114; *Manchester Guardian*, 25 September 1959.
11. Butler, *Trials*, Vol. 5, p. 114; Winter, *Der Teufel*, p. 271.
12. *The Times*, 25 September 1959; *Manchester Guardian*, 25 September 1959.
13. *News Chronicle*, 25 September 1959; *Daily Mail*, 29 September 1959.
14. Butler, *Trials*, Vol. 5, pp. 114–15.
15. *News of the World*, 27 September 1959.
16. Butler, *Trials*, Vol. 5, p. 115.

17. Winter, *Der Teufel*, pp. 273, 276, 286.
18. Butler, *Trials*, Vol. 5, p. 115.
19. Ibid., pp. 115–16.
20. *The Times*, 25 September 1959.
21. *News of the World*, 27 September 1959.
22. Ibid.
23. Butler, *Trials*, Vol. 5, p. 113n.
24. Ibid., p. 116; *Manchester Guardian*, 26 September 1959.
25. Butler, *Trials*, Vol. 5, pp. 117–18.
26. Furneaux, *Famous Criminal Cases*, VI, pp. 80–1.
27. Ibid., pp. 81–2.
28. Ibid., pp. 82–3.
29. Ibid., p. 84.
30. *The Times*, 26 September 1959.
31. Furneaux, *Famous Criminal Cases*, VI, p. 86; Butler, *Trials*, Vol. 5, p. 118; *Manchester Guardian*, 29 September 1959.
32. *Manchester Guardian*, 29 September 1959.
33. Butler, *Trials*, Vol. 5, pp. 119–20.
34. Furneaux, *Famous Criminal Cases*, VI, p. 87; *The Times*, 30 September 1959.
35. Furneaux, *Famous Criminal Cases*, VI, pp. 87–8; *Glasgow Herald*, 30 September 1959.
36. *The Times*, 30 September 1959.
37. Furneaux, *Famous Criminal Cases*, VI, p. 89.
38. Ibid.; *The Times*, 30 September 1959.
39. *Sunday Pictorial*, October 1959; *News Chronicle*, 1 October 1959.
40. *Sunday Pictorial*, October 1959.
41. Ibid.
42. Ibid.
43. Ibid.
44. Ibid.; Molloy, *Happy Hack*, p. 23.
45. Butler, *Trials*, Vol. 5, p. 121; *The Times*, 1 October 1959.
46. Furneaux, *Famous Criminal Cases*, VI, p. 90; *The Times*, 23 December 1969; *Manchester Guardian*, 1 October 1959.
47. *Daily Mail*, 1 October 1959.
48. *News Chronicle*, 1 October 1959; *Manchester Guardian*, 3 October 1959.
49. *News of the World*, 4 October 1959.
50. Williams, *Hume*, p. 17.

Chapter 11

1. *Sunday Pictorial*, 15 November 1959; *Daily Mail*, 29 September 1959.
2. Playfair and Sington, 'International Psychopath', p. 5.
3. *Manchester Guardian*, 2 October 1959; *News Chronicle*, 25–6 September 1959; *Neue Zurcher Zeitung*, 20 October 2016; G. Playfair and J. Sington, *Crime, Punishment and Cure* (1965), p. 150.
4. *The Times*, 28 May 1960.
5. Ibid., 1 June 1960.
6. Ibid., 3 June 1960; Playfair and Sington, 'International Psychopath', p. 5.
7. *Manchester Guardian*, 28 June 1960.
8. Williams, *Hume*, pp. 188–9.
9. Ibid., p. 189.
10. Ibid., pp. 189 90.
11. *Neue Zurcher Zeitung*, 20 October 2016.

12. Williams, *Hume*, p. 190.
13. *Sydney Morning Herald*, 24 January 1959.
14. TNA, DPP2/2906.
15. Ibid.
16. *Sydney Morning Herald*, 24 January 1965.
17. *Daily Express*, 8 May 1965.
18. *Daily Telegraph*, 21 August 1976.
19. *Sydney Morning Herald*, 13 October 1963.
20. Ibid.
21. *Sydney Morning Herald*, 24 January 1965.
22. *Murder Casebook 30: Hume the Deadly Fantasist* (1990), p. 1075.
23. TNA, CAB143/22.
24. Playfair and Sington, 'International Psychopath', p. 11.
25. *People*, 4 October 1970.
26. Ibid.
27. Ibid.
28. *Neue Zurcher Zeitung*, 20 October 2016.
29. *Die Weltwoche*, 13 November 1970.
30. *Manchester Guardian*, 1 March 1963.
31. *People*, 4 October 1970.
32. Ibid.
33. Ibid.; *Neue Zurcher Zeitung*, 3 February 1959.
34. TNA, HO343/117.
35. *Daily Express*, 3 May 1965.
36. TNA, HO343/117.
37. *Sunday Express*, 22 February 1976.
38. *Manchester Guardian*, 1 March 1963 and 21 August 1976.
39. TNA, HO343/117.
40. Ibid.
41. Ibid.
42. Ibid.
43. Ibid.; *Sunday Telegraph*, 21 August 1976; *Daily Mail*, 21 August 1976.
44. *The Times*, 21 August 1976; TNA, DPP2/2906.
45. R. Kray, *My Story* (1993), pp. 76–7.
46. Ibid., p. 77.
47. Ibid., pp. 77–8.
48. Ibid., p. 78.
49. Ibid., p. 79.
50. A. Holden, *The St. Albans' Poisoner: The Life and Crimes of Graham Young* (1974), pp. 38–40; *The Times*, 1 July 1985.
51. Berkshire Record Office, D/H14/D3/6/2.
52. Kray, *My Story*, p. 85.
53. Ibid., pp. 85–7.
54. Berkshire Record Office, D/H14/D3/6/2.
55. C. Bronson, *Broadmoor: My Journey into Hell* (2015), pp. xvii, 13, 19, 30, 61.
56. Kray, *My Story*, p. 171.
57. Ibid., p. 137.
58. C. Bronson and S. Richards, *Legends* (2000), pp. 54, 57.
59. Information given to the author on 13 December 2015.
60. Ibid.
61. *Daily Mail*, 24 August 1976; *Sunday Telegraph*, 22 August 1976; *Sunday Express*, 22 August 1976.

62. *Daily Mail*, 24 August 1976.
63. *Sunday Express*, 27 March 1977.
64. Ibid.
65. *Daily Mail*, 19 December 1982.
66. *The Times*, 2 July 1985.
67. *Daily Express*, 18 January 1978.
68. F. Dinenage (ed.), *Our Story: Ron and Reg Kray* (1995), pp. 207–13.
69. Ibid.; Berkshire Record Office, D/H14/D4/1/36.
70. TNA, DPP2/2906.
71. Ibid.
72. Metropolitan Police: CRO Files: Hume.
73. TNA, MEPO26/234, DPP2/2906.
74. TNA, DPP2/2906.
75. Ibid.
76. Ibid.
77. *Independent*, 3 October 1994.
78. *Southall Gazette*, 22 April 1988; *Daily Telegraph*, 20 April 1988.
79. *St. Bernard's Hospital Information Handbook*, pp. 6, 8, 12; *St. Bernard's Hospital Patients' Handbook*, p. 13.
80. *St. Bernard's Hospital Information Handbook*, p. 5; *St. Bernard's Hospital Patients' Handbook*, pp. 9, 13.
81. Information, Mr Lang.
82. Kensington electoral registers, 1992–8.
83. *Gazette: Basingstoke and North Hampshire*, 20 July 1998.
84. Ibid.; *Sunday Mirror*, 19 July 1998.
85. Hume's death certificate.
86. *Gazette: Basingstoke and North Hampshire*, 20 July 1998.
87. Grant of Donald Brown.
88. Butler, *Trials*, Vol. 5, p. 124.
89. *Ibid.*, p. 125.
90. Furneaux, *Famous Criminal Cases, VI*, pp. 90–1.
91. Playfair and Sington, 'International Psychopath', pp. 5, 18–19.
92. A. Garve, 'The Strange Case of Stanley Setty', in Eric Ambler (ed.), *Great Cases of Scotland Yard, Vol. 1* (1978), pp. 244–5.

Last Words

1. *Sunday Pictorial*, 8 June 1958.

Bibliography

Primary Sources

Archival

The National Archives
BT226/5547
CRIM1/2033
CRIM4/1687
CRIM5/13
DPP2 /2906, 2/2889
HO334/1102/79338
HO343/117 (partial)
HO405/48518
KV2/2902-3
MEPO3/3144 (partial), 26/234

Barnet Local Studies
Hendon Education Committee Minute Book, 1911–1913

Berkshire Record Office
D/H14/D3/6/2
D/H14/D4/1/35-37

Islington Local Studies Library
Diary of Gladys Langford, 1949–50

Hampshire Record Office
Basingstoke Grammar School Pupil List
Herriard School Managers' Meetings Minute Book
Longparish marriage registers

Wakefield Archives
C118/226 and 224/A/2

Metropolitan Police
CRO File: Donald Hume
CRO File: Stanley Setty

Printed

Newspapers

Andover Advertiser, 1944, 1950
Brentford and Chiswick Times, 1958
Cheltenham Chronicle, 1928
Daily Express, 1949, 1950, 1958, 1959
Daily Mail, 1949, 1959, 1976, 1982
Daily Telegraph, 1949–50, 1959
Dundee Courier, 1949
Empire News, 1950, 1959
Evening Standard, 1949–50, 1959
Gazette: Basingstoke and North Hampshire, 1998
Glasgow Herald, 1959
Hampstead and Highgate Express, 1912
Hereford Times, 1949
Independent, 1994
London Gazette, 1947, 1950
Manchester Guardian, 1928, 1938, 1950, 1958, 1959, 1963, 1965, 1976
Middlesex County Times, 1958
Neue Zurcher Zeitung, 1959, 2016
News Chronicle, 1950, 1959
News of the World, 1949–50, 1959
People, 1949–50, 1959, 1970
Picture Post, 1949
Portsmouth Evening Post, 1951
Southall Gazette, 1988
Southend Standard, 1958
Spectator, 1962
Sunday Express, 1976-7
Sunday Graphic, 1950, 1959
Sunday Mirror, 1998
Sunday Pictorial, 1949–50, 1958–9
Sunday Telegraph, 1976
Sydney Morning Herald, 1957, 1963, 1965
The Times, 1912, 1949–50, 1958–60, 1969, 1976, 1988
Time Magazine, 1959
Die Weltwoche, 1970
Western Morning News, 1949
Yorkshire Evening Post, 1951
Yorkshire Post, 1928, 1949

Other

Arlott, J., *Basingstoke Boy: The Autobiography* (1990)
Bixley, W., *The Innocent and the Guilty* (1957)
Brabin, D., *Rillington Place* (1966)
Bronson, C., *Broadmoor: My Journey into Hell* (2015)

Bronson, C. and S. Richards, *Legends* (2000)

Butler, I., *The Trials of Brian Donald Hume*, Vol. 5, *Celebrated British Trials* series (1976)

Camps, F. and H. Holden, 'The Case of Stanley Setty', *Medico-Legal Journal*, Vol. 19/1 (1951)

Dinenage, F. (ed.), *Our Story: Reg and Ron Kray* (2015)

Directories – Hampshire, Hendon, Manchester and London

Electoral registers – Basingstoke, Kensington, Hampshire and Dorset

Furneaux, R., *Famous Criminal Cases, VI* (1961)

Howe, R., *The Pursuit of Crime* (1961)

Hume's birth and death certificates

Hume's grant, 1998

Humphreys, C., *Both Sides of the Circle* (1978)

Kray, R., *My Story* (1993)

Molloy, M., *The Happy Hack: A Memoir of Fleet Street in its Heyday* (2016)

St. Bernard's Hospital Information Handbook

St. Bernard's Hospital Patients' Handbook

Scott, Sir H., *Scotland Yard* (1955)

Simpson, K., *Forty Years of Murder* (1978)

Tennyson-Jesse, F., *The Trials of Evans and Christie* (1957)

Totterdell, G.H., *Country Copper* (1958)

Webb, D., *Crime is my Business* (1953)

Webb, D., *Deadline for Crime* (1955)

West, R., *Train of Powder* (1954)

Wildeblood, P., *Against the Law* (1955)

Williams, J., *Hume: Portrait of a Double Murderer* (1960)

Oral History Reminiscences

Charles Bronson/Salvator (Broadmoor)

Paul Howard Lang (St Bernard's Hospital)

Secondary Sources

Books and Chapters

Dahl, R., *Going Solo* (1986)

Garve, A., 'The Strange Case of Stanley Setty', in Eric Ambler (ed.), *Great Cases of Scotland Yard, Vol. 1* (1978)

Holden, A., *The St. Albans' Poisoner: The Life and Crimes of Graham Young* (1974)

Jackson, R., *Dr Francis Camps* (1975)

Kynaston, D., *Austerity Britain, 1945–1951* (2006)

Miller, Mervyn, *English Garden Cities: An Introduction* (2010)

Murder Casebook 30: the Deadly Fantasist (1990)

Oxford Dictionary of National Biography (2004)

Pitcher, A., *Herriard and Lasham* (n.d.)

Pitcher, A., *Mapledurwell, Up Nateley and Andwell* (n.d.)

Playfair, G. and J. Sington, *Crime, Punishment and Cure* (1965)

Thorowald, J., *Dead Men Tell Tales* (1966)

White, P. (ed.), *Crime Scene to Court: The Essentials of Forensic Science* (1998)

Who Was Who, 1971–1980
Winter, Curt Cäsar, *Der Teufel kam nach Zurich* (1961)

Journal Articles

Playfair, G. and J. Sington, 'International Psychopath: The Case of Donald Hume', *Encounter*, 104, May 1962

Mayes, R., 'Alcohol Discovered in the urine after death; Ante-mortem ingestion or post-mortem artefact', *Medical Science Law*, 45/3 (2005)

Murphy, G.K., 'The Case of Stanley Setty', *The American Journal of Forensic Medicine and Pathology*, 1/3 (1980)

Electronic Sources

Ancestry – census returns, indexes to birth, electoral registers, births, marriage and death certificates

Findmypast – 1939 registers

Index